NEW MEXICO
GHOST STORIES

VOL. I

ANTONIO R. GARCEZ

RED RABBIT PRESS, LLC
NEW MEXICO

Printing History
First published as the Adobe Angels New Mexico Series.

3rd edition—2008
ISBN 0-9634029-9-4

4th edition—2015
ISBN 978-0-9898985-2-2

The author may be contacted through:
Red Rabbit Press, LLC
GhostBooks.Biz

Some of the places that appear in these stories have changed ownership or names since the first printing of this book. Some of the individuals whose stories appear in this book have, since its first printing, moved on, either in this world, or to the next. Their stories appear here as they were directly related to the author at the time they were interviewed.

Praises for NEW MEXICO GHOST STORIES VOL. I
by Antonio R. Garcez

"This collection of personal encounters with the 'spiritual,' or 'supernatural,' certainly supported some of my own experiences. These stories are made more frightening by their very proximity."
—*Stephanie Gonzales, former NM Secretary of State*

"I highly recommend that both local citizens and visitors to Santa Fe read this book!"
—*Sam Pick, former Mayor–Santa Fe, NM*

"Fascinating to read . . . offers the reader insight into our town's unique traditions, folklore, and history; don't miss it!"
—*Frederick A. Peralta, former Mayor–Town of Taos*

"Important documentation of the people and history of northern New Mexico. Keep writing!"
—*Kathleen Knoth, Librarian, Millicent Rogers Museum, Taos, NM*

"At last someone has written a book about the ghost tales people have been telling here for years!"
—*Tom Sharpe, Albuquerque Journal*

"It's enough to send shivers right up your spine! An excellent effort by Antonio Garcez, and I anxiously await his next book!"
—*Dale Kaczmarek, Ghost Research Society*

"If you're a lover of the supernatural, get cozy in an easy chair and prepare yourself for the inevitable. Eyewitness accounts told in a straightforward manner!"
—*Tim Palmieri, Western Outlaw-Lawman History Association*

"Another terrifying book from Garcez . . .!"
　　　　—*Chris Woodyard, Invisible Ink–Books on Ghosts Hauntings*

"Highly entertaining!"
　　　　—*Mary A. Sarber, Texas Book Columnist, Herald-Post, El Paso, TX*

Praises for ARIZONA GHOST STORIES by Antonio R. Garcez

"*Arizona Ghost Stories* gives a hauntingly accurate overview of the many reports of haunted sites all over the state. It not only lists the places from north to south, but quotes the interviews of eyewitnesses, giving a remarkable feeling of being there with them as they encounter the unknown. Such sites as the Copper Queen Hotel in Bisbee to the Jerome Inn come to life in Mr. Garcez's investigations. His chapter on the reports of ghosts at Tombstone is perhaps one of the best accounts I have seen on this subject."

—*Richard Senate*

"The accounts range from sweetly sentimental to truly terrifying, but all share the benefit of Antonio's sensitivity and attention to detail. He shows respect for the tales, and those who tell them, and understands that history and culture are inextricably bound to all folklore."

—*Jo-Anne Christensen*

"Arizona could not have asked for a better chronicler of its supernatural landscape than Antonio R. Garcez. From Arivaca to Yuma, Arizona's most haunted places are all here! These stories will send shivers up your spine, and rightly so—they all really took place! If you have ever wanted to experience something paranormal, let this book be your guide!"

—*Dennis William Hauck*

"These are not long-ago cowboy yarns, but very real, very current ghost stories from a rich and chilling mix of voices. Antonio has a rare talent for telling detail; he paints unforgettably creepy images that linger long after the book is done."

—*Chris Woodyard*

"The reader is transported into the world of the supernatural, by a great storyteller who weaves history and personal interviews into a series of riveting tales, sure to make your skin crawl! Here, restless spirits of the past meet present-day skeptics head-on. Memories come to life in the stories from 19 diverse Arizona counties. The thoughtfully told, well-researched stories are sometimes frightening, oftentimes chilling, and always fascinating."

—*Rob & Anne Wlodarski*

Table of Contents

DEDICATION
To my ancestors

And to my life partner, Hank Estrada,
who dreams with me.

And to Civil Rights leader Cesar E. Chavez (1927–1993),
who founded the United Farm Workers of America, AFL-CIO.
A tireless advocate for all people, he dedicated his
life to working in the service of others.

Cesar Chavez and me.

PREFACE

One of the major motivating factors in completing this book was my discovery several years ago that no book existed on the sole subject of New Mexico's ghosts. This omission surprised me, because New Mexico has a well-known reputation within its native population for supernatural occurrences.

My interviews provided me with the eye-opening experience of witnessing the aftereffects of encounters with the weird, eerie, spooky—and at times—evil. My childhood experiences taught me to be sensitive to the unexplainable, yet real, examples of a life beyond the tangible. In my family, we did not make fun of such subjects as ghosts, hauntings, or brushes with the supernatural. On the contrary, my mother taught us to maintain a cautious respect for spirits, folk healers, witches, and forces considered to be occult in origin. Undoubtedly, my Mescalero Apache grandfather, who was brought to Santa Fe as a child to be "educated" at the Indian School, provided his daughter—my mother—with the basis for such a positive and respectful view of the paranormal.

My parents were healers who were able to draw upon the after-death sphere. As a child, I accompanied them on their frequent visits to households blemished by the misfortunes of illness or the troubles of misguided spirits. Through this personal apprenticeship, I witnessed both the positive and negative aspects of spirits. The important learning tools I acquired from my family were understanding and respect for spirits and their energies.

However, my personal perplexities regarding the interviews presented an additional hurdle: Would the individuals—the Native Americans, Hispanics, seniors, and religiously pious I chose to interview—grant me the privilege? I decided at the onset of the project to maintain respect for the personal thoughts and beliefs of each person interviewed. Furthermore, I decided that if there was ever a time during any interview when I felt I might be crossing the border of sensitivity, cultural or

My mother's "Mescalero Apache" father, my grandfather Juan Ramirez, who sang and played Apache songs on his harmonica.

otherwise, I would not press the issue. Happily, my own Native American background (Otomi, Mescalero Apache) afforded me the instinctive moral and intellectual understanding to recognize when I was about to enter another person's "space."

During my interviews with the area's residents, occasionally I touched upon intimate topics such as family structures, love relationships, money, religious attitudes, and personal definitions of death and the afterlife. I was repeatedly surprised at the ease with which people discussed their experiences with me. Although some people were understandably hesitant, overall I met with little resistance. The people I interviewed were not unusual or particularly exceptional in their spiritual or religious capacities. They represent a cross-section of city folk: administrators, janitors, laborers, nurses, and professionals. Some could trace their family roots in Santa Fe and Taos back four or more generations. In addition, I interviewed several Pueblo Native Americans, and contrary to popular belief, it is not necessarily true that Native Americans will not discuss stories of ghosts. However, it does not hurt to know the culture's rules of decorum, both spoken and unspoken. I am convinced that my sensitivity and personal knowledge of Native American culture have been definite assets.

I learned that people are both fascinated and very serious about the subject of ghosts. At this point, I must emphasize that the stories contained within these pages are not intended simply to amuse. They are not fanciful tales to be recounted on stormy nights to groups of wide-eyed Boy Scouts. The people who confided their personal experiences to me deserve courteous respect. They remain confident and secure in the knowledge that they are not conjuring up experiences from their own imaginations; rather, they maintain with personal honesty that their experiences truly happened. In addition, not only did these events happen, they may happen again—to you. Whenever possible, I have given detailed descriptions of the places where these events occurred. You are welcome to visit these places, but please respect the privacy and property of the inhabitants/informants. Please use common sense and discretion.

My father's "Otomi" mother, my grandmother, Maria Camargo Garcez Rios, who once told me, "Never forget that your umbilical cord is attached to this land, so you will always be."

I find it personally gratifying to know that amid the silver and turquoise shops, the upscale art galleries, and the posh restaurants, and deep within the earthen walls of these timeworn cities, the souls of the dead refuse to be forgotten.

The interviews required a considerable amount of editing. As anyone knows who has conducted interviews by transcribing from tape recordings to paper, the process is not as simple as it might appear to be. Careful attention must be paid in order to keep the right "feeling" of the interview. Arranging and giving the proper emphasis where it was obvious, keeping the subject matter in context, attempting to describe facial expressions and hand gestures, among other human characteristics, can be challenging, but is not impossible. I attempted to keep the narrative flow and the mental image of the interview as close to genuine as possible. I must confess, however, sometimes I needed to change a sentence for the story to proceed smoothly and to be understood clearly. This editing was necessary, but does not detract from the story's principal subject matter. The stories speak for themselves.

The stories, I believe, provide more questions than answers to thoughts the reader may have about the existence of ghosts. For example: What is a ghost? Do ghosts harm, or do they provide a positive direction for the living? Can a ghost be an angel, fallen or otherwise? Do animals have spirits? Enduring questions are raised about how we as human beings see ourselves, and how we interpret life and death.

It would be presumptuous of me or anyone else, for that matter, to claim to have the answers for or against the existence of ghosts. Culturally, what is our focus regarding death, and how does this cultural view differ from our personal view? In Western nations death is assigned to a profession of licensed artists known as morticians. Their attempts to keep death clean and to make them look as lifelike as possible are all in vain. Ultimately, death wins. Death is patient, and death can be kind. It can end pain, it can cause much pain. Death can change the course of history. Above all, death must be respected. The twin sister of life is death. Death welcomes you no matter who or what you believe in, how much money you make, or what color you are. Death is an equal-opportunity collector. Given all this, where do ghosts fit into the web of death? Perhaps these questions can be answered only through our customs and traditions. Then again, perhaps not.

Ghosts provide the living with not only curious and sometimes strange fodder for stories and folklore, but also insight into another world in which time and space cease to exist. Within these pages this book will provide stories that make for engaging reading, and a little history lesson as well.

The stories of the ghosts of New Mexico will forever remain unfinished. We owe it to ourselves to listen with our hearts, to reach across space, and to hear the voices of what will one day prove to be our own.

Death may be eternal, but life is not. It's time we treated each other as the precious spirits we truly are.

—*Antonio R. Garcez*—

ACKNOWLEDGMENTS

I wish to thank the following for their
support and assistance:

Louise Walter, *Grant Corner Inn History*

Skip Keith Miller, *Hacienda Martinez History*

Taos Art Association, *Stables Art Center History*

Nola Scott, *Ghost Ranch History*

Carol Mackey/Silvia Deaver, *Georgia O'Keeffe at*
Ghost Ranch & Ghost Ranch Logo Histories

Salinas Pueblo Missions National Monument/
National Park Service, *History of the Salinas Pueblo*

Ellyn Bigrope, Curator, Mescalero Cultural Center,
History of the Mescalero Apache

Carlsbad Public Library/
The Old Mesilla Association, *History of Mesilla*

Catherine E. Wanek, *History of the Black Range Lodge*

Charles W. "Buddy" Ritter, *History of the Double Eagle*

David A. Vigil, *History of Lincoln and
The Ellis Store Bed and Breakfast*

Linda Goodwin, *History of The Lodge, Cloudcroft*

Ruth Birdsong, *History of White Oaks*

*. . . and especially to every person who
I interviewed for this book.*

Death is not a period but a comma in the story of life.

SANTA FE

SANTA FE
ON THE CAMINO REAL

Population 58,000 · Elevation 7,045

Santa Fe, the oldest capital city
in the United States, was established in 1610 as the seat of Spanish colonial government for the
Province of New Mexico. The
Palace of the Governors, used by
Spanish, Mexican, and Territorial
governors, has flanked the historic plaza since its construction
in 1610, and now comprises part
of the Museum of New Mexico.

SANTA FE, THE CITY DIFFERENT

Santa Fe. Rich in cultural heritage, natural beauty, and legendary myth. Many beings have left their spiritual mark on its soil. Be they Native Americans, Spanish explorers, or, most recently, the descendants of European Caucasians. They have all shaped the landscape and the traditions of this mud-walled city. Today's visitors experience the awe-inspiring culture of the Southwest, witness firsthand the land-scape Georgia O'Keeffe set on canvas, wonder at the

unique adobe architecture and its preeminent art galleries, and savor the flavors and aromas of its northern New Mexico cuisine. Most people, however, rarely share one of the most interesting aspects of this city—the inhabitants who once were, yet continue to be, important parts of the community—the ghosts.

Ghosts continuously make their presence known throughout Santa Fe, some in a positive manner, others in evil and sinister manifestations. In Santa Fe, as in communities throughout New Mexico, sincere and saintly healers, when called upon, confront and battle against these spiritual foes. Ghosts are manipulated to do the bidding of the living, either to cause harm or to direct goodness. Here you will read about a fierce wind that drove a demon through one family's living-room window; you will read about a young man so involved with Satanism he killed a neighbor's dog and then committed suicide. But, at the opposite end of the spectrum, you will read about spirits who traversed the hallways of popular hotels at night, who want nothing more than to be acknowledged and recognized. And you will read about the woman's spirit that wanders the banks of the Santa Fe River, beseeching forgiveness for some ancient transgression.

The many picturesque sections of Santa Fe—its buildings, houses, and thoroughfares where these past events occurred—still endure supernatural manifestations. You'll soon come to realize that not all the past remnants of Santa Fe are in its museums.

At dusk, as the piñon and juniper-wood smoke rises up the adobe chimneys of this ancient, high desert town, as the cool night wind rustles through the leaves of its majestic cottonwoods, some of you might even experience the unusually fearful presence of "something" following you. As its eyes follow your every footstep, your mind wrestles between amusement and terror. What you are experiencing is not artistic inspiration of the imagination; no, no, this is horror manifested.

Welcome to the abode of the ghosts of Santa Fe.

SISTER GEORGE

THE THREE SISTERS

The Three Sisters Boutique, 211 Old Santa Fe Trail, Santa Fe, New Mexico, had a well-known reputation for strange goings-on. The store specialized in Western wear "à la Santa Fe." June Keys was one of the many people who experienced the benevolent manifestations of Sister George's ghost on the property.

Several decades ago, on the site of the boutique, Sister George, along with several other nuns, ran a school for the physically and mentally challenged children of the city. The nuns belonged to the Catholic order known as the Sisters of Loretto. The members of this order were responsible for building the famous Loretto Chapel, located in the heart of Santa Fe.

In 1970, what remained of the original school closed and the building was sold to the Best Western Corporation. The corporation tore down the adobe school buildings, except for a portion along Alameda Street, which had been used for various purposes—horse stable, chicken coop, storage area. At one time, this section of the original buildings had housed the Opportunity School, codirected by Sister Harold and Sister George.

Sister Harold (left) and Sister Miriam George Simon (right) with students of the Santa Fe Opportunity School, 1948.

The two nuns had raised the necessary finances for the school's upkeep and its supplies by organizing large community barbecues. Sister George also had marshaled the help of the New Mexico State Penitentiary for the much-needed repair of the school's classroom floors. In addition, she was very active as a community networker and teacher. She cared for the children of the Opportunity School until a devastating fire destroyed most of the school building in the late 1960s. A few years later, Sister George died.

Because of the historical and sentimental importance of the site, the new owners preserved two of the original structures—the beautiful Loretto Chapel and Sister George's Opportunity School building.

Once the hotel corporation built the Loretto Inn, the modest schoolhouse became a valuable piece of real estate and was leased as commercial property. Sometime in the 1970s, the first business to occupy the schoolhouse was the Copy Company, owned by James Kirkpatrick. One of his employees, Blue Rogers, who did everything from building shelves and counters to painting, was the first person to experience the ghost of Sister George. Rogers stated that he heard footsteps in empty rooms, saw lights blink on and off without explanation, and saw office machines that

Portrait of Sister George.

would turn on and off by themselves. He also attests that large reams of office paper would be moved from their original positions in a matter of a few minutes.

It all came to a head one day when the owner, Kirkpatrick, experienced the office paper being moved from one room to another. He announced in a disturbed and irritated voice, "Enough is enough!" Apparently this was enough to startle the ghost, because there were no further disturbances for several months. Then, one night when Rogers was alone, working after hours at the rear of the store, he heard a woman singing in a pleasantly high-pitched voice. The singing was soft and pealing like a bell. Not unlike a song that would be sung in church. The sound seemed to be coming from the front of the store, and although he had carefully closed and locked the doors for the evening, Rogers decided to investigate. As he approached the front room, the singing ceased. He turned on the lights and saw nothing out of the ordinary, so he switched them off and made his way back to his work area.

A few minutes later, he heard the singing again. After two more fruitless investigations, Rogers decided to ignore the whole situation. The singing lasted for a total of two hours. A local visiting nun mentioned to Kirkpatrick that the spirit of Sister George might be still looking after her old schoolhouse.

There are several rooms in the building that were originally used as classrooms by Sister George. Kirkpatrick's sisters-in-law rented both these rooms, and turned them into the first business to occupy the property, a variety shop called The Santa Fe Store. Later, a second business occupied the space, The Three Sisters Boutique. It was stocked with souvenirs and Santa Fe–style clothing. The sisters-in-law reported that after hours, when the store was closed, they would hear the clothes hangers sliding along the metal racks—by themselves. Hangers with clothing on them would move back and forth on the racks, as if someone was physically moving each hanger. Seeing the lights in empty rooms switch on and off was another frequent occurrence. This was such a frequent occurrence that the owners simply got used to it. Electricians were called, but nothing unusual was discovered with the electrical wiring.

Another strange incident at The Santa Fe Store occurred during the first week of operations. Each morning, when the two women checked their cash register, they invariably found an extra $10 bill that they could not account for. A nun from the Loretto Chapel theorized that it was Sister George giving the ladies her blessing. Since Sister George had been known as a "harvester" of donations, it was thought she could be making a contribution to help the ladies' new business get off the ground.

★ ★ ★

The following two interviews describe detailed accounts of Sister George's ghostly activities during that time. The first interview was with June Keys, the co-owner of The Three Sisters Boutique, and the second was with a woman I will call "Sandra," who wished to remain anonymous.

JUNE KEYS'S STORY

I had been told by a friend that the building was haunted by the ghost of a nun named Sister George, but I didn't give it much thought at all. Then about two years ago, when I first opened the business, I experienced several strange occurrences. I always open up early and go directly to my office in the rear of the building to begin the paperwork for the previous day's sales. One morning, I recall feeling a "presence," as if someone had come into the store with me, even though I was alone and had made sure I had locked the door behind me. But the strong feeling that someone's eyes were staring at me was impossible to ignore. I felt uncomfortable. This is how my experience with Sister George's ghost began.

June Keys, former co-owner, The Three Sisters Boutique.

A few days later, after an extremely busy day, I went to the storeroom that was located in the rear of the shop, to unpack and arrange some new clothes on a wooden frame I used as a clothes rack. I imagine this frame was what was left of an old classroom chalkboard. I had found it under some cardboard boxes, along with moldy clothing, boxes of used pencils, and school supply debris in the storeroom. After I had cleaned it up, I decided it would make a nice, temporary clothes rack.

I've been in the retail clothing business for several years and have adopted my own way of doing things. One fanatical habit I have is to hang clothes on racks with the hangers facing the wall. I have been hanging clothes in this manner for years; it has become my personal style. Well, the following morning, when I arrived at the store, I decided to move the new clothes I had hung on the rack in the back storeroom to an empty clothes rack in the showroom. When I entered the storeroom, I discovered that all the clothes and hangers I had painstakingly arranged on the wooden rack the night before had been reversed!

I became very upset, thinking that someone had broken into the store and ransacked the clothing. When my assistant arrived, I questioned her, but she assured me that she had not been in the store since the previous day and had certainly not moved the clothes. Now I was bewildered.

A few days later, a strange incident occurred involving two customers. One woman entered the small dressing room and immediately came out, saying, "Something is in there, I know it, something is watching me." Later, another visibly shaken woman returned to the counter with her blouse, and told me someone had just touched her. She showed me her arms—they were covered with goosebumps. Needless to say, she was no longer in the mood for shopping.

I have had no further incidents regarding what I believe is the ghost of Sister George. The spirit has never hurt anyone. I believe that she makes her presence known only to keep us aware that she had put a lot of time and love into her school and to remind us of her good works in Santa Fe and especially for the children of her school.

SANDRA'S STORY

Several years ago, when I worked at The Santa Fe Store, I had an experience that made me believe, without question, in the existence of ghosts. I have not discussed the experience with anyone for more than a year because I was afraid to recall the whole thing. It was something I did not welcome, and do not wish to experience again.

One morning, about 8 a.m., I was in the back room, the storeroom of the store. I was arranging various boxes on the shelves when I heard the sound of footsteps in the showroom. I thought at first it was a delivery boy, but I realized that I had locked the door behind me when I entered. I decided to see what was going on.

I took one step into the well-lit showroom and noticed a rack of clothes move at the far end. The clothes swayed back and forth as I watched for a second or two. Then, the whole rack, which was over six feet long and loaded with dresses and blouses, lifted on end and rose toward the ceiling. I stood, frozen with fright. The rack came back down then rose up again—three separate times.

Talk about cold chills and hot flashes—I was gripped with terror. I knew the doors and windows were closed. But even a strong gust of wind could not have lifted that rack and left everything else in the room undisturbed. And there was something else unusual—

"Then the whole rack . . . lifted on end and rose toward the ceiling."

when the rack settled, after the third time, the clothes were absolutely still. They did not wiggle as one would expect, but came to a dead stop as if some unknown force held each stitch of clothing in place.

Even though I saw plainly that there was not another living soul in the small room, I decided to make sure. I gathered my courage and searched the room, pushing the clothes aside. I found no one hiding among the racks.

I must admit I was visibly shaken, and I was unable to speak to anyone about this incident. I quickly made my way to the front door and left for the remainder of the day. As I think back, I believe it was the ghost of Sister George. Maybe she was trying to get my attention or even playing with me. Soon after that incident, I leased the building and moved into another shop within the Loretto Inn compound, closer to the chapel.

Sadly, The Three Sisters Boutique is no longer in existence, but who can say what "unusual" occurrences might be going on at the property today. Both women's stories leave no doubt about Sister George's desire to remain an important part of the present activities in "her" building. My guess is that she will continue to be as vital a member of the Santa Fe community as she certainly has been in its past.

SISTER GEORGE: A CHRONOLOGY

June 24, 1909	Born, Pirtleville, Arizona, to George Simon and Miriam Shamas (Syrian for Simon); both parents were Syrians and Catholics.
March 17, 1910	Baptized at Immaculate Conception Church, Douglas, Arizona. Most of elementary and secondary education received in public school, Douglas, Arizona.
August 14, 1931	Confirmed by Archbishop Daeger.
February 1926	Entered the Loretto Community.
August 15, 1926	Received the habit of the Sisters of Loretto.
August 16, 1927	Took her first vows.
May 30, 1976	Died; 50th year of religious life.

Teaching Assignments

1927	St. Francis Cathedral, Santa Fe, New Mexico.
1930	Our Lady of Sorrows, West Las Vegas, New Mexico.
1933	Loretto Academy, Las Cruces, New Mexico.
1935	St. Francis Cathedral, Santa Fe, New Mexico.
1940	Opportunity School, Santa Fe, New Mexico.
1970	Retired.
1975	Moved to Nazareth Hall, El Paso, Texas.

GRANT CORNER INN

In 1905, a colonial-style home of the "railroad era" was constructed on the corner of Johnson Street and Grant Avenue for a wealthy New Mexican ranching family named Winsor. The Winsors lived in the home for a short time (possibly a year) before it was acquired by the

First Presbyterian minister of Grant Avenue's church, Reverend Moore. Shortly thereafter, Reverend Moore passed away, leaving the house to his widow, Ada Peacock Moore, and their four children, Eta, Ada, Ruth, and Mary.

Ada Peacock then married Arthur Robinson, well known in Santa Fe for his spunk and eccentricities. The rumor goes that he was fired from his job at the post office for stealing stamps, which earned him a jail sentence. Other stories include Arthur Robinson throwing rocks and chasing children away from the house, stealing milk from the Safeway market located directly across the street, and maintaining a fully lit and decorated Christmas tree in the window all year long! Ada helped the family income by teaching piano in what is now the bathroom in guest room number eight. Arthur (after his scrape with the law) miraculously became Justice of the Peace, and maintained an office in what is currently Grant Corner Inn's office. Many Santa Feans reminisce about marriages in the parlor and payment of traffic fines in this office. Many of these residents remember the judge as being most fair and with a jovial disposition. After Ada's death, the judge began to take in boarders. He also converted the back second-story porch into a "sleeping porch" where he slept. (This room is Grant Corner Inn's guest room number four.)

After Judge Robinson's death in the 1950s, the house became "La Corte Building." The owners, Leroy Ramirez and Albert Gonzales, then offered office space for lease in the large house. Each bedroom, as well as the living and dining rooms, became offices. Also, The Santa Fe Chamber Music offices at one time occupied most of the rooms on the second floor.

In April 1982, the Walter family purchased La Corte Building and moved from Phoenix to begin work on their bed-and-breakfast inn. A nine-month renovation period included new plumbing and electrical wiring, a gazebo and picket fence with tree plantings, a new front roof line with new porch colonnades, and the addition of a downstairs commercial kitchen and outdoor back staircase and porch. The woodwork in the office, the banister, and the mantel as well as all the wood floors were totally refurbished. Pat, a builder, and Louise, an interior designer, did much of the work on the house themselves. With the addition of their collections of artwork and furnishings, the old house became a home again and opened as the Grant Corner Inn on December 15, 1982.

★ ★ ★

I interviewed Art Garcia at his home for this story. He described to me his experience at the three-story home, which is now known as the Grant Corner Inn. The unpleasantness of living through the events that he described still remains with Art. For instance, as Art described his series of ghostly encounters, his facial expression and nervous voice gave away an emotional level of character that seemingly only a person who had directly witnessed and experienced the realm of ghosts could give. I'm doubtful that Art can ever totally forget his stay on the third floor of the house. But for now, Art is content to pursue the daily activities of life in Santa Fe without dwelling too much on the past.

ART GARCIA'S STORY

In 1980, I was just out of college and living in Seattle, Washington, when I decided to return to my hometown, Santa Fe, New Mexico. Soon after my arrival, I met the owners of a three-storied house on Grant Street. The owners offered me a job as custodian of the building, and for this, they provided me with the third floor for my living  quarters. I moved into my new apartment during the month of March. My mother offered to help with the cleaning, and we both began the arduous task of cleaning and dusting the entire house. It took us over three weeks to make the place spotless.

Eventually, the second floor was rented to some art students who used the bedrooms as storage and workspace. They rarely stayed more than a few hours at a time, and always let me know when they were in the house. Both floors had telephones, so when they were in the house, either I called them or they called me—as a courtesy.

One evening, I attended a function at the Santa Fe Community College and did not arrive home until about 11 p.m. I walked up to the third floor, passing through the second floor, which was in total darkness. There was no sign of anyone in the whole house. Once in my room, I turned on the television set and made myself a snack.

Just as I had finished my sandwich, I heard some loud noises that seemed to be coming from the floor below. I thought the noises were coming from outside, maybe from someone on the sidewalk, but soon the sounds increased in volume and took on a piercing, roaring quality. I thought it might be the art students using power tools to build some sort of art project, but I knew them and was certain they would not make such a commotion at such a late hour. Furthermore, they had never worked during the night.

After about 10 minutes of listening to the sound of doors opening and slamming shut and large, heavy objects dropping on the floor, I had had enough. I telephoned the students below to ask about the noise. The phone just rang and rang—I could even hear the ringing through the floor. When there was no answer, I decided it must be burglars, so I hung up the phone and nervously switched off the television. I thought of escaping from my third-floor apartment, but from my floor, there was no way out except by jumping through the window. I sat tight.

I decided to call my father, and as I was describing the experience to him, the noises began again. But the sounds were now overhead, on the roof. The noise was deafening—constant pounding that reverberated throughout the third floor. My father said he'd be right over, so I hung up and listened to what sounded like someone walking on the roof. The footsteps were so loud that when I attempted to make another call to the police, I could not hear the voice at the other end of the telephone. By this time, the sounds were enveloping the entire third floor.

When the noise subsided some, I called my parents' home again. My mother told me that my father was on his way over. I then telephoned the police once more and luckily got through. I reported a burglary in progress, and the dispatcher assured me that a police car would be right over. Soon, I saw the flashing blue-and-red lights of a patrol car pulling up in front of the building. As I withdrew from the window and turned in the direction of the stairwell leading below, I smelled a faint, yet extremely foul, odor. The scent grew stronger, until I had to place my hand over my mouth to keep from disgorging the contents of my stomach.

I made my way two steps down the stairwell when I heard the sound of a door on the second floor open and slam shut. I stopped, grabbed hold of the handrail, and peeked over to the floor below. I waited, expecting to see the police officer, but instead I heard the sound of footsteps approaching the stairs. The footsteps stopped, and then suddenly began ascending the stairs—towards me. I stared in the direction of the sound, but saw nothing. The footsteps were loud, and the sounds echoed off the walls. I froze.

All at once, I felt a cold, bone-chilling rush of air speed past me, followed by the overpowering stench of rotted meat. It smelled as if the large carcass of a decomposing animal was lying on the stairs below. This wafting, invisible fog of decay became stronger as each footstep approached me. Soon, it seemed as though the footsteps were just a few feet in front of me. Then suddenly, something shoved my shoulder with tremendous force, as if pushing me out of the way.

I grabbed the banister to steady myself and then decided to make my escape. I ran down the stairs to the front door where I met the police—who were just about to ring the doorbell. The police entered and searched every room in the house. They discovered nothing. Soon my father arrived, and helped me lock every door and window. Then my dad drove me to my family's house where I spent the night.

The following day, I returned to the house on Grant Street, but for my own peace of mind, I brought my parents along. We walked through the house together, checking everything. As I began the climb to the third floor, I noticed that all of the beautiful, large potted plants I had been caring for, that were located on the stairs, were completely wilted. I looked closer and realized that the leaves and stems had frozen. I was completely baffled. I had left several steam heaters on overnight, and the house was comfortably warm. In my bedroom, the large tropical plants now resembled defrosted frozen vegetables—limp and soggy. I searched throughout the third floor for a draft or some other source, but found nothing.

That evening I turned the television on to watch a favorite comedy show. At approximately 11 p.m., again I heard movement on the floor below me. I immediately turned the television off. There was no doubt—the noises from the night before were back, but this time the sounds started up very quickly and pronounced—in a direct, purposeful manner. I began to also hear a malicious sort of laughter. This laughter convinced me that there was a ghost in the house. Soon the sounds were deafening—the loud slamming of doors and pounding on the walls. I had to do something, so I phoned the police. I was not about to report a ghost, so I said that a burglar was in the house. As the noises reached a climax, I decided not to stay a minute longer. I made my way down the stairs and out the front door to my car. In the car, I felt safe. Once again, I spent the night at my parents' home.

In the safety of my parents' living room, I phoned the police department and asked to speak to the officer who had responded to my burglary call. The officer informed me that as he had approached the house, he had seen blinking lights on both the first and second floors. Lights seemed to be moving rapidly from room to room as if someone were carrying them.

For five more nights, I attempted, with all of my willpower, to spend a quiet, normal evening at home. But as soon as the eleventh hour struck, the slamming and pounding commenced. And once again I would take off to the comfort and safety of my parents' home.

My nerves were frayed, but I felt I had to prove to myself that I had some semblance of courage remaining. On the sixth night, I turned on all the lights on my floor and waited for the loathsome sounds—nothing happened. For a week after that, I experienced continued peace. But then, abruptly, the noises started up again, and I questioned my own sanity. I thought that I might be having a nervous breakdown. Maybe I was imagining the whole thing. I would lie awake at night for hours, anticipating another ghostly visit, until my fatigued body would finally doze off from exhaustion.

Each morning it took all of the strength I could muster just to get out of bed. I would arrive at work with dark circles under my eyes. My co-workers and friends began inquiring about my health. At this point, I consulted a psychiatrist. The psychiatrist said I appeared to be under a tremendous amount of stress, but that there was no pathological problem. He felt I was quite normal.

As the days and nights passed, I decided to get roommates, and a short time later, two friends of mine moved in. Soon, we all began to see and hear unexplainable phenomena. Sometimes, lights would turn off and on in empty rooms. At all hours of the day and night we heard the sound of several human voices coming from the empty floor below. Often, we heard loud laughter in empty rooms on our own floor. From the second floor, we heard the toilet flush and doors opening and closing. At times, the scent of a rancid, flowery perfume preceded the unexplained sounds. Whenever I recall that odor, I still get goosebumps.

My brother, who at that time was a city police officer, visited me several times and personally witnessed these happenings. On the first and second floors, several times we actually saw a doorknob turn and the door open, only to slam shut—all on its own.

On several occasions, knowing no one else was in the apartment, my mother would grab a doorknob to open a door, and feel the door being pulled away from her. Given all the ghostly activity in the house, and my mother's strong personality being what it is, she would shout, "You're not going to win this one!" Then she'd pull with all her strength, using two hands, until the door gave. My roommates had similar experiences, but they were not as insistent in pursuing a ghostly tug-of-war.

One day, by chance, I met a couple in town who had lived in the house before I did. When they had lived there, they had had a young child. They told me that they had experienced similar phenomena. The unearthly experiences finally had driven them to move out, at which point a very strange thing had happened, as they had begun packing room by room. As they completed one room, neatly stacking the filled boxes, they moved on to another, but when they returned to the finished room, they found their boxes emptied and the contents strewn about the room. Eventually, and with much courage, they packed their belongings, and moved out.

Initially, my two housemates found the unusual ghostly incidents amusing; however, they too grew tired, from a lack of sleep and the occasional scare. They both decided to seek other living quarters, and moved out. The day they moved out, another friend, Ken, and his cat, Missie, moved in.

On several occasions, Ken and I observed Missie walk into a room and then suddenly arch her back and hiss loudly at an invisible enemy. As every hair on her body and tail stood out straight, Missie backed her way out of the room. Ken and I looked at each other, but said nothing.

At other times, I would put a record on the stereo, but soon the arm would be lifted off the record and the stereo turned off. Another time, when I was watching television one evening, a gust of wind suddenly and violently swung all the hanging plants and light fixtures. Loose papers flew in all directions. Then, as suddenly as it had begun, the wind ceased. I checked all the windows, but each was shut tight. I found no way that a wind with such force could have entered the room.

A new series of incidents began when I was taking a shower. I suddenly heard a woman's voice laughing loudly and harshly. I immediately parted the shower curtain and peeked out, but saw nothing out of place. However, there was another time when I did see something out of place. I had been asleep, but was awakened by a noise in the bedroom. I slowly opened my eyes and saw a white shadowy figure moving along the wall. I did not move a muscle. I stared at the figure, and it began to laugh. It was the same laughter I had heard before, while in the shower. The figure laughed, but made no movement within its form. Then the laughter suddenly turned to crying, and the figure moved closer to my bed. As it stood next to my bed, it slowly dissolved until it had totally vanished. But, as soon as it disappeared, I felt the mattress at the foot of the bed depress as if someone were sitting down on it. I grabbed the blankets and covered my head. My heart was pounding hard in my chest. This was more frightening than anything I had experienced before.

Not long after that experience, I received a call from a priest from the local Guadalupe parish. He said my aunt, Ruby Sandoval, had discussed my situation with him and had asked him to talk with me because she was concerned for my safety. I agreed to meet him, and he agreed to keep our conversation in strictest confidence.

He started by asking me questions about my personal beliefs and whether I had ever studied or was interested in demonology, Satanism, witchcraft, or the occult. I confidently told him no. Then he questioned me about the events I had experienced in the house on Grant Street. I divulged everything—the sounds, the ghostly laughter, everything. At the close of our visit, he said he would like to conduct a blessing in the house. I had no problems with his suggestion and agreed to an appointment for the following evening.

At work the next day, I described my meeting with the priest to a co-worker, Jean. When she heard about the happenings at the house and the planned blessing, she asked to be present. Jean said she had always been interested in the occult and wanted to witness such a house blessing. I agreed, and that evening both Jean and I sat in the apartment bedroom awaiting the priest's arrival.

We didn't have long to wait, because soon a car pulled up. The priest had arrived. We hurried downstairs and met him as he was walking up the front porch steps. As soon as he entered my apartment, he began dressing for the ceremony. He put on his chasuble and vestment stole. Next, he brought out holy water and began sprinkling the room, and reciting prayer after prayer. The moment he sprinkled the water towards the living room wall, we heard a loud cracking sound, like splitting wood, followed by a loud bang. Jean and I looked at each other, not masking our astonishment and fear. I felt as if I was in a movie, something like *The Exorcist*. The priest performed the blessing, moving solemnly from room to room throughout the entire house—from attic to basement. Eventually, after about an hour, ending prayers were recited, and he left.

Since the night of the blessing, I have had no more negative experiences with slamming doors, poundings on the walls, or rotten odors. I became convinced that the blessing had removed or quieted whatever had been in the house. I enjoyed the peace that prevailed throughout the house.

Several weeks later, I left for the West Coast to visit friends, and my parents assumed the task of checking on the empty house on Grant Street. Each night, between 9 and 10 p.m., they drove by the building to make certain all was well.

When I returned, I contacted my parents and asked about the welfare of the building. My mother's voice became quite concerned as she described what they had seen. On several occasions, as my parents drove by the house, they saw the figure of a man standing in one of the windows on the third floor. He seemed to be staring at the street. One night, my parents called my brother, the police officer. When he arrived, he too saw the figure. My brother and parents entered the building to investigate, but found no one and nothing out of place. All the doors and windows were locked, as they had been left.

About three weeks after I returned from my trip, a woman who claimed to be a clairvoyant visited me. She just knocked on my door one day. After she had told me of her world-renowned history as a medium, I invited her in. As soon as she entered the building, she said she felt vibrations. I led her to the first-floor living room and we sat down. She began to breathe slowly and deeply. Then she paused and, with closed eyes, began describing people she identified as being lost souls existing in the house. These souls or spirits, as she explained, are without knowledge of their deaths, and are lost, forever searching for a home. She said she was seeing two female figures and a male figure standing off to one side, observing things. The older female appeared to be angry, due to her facial expressions and arm movements. The medium explained that the figure was screaming and slapping her hands to her body. The clairvoyant said that she could not understand what the younger woman and the man were saying, but the older woman told her that she had been trapped on the second floor—no matter what she did she could not free herself from that floor. Soon, the clairvoyant opened her eyes and told me that the spirits needed help in order to understand that they must go on with the process of death. She said they were attempting to relive their past lives by staying in the house. Abruptly, the clairvoyant excused herself, left the house, and never returned. I have had no further contact with her, and to this day I do not know her name.

For days, I continued to dwell on what the clairvoyant had told me. Finally, I decided to move out of the house. I gathered boxes and packed my belongings. I stacked the boxes in the middle of the bedroom and left to get some lunch. An hour later, when I returned, I found the boxes had been opened and the contents tossed about the room—except for my books. They had been neatly stacked into small piles on the floor beside the empty boxes. I recalled the experience of the former family as they tried to leave the house. As you can imagine, I became even more determined to move. I finally settled on the west side of Santa Fe, where I live now.

Years later, I learned something very interesting about the original owners of the house on Grant Street. The husband was a postal worker, and he had kept his wife, a paraplegic, on the second floor. I cannot verify the accuracy of this information, but it does coincide with what the clairvoyant had said. I also learned that the owner's adult daughter, who had lived in the house until the 1970s, was killed with her husband in an automobile accident on the highway somewhere north of Santa

Fe. There was snow on the road, and either a car hit them or they drove off the road, down into a canyon.

Since the day I moved out, I have never returned to that house. I have no desire to go back. The memories of my experiences there remain very fresh in my mind. I am pleased that the present owners have transformed the house into a luxurious bed-and-breakfast, because it was a beautiful home, and now it is even more special. Along with my memories, today I occasionally dream about the time I lived at the house. I realize that I had to live with the fear of knowing that someone or something had been watching me.

DOÑA LETICIA

One hot August day, I interviewed Alberto Serna. We sat on his front porch, and as we talked, Daniel, Alberto's 17-year-old son, sat with us and listened intently to his father's story of Doña Leticia, a witch. Frequently, Alberto would pause and reflect upon other memories awakened as he related his story. At these times, Daniel would ask his father to explain further, to provide small details of these family memories. I enjoyed those moments and appreciated being present as an oral tradition was transferred from one generation to another.

Now in his 50s, Alberto recalled a brief incident that had occurred six years before when he returned to his old neighborhood. On that day, in place of the former homes of his neighbors—including that of Doña Leticia's house—he found scattered bushes of Chamisa and dust. But as he walked back to his car, he spotted a large black raven standing on a boulder. It cawed several times then abruptly lifted off and flew away.

When I asked Alberto what he thought this meant, he answered, "I know it was just that old witch letting me know she's still around—to this very day!"

★   ★   ★

ALBERTO SERNA'S STORY

My name is Alberto Serna, and I am the oldest of four brothers. My family and I once lived in a little settlement three miles northeast of Santa Fe. My grandfather had built our home of adobe in 1918, and when he died in 1953, he passed it to my mother, who already had a growing family. This home, along with Doña Leticia's house, was demolished soon after the family sold the land to the New Mexico Highway Department. Presently, I live on the west side of Santa Fe and have two sons.

By the age of 15, I had acquired a great knowledge of ghosts and witches through the spoken stories told to me by my grandparents, and uncles and aunts, including stories of the famous La Llorona. So when my father took me aside and told me of Doña Leticia, a neighbor who lived about a quarter of a mile east of our home, I was not surprised by my father's lecture. He warned me to avoid the old spinster and stay away from her home. When I asked why, he replied simply, "*Es una bruja.*" ("She is a witch.")

My father told me that he had always suspected that she had evil powers, but hadn't any proof until his friend Juan told him how Doña Leticia had given his brother *el mal ojo* (the evil eye). My father said that soon Juan's brother became bedridden and remained that way for a month until his wife tearfully beseeched Doña Leticia and offered her cash to remove the spell.

My father also told me that Doña Leticia had a small wooden box in which she kept some sort of animal that she could manipulate to work her magic. The witch fed the animal a concoction of herbs, threads from an intended victim's clothes or strands of hair, and drops of Leticia's own blood.

I listened intently to my father's words and promised never to go near the witch's house.

About a month later, neighbors received the news that, while en route to Albuquerque with a close friend, Doña Leticia's cart had turned over and she had broken her back. She died the following day.

Because my parents were held in high regard in our community, Doña Leticia's only surviving relative, a 73-year-old brother from Taos, gave them the opportunity to buy Doña Leticia's house and land for a reduced price. None of the neighbors wanted anything to do with the place, so, since my parents had saved up a few extra dollars, they purchased Doña Leticia's small homestead with the intention of fixing it up and renting it.

Once Doña Leticia's brother had removed most of her belongings and left for Taos, my parents and I entered the house. Apparently, in his haste, the brother had disturbed a floorboard in the bedroom. I removed the board and found a small wooden box painted in a faded green patina. I retrieved the box and undid the tight twine holding the lid in place. The inside of the box was lined in red cloth and lying on the cloth was a black, coiled, and shriveled worm. I assumed that this was the animal my father had told me about.

When I showed the box to my parents, my mother immediately made the sign of the cross and ordered me to "take that thing outside!" My father followed me out of the house and around to the back. Then he gathered some old boards that were lying in the yard and built a fire. Once the fire was roaring, he threw the box into the flames. I watched the flames of the fire consume the green box and its twisted, black contents.

Many months later, after painting, fixing the plumbing, and sprucing up the property, my parents finally rented the house to an older couple from Colorado. For the first few days, they seemed to be enjoying the place, but within two weeks they had moved out. The woman said she was being bothered by horrible nightmares, and would awaken with the sense that someone was choking her.

Just a few days later, a group of family members and friends from the Chama area came to visit, so my mother offered to put them up at our house while my brother and I slept in Doña Leticia's house. I must admit I was a bit nervous about entering the house, but my parents reassured me that everything would be fine, and, after all, my brother would be with me.

That night, my brother and I went off to the old witch's house. My father said he would join us later. We spent the early part of the evening listening to an old radio, but as the night grew darker, I heard a soft crying sound coming from the bedroom. I lowered the volume on the radio to hear better, and we both clearly heard the sound of a baby crying in the bedroom. As I got up to investigate, I saw on the wall of the hallway the shadows of three tall cats—standing upright. As I approached the shadows, they glided across the wall. I stood still. Then I heard what seemed to be an argument among the cats, but they were speaking in women's voices. I ran back to the living room, grabbed my brother's hand, and dashed home.

I was shaking and sobbing when I reached our house and told my mother, in front of all our visitors, what I had experienced. My father, his brother, and my godfather decided to spend the night at the old woman's house.

Later that night, I was awakened by my father's voice. Then he and my mother grabbed blankets and set the men up on the floor of our house.

In the morning, my father told me the whole story. He said that the three men were joking and preparing their beds when they heard what sounded like a large dog scratching at the front door. My father opened the door slightly, but saw nothing. However, as he turned toward the other men, something large and dark streaked into the house through the partially opened door. All three men saw a flash of black head for the bedroom. As they followed it, they suddenly heard the loud, piercing scream of a woman.

"*Fuera de mi casa. Fuera de mi casa!*" ("Out of my house . . ."), she yelled.

Then the men saw the dark shadowy figure of a woman materialize and approach them, as a cold rush of air pushed them out of the bedroom. They all scrambled out the front door and ran to our house, and that's when my father's voice and the loud conversation of the others woke me up.

After that night, our family only ventured to Doña Leticia's house during the day. Unable and unwilling to use the house for family, my parents have rented it several times throughout the years, but inevitably the renters have left. Sometimes they would cite strange happenings, other times they claimed they saw or heard an unknown woman in the house.

Once, my parents brought a medicine man from San Juan Pueblo to perform a blessing ceremony on the house. This settled things down for a while. But we'll never know if Doña Leticia's presence has been removed, because soon after that my parents sold the house to the New Mexico Highway Department and it was razed. I hope the bulldozers destroyed Doña Leticia's evil presence along with the house. We haven't heard of any further strange occurrences taking place on the land, so I hope her power has finally gone.

THE HOUSE ON APODACA HILL

When I consider the stories of the people I have interviewed for this book, I believe that this particular interview with Patricia Camacho will prove to be the most puzzling for the reader, because of the overt malevolence and the downright tenacious nature of the ghosts. Camacho presented her story in a calm manner, never giving an emotional reaction to the bizarre atmosphere surrounding what she, her family, and friends experienced at 507 Apodaca Hill.

Stranger still—and most difficult to understand—is why she remains in this house. The mischievous incidents continue to this day. Experiencing just one sample of what Camacho goes through would send most people packing in a matter of minutes. Apparently, Camacho is a breed of woman who will stand her ground rather than forfeit her courage.

Patricia, it is my hope that you succeed.

★   ★   ★

PATRICIA'S STORY

The house I am presently renting is over 70 years old. The landlord told me that it used to be a brothel and an illegal gambling hall in the 1920s. The house is divided into two sections, with the bedrooms below ground level and the kitchen and living room above. The upper section was added in the 1950s, and solidly constructed of adobe bricks in the Pueblo style, which is very distinctive of Santa Fe.

Within the first few days of moving in—about three years ago—I had many unusual experiences. One time, when I was walking down the stairs to my bedroom, I suddenly felt a hand grab my ankle. Whoever, or whatever, it was, was trying to trip me on the stairs. I actually felt a large hand hold tight on my ankle. This sensation disappeared as soon as I struggled free.

Several days later I was not so fortunate. In the following weeks, I had many falls. My legs and arms became bruised as a result. I also experienced nights when I was awakened by the touch of fingers on my face—this happened in the daytime as well. As I was going about my housecleaning, I often felt something brush against my face. At first, I thought it was a bit of feather or a strand of spider web that was floating freely in the air and had landed on my face, but a look in the mirror revealed nothing.

Soon, the pressure of what was brushing against my face increased, and strands of my own hair would be lifted up into the air. It felt as if an invisible hand was caressing my face and hair. This

Patricia Camacho.

continued for several days and nights, but I just shook my head and tried to go about my business.

"Miko."

There were also evenings when I was sitting up in bed reading and I noticed movement at the foot of the bed. I saw and felt the blankets slide across my feet, and then saw the impression of a body sitting down on the bed. The mattress actually depressed with the circular impression of someone's behind on the comforter. As I slowly lifted the blankets to get out of bed, I clearly saw the mattress puff up, returning to its original form.

About two months ago, I was awakened in the middle of the night by my dog, Miko, barking. As I awoke, I heard the loud pounding noise of someone hitting the wall area beside my head . . . then the whole bed shook as if someone wanted me out of bed. Miko growled, and ran to the door to be let out.

Another strange phenomenon is the appearance of "cold spots" in several areas of the house. As I walk from one room to another, I often pass through an area of extreme cold, much colder than the surrounding temperature of the room I happen to be in. It seems as if there is a long vertical tube of frigid air that I pass through without warning—until I am in it.

These things happened within the first few months of moving into the house, but as the months passed, things took on a new approach. During the night, I would be awakened by a variety of noises. I would open my eyes and gaze at the darkened ceiling, listening to the sounds of bottles being moved about, and of voices of people deep in conversation. The sounds seemed to be coming from the basement. I was able to detect the source of the sounds because the house is not very large and I am familiar with the rooms.

Most nights, the voices sounded like a group of people, but on some nights, I was awakened by the harsh voice of a man and the sound of a woman responding loudly. It was difficult to make out what they were saying, even though the language was English. The voices were muffled, but the intensity and the anger were very clear. I heard these voices only at night, but both night and day I heard the sounds of bottles being moved and sometimes broken.

Sometimes, when I was in one room like the kitchen, I would hear the sound of a breaking plate or vase coming from another room. At this, Miko would run in circles and bark wildly. Then, I would run into the room expecting to see a mess of pottery on the floor. I would find only Miko, and I would have to let her out immediately, because of her extreme nervousness.

These smashing sounds could occur in any room at any time throughout the house. People who have spent the night with me have reported hearing the sounds of breaking glass and feeling both the extreme cold and weblike fingers brush against their skin. One visitor heard the sound of someone chopping wood at 3 a.m. Other visitors reported seeing framed pictures lift off their nails and crash on the floor, articles of clothing move about or disappear, and jewelry or coffee cups disappear at the turn of a head.

One day, a friend, who was enjoying a hot cup of coffee in the living room, rose from her chair and left the room for a moment. When she returned, the cup was gone. To this day we have not found the cup. Friends and family, who have spent the night, awake in the morning and reach for their clothing only to find a shirt, or a shoe, or a sock missing.

My son, Chris, visited me on two occasions, and both times he lost items of clothing. The first time, during the summer, he slept on the couch in the living room for three nights. He said that each night he felt a touch on his face or on his leg. On the last night of his stay, he just could not take it anymore. He was awakened by the feeling of being shaken violently and the sound of a man's voice yelling at him, demanding he get up and go to church. Chris was caught off guard by this experience, but got a good look at an older man with long blond, or gray-colored, hair and a moustache. This man was wearing dark clothes and soon disappeared. After that experience, my son returned to his own home.

Several months later, Chris came for another overnight stay. It was Christmastime, so I guess he felt compelled to spend a few nights— ghost or not. Each morning he told me of his unusual experiences. On the first two nights, he felt extremely cold gusts of air moving past him, and he heard a noise that he described as a bottle rolling on the floor. Not much else happened, so he began to relax.

However, during the last night of his stay, all hell broke loose. I was making my way downstairs to one of the bedrooms, and my son was watching television in the living room with Miko at his side. All of a sudden, we heard the tremendous sound of breaking glass and furniture being thrown about in the bedrooms. Miko began howling and ran to the basement. My son and I remained in our places, motionless. Then Miko's bark changed; she began barking as if someone were attacking her. Before I took one step down the stairs, the dog ran back upstairs and began running in circles. My son said he had had enough and went to a motel.

Ten minutes after my son had left the house, the sounds started up again. As usual, when I went to the bedrooms to investigate, I found nothing broken or disturbed. The only evidence to suggest that someone had been in the rooms was the strong, musky scent of a man's cologne.

My friend Jonathan, who visits often from Cochiti Pueblo, has heard the now-common noises emanating from the basement. He reports hearing a high-pitched woman's voice screaming at someone to leave her alone and the response of a man's voice, which Jonathan cannot clearly make out. Jonathan has also heard the sounds of furniture being thrown against the walls.

One night, he was awakened by having his mattress shaken violently. When he opened his eyes and sat up, a loud thumping commenced on the wall next to his head. A Native American, Jonathan wears his hair long. He told me that he has felt an invisible hand stroking his hair, and several strands have been lifted up into the air by themselves. At these times, Jonathan has distinctly felt a presence standing beside him.

Another friend, Joe, from Taos Pueblo, who is a medicine man, visited me and immediately said, "You've got something very bad in this house, Patricia."

Joe's son, Standing Deer, who was with him, said that he felt covered in a cold chill and felt hands touching him.

Joe proceeded to make a small medicine bag for me, which I now carry at all times. Joe also burned sage incense and blessed the house to clear it of its bad spirits. For a few months after that, I had no problems.

But, not long after Joe's visit, a friend came from California to spend a week with me. One afternoon she was standing in the living room while I was in the kitchen. We were conversing between the rooms when, suddenly, she did not answer. I turned toward her and saw that her eyes were as large and as round as saucers. She stood there motionless, gazing at me as if she were in shock.

Then she yelled, "Oh my God! Someone is touching me!"

I went up to her and grabbed her arm. Her skin was ice cold, and her arms were covered in goosebumps. Because of my own experiences, I knew what was happening. I spoke loudly to her, attempting to break through the fright and horror. She responded in a shaky voice.

She said that a coldness had approached her and enveloped her, petrifying her senses. Very quickly, the coldness had entered her body and soon she became hysterical, pleading with me to make the "thing" leave her alone. I hugged her and tried to settle her down. I told her to extend her hands, palms up, and I held my hands over hers—palms down. Then I concentrated and demanded that whatever was taking over her body leave her. Soon after that, I felt the cold chill creep from my fingertips up my arms and throughout my body. Seconds later, the coldness left me and we hugged each other again.

At times, I have considered seeking the help of a medium, perhaps to perform an exorcism, but I just haven't gotten around to it. A recent incident, however, may have convinced me. I was sitting at the kitchen table mulling over my thoughts, when suddenly one of the lower cabinet doors swung open and a glass baking dish flew out. I watched as the dish sped across the floor and hit the opposite wall with a tremendous crash, sending shards of glass in all directions. The sight was mentally staggering. I could not imagine how the door had opened or the dish had flown out. The dish had been set on the lower shelf of the cabinet. Immediately after the dish shattered, Miko began barking and ran to the front door to be let out.

I felt it was time to find out more about this house, so I asked my landlord, Hank, if he or his family had experienced anything unusual when they had lived here. He told me his children had used the basement for their bedrooms, and they had placed a small television set on top of one of the dressers. He said that often the children would run upstairs shouting that a man had walked into the room and turned off the TV. Then, this strange man simply walked into the wall and disappeared.

At other times, his children told of being awakened in the middle of the night by skeletons walking about on their beds. Like the strange man, the skeletons also disappeared through the wall. Hank's oldest son corroborated these statements.

Hank admits that he too heard loud noises, felt the cold spots throughout the house, and had "lost" various items.

Just two nights ago, while sitting in the upstairs living room, Miko started barking, ran to the bedroom, and jumped up on my bed. She continued barking, facing the wall where my pillow is. I saw nothing unusual. Then she stopped barking and just stared at the wall—as though she did not want to miss anything that might happen. Suddenly, she began to bark uncontrollably, and try as I might, I could not stop her. Then she dashed to the living room door and scratched to be let out. She spent the remainder of the night outside, refusing to enter the house.

Well, I'm not sure what to do. Considering all that has taken place, I guess people might think I'm crazy to stay at the house. I'll just stay put for the time being. I enjoy the house and the neighborhood, so a ghost or two is not going to make me start looking for a new place anytime soon.

★   ★   ★

Jonathan Loretto is a young man from the Cochiti Pueblo, about 20 miles south of Santa Fe. He designs and produces stunningly beautiful pieces of silver and turquoise jewelry. At the home of Patricia Camacho, Jonathan maintains a workbench and jewelry-making studio in the basement. He believes the spirits he encountered here intended no harm. You be the judge.

JONATHAN'S STORY

Patricia Camacho and I have been good friends for a long time, so when she offered her basement area for me to use as a workshop, I jumped at the chance. Although I did not notice anything out of the ordinary at first, Patricia informed me that there might be some strange noises or goings-on. But I was not expecting anything paranormal—or ghostly—to happen.

About a year ago, I was down in the basement working on a delicate woman's silver ring when I felt a presence in the room. I thought that it might be Patricia paying me a visit, so I turned away from my work and glanced around the room. I saw no one, so I went back to work.

A few minutes later, I felt the pressure of a hand caressing the back of my head. Immediately, I stopped working and sat motionless on my chair. I knew no one was in the room. Tied loosely with a strand of yarn, my long hair hung down my back. As I sat there, I again felt the pressure of a hand on my hair, and then I felt—and saw—some strands of my hair rise up into the air as if someone were lifting them.

Quickly, I stood up and moved away from the workbench, but again strands of my hair floated up. I waved my right hand to slap what was teasing me. Then I ran toward the stairs leading to the living room. Halfway up the stairs, I felt something grab hold of a large mass of my hair and jerk my head backwards. Without a moment's thought I pulled away, and quickly made my way up the stairs to the living room and out the door! I waited outside until Patricia drove up to the house and saw me standing by the fence.

When I told Patricia of my experience, she admitted that other visitors had been similarly accosted.

After that night, I had second thoughts about working in the basement, but I tried to put them aside. Then, one day, in the middle of my work I stopped to go upstairs for a drink. As I made my way back down the basement stairs, I suddenly felt a chilling coldness descend upon me, and I clearly heard the sound of loud, harsh laughter. It was the laughter of a mad, hysterical woman, and it was coming from the basement. I ran back upstairs and outside to the comfort of the warm afternoon sun.

A few minutes later I returned to the house but decided to stay in the living room and watch television—something to distract me. But as I sat on the couch, I again felt the cold chill and knew someone—or something—was in the room with me. The curtains were drawn open, filling the room with daylight. I looked in the direction where I thought the presence was and distinctly saw one of the couch cushions slowly depress. . . as if someone were sitting down on it. That was all I needed. I jumped up, did an "about face," and headed for the door.

Another curious incident occurred when I stayed overnight at the house. I had removed my favorite "L.A. Raiders" T-shirt and draped it over a nearby chair, then went to sleep on the couch. The next morning, I reached for the shirt, but it was gone. I searched everywhere. There had been no visitors, and I had locked the doors myself. I never found the shirt.

These days, I stay in the house only when someone else is there. I don't even want to think about the ghosts starting up again. I don't know what took place to make them hang around at the house, but I just wish they would go away.

GUADALUPE AND LA LLORONA

Guadalupe was born to a family that consisted of her parents and five older brothers. Because of the harsh conditions of rural life in the 1920s, and the lack of proper medical care, three of her brothers had died by the time she celebrated her eighth birthday.

At the time of this interview, Guadalupe was 70 years old and in good health. She told me of many childhood experiences in Santa Fe, and she described the difficulties of daily existence without the aid of a telephone, automobile, or washing machine. As of seven years ago, Guadalupe was still practicing her "gifts" as curandera (healer) and midwife. To this day, the elder Hispanic people of the city seek her counsel. During my interview, we sat in her kitchen sipping coffee.

Guadalupe clasped her hands daintily in her lap and closed her hazel eyes in concentration, accenting the tiny wrinkles of her face. Then she told the story of her encounter with one of New Mexico's most famous spirits, La Llorona (The Weeping Woman).

★   ★   ★

GUADALUPE'S STORY

It happened one hot day in 1931, when I went with my brothers and a few neighborhood friends to the Santa Fe River. Even though it was four miles away, we didn't mind the walk because we knew that the refreshing cool river awaited us. Before leaving, I gathered up my white puppy, Peewee, who had been resting in the shade of a piñon tree, and then ran to catch up with the others.

When we reached the river, my brothers began throwing small stones into the swirling eddies. I placed Peewee on the ground and joined in the game. After a few minutes, the sun beating down on my exposed head made me nauseous and I sought shade under some nearby willow trees. My puppy joined me as I dug up the reddish-brown mud from the water's edge to make "mud people." I fashioned the bodies out of mud, used twigs for the arms and legs, leaves for dresses, and small, flat stones for boys' hats. I could see and hear my brothers and their friends laughing and carrying on, but I was content to play house with my mud dolls and my puppy. Suddenly, while I was arranging the dolls in a circle, a strong gust of wind enveloped me and the surrounding cattails and tall weeds swayed violently. Then I heard the sweet tinkling sound of bells. Captivated by the ringing, I stopped playing and listened.

As I turned to tell my brothers about the bells, I noticed that they had also heard the sounds, for they were standing silently just gazing at the sky. The sound of the bells got louder and louder, and my puppy, who stood at my side, began to bark and then ran off into a large clump of cattails. I tried to go after him, but discovered that I could not move a muscle. I was mesmerized by the sound of the bells for at least a minute.

Then the tinkle of the bells subsided, and in the sudden silence, I heard a woman gently sobbing and calling, "*Mija, mija.*" ("Daughter, daughter.") Suddenly, I was able to move, so I stood up and called to my brothers. They rushed to my side and took me by the hand. From the feeling of fear that gripped me, I knew this was something evil. We all raced home.

I soon learned that my brothers and the other children had also heard the woman crying and beseeching. But to them she had called out, "*Mis hijos, mis hijos.*" ("My sons, my sons.")

Once I was safe at home, I realized that I had lost my puppy, and I cried because I was certain it had drowned. After we explained what had happened, my mother said we had done the right thing by leaving.

From what we told her, she believed something evil had happened. My parents decided to make a visit to the spot where we had heard the weeping. I was apprehensive about returning, but at the same time, I was anxious to find my puppy.

As my father was getting the horses ready, I heard my mother whisper to him, "*La Llorona.*" ("The Weeping Woman.")

When we arrived at the river, the sun was hanging heavy and tired in the western sky, and as we approached the river's edge, we all heard the woman's voice and felt the sense of urgency as she cried loudly for her children, "*Mis hijos, mis hijos.*"

My father called out to her, "*¿Quien es. En donde estas. Que quieres?*" ("Who are you? Where are you? What do you want?")

He received no reply, so my mother shouted, "*Deje a mis hijos solos, hija del demonio!*" ("Leave my children alone, daughter of the devil!") Then she made the sign of the cross and called to us, "*Vamonos!*" ("Let's go!") And off we went.

But in our haste, my mother's horse, which she and I were riding, tripped, and I fell off into the mud, hands first. As both of my parents came to help me, one of my brothers shouted for us to look at the river. We all turned and saw the apparition of the woman walking toward us with her arms outstretched.

The setting sun had cast a deep red, orange, gold glow on the river, and we clearly saw this woman walking on its surface. My father yelled for us to hurry, and we quickly made our way back home. As soon as we got back, my parents alerted the neighborhood to the danger at the river. They told everyone what we had witnessed and warned people to keep a close watch on their children.

Most people think La Llorona makes her presence known only at night, but I am here to tell everyone that evil can choose any time to come forth. To this day, I clearly recall that phantom woman walking on the water and crying for her children.

CANYON ROAD

Before the arrival of the conquistadores, Canyon Road was already a well-traveled trail. Used by the Native Americans of the Rio Grande Valley, it was the principal route to the Pecos Pueblo.

Later, Canyon Road served as a route for firewood-laden burros arriving from the surrounding hills to their destination on the Santa Fe Plaza. Presently, this former footpath is the center of the city's art colony.

★   ★   ★

William Auclair, once owner of Night Sky Gallery at 826 Canyon Road, presented me with this unusual account of his family's experience with a "past occupant." The current property now houses the Rod Hubble Gallery.

WILLIAM AUCLAIR'S STORY

In 1986, I bought this house from an obstetrician, Dr. Moskowitz. My wife and I intended to remodel the interior of the house and use the front portion, facing the street, as an art gallery, maintaining the rear for our private residence. Prior to our purchase, the house had been occupied by renters for close to five years, but before he rented it out, the doctor had lived in the rear of the house and used a large front bedroom as a birthing room.

Two years after we had completed our remodeling efforts, Dr. Moskowitz paid us a visit. During our conversation the doctor casually remarked, "Have you had or heard anything unusual in the house?"

William Auclair.

I said, "Like what? I'm not sure what you mean."

Then he explained that the renters had complained from time to time that they heard human voices and unusual, unexplained sounds in some of the rooms. When I questioned him further, he admitted that the renters had insisted the house was haunted.

This made me think of some of the strange sounds my wife and I had heard. So I told Dr. Moskowitz about the "voice." Often we had heard the sound of a woman's voice speaking a mix of Spanish and broken English. The voice came from the old birthing room. Usually between 3 and 4 a.m. we'd hear our dog, Neema, who never barks, begin to growl and walk nervously towards the door of the room. Then, minutes later, we'd hear the woman's voice.

This scenario happens so often that we have grown to expect it every week or so. The sounds and Neema's growling always wake us up, and either my wife or I open the door and peer into the empty, darkened room. Immediately the voice stops, and for the remainder of the night things remain quiet. Strangely, we've noticed that we hear the voice only during the winter months. We also get the impression that the spirit is not contentious or malicious. In fact, the voice is quite soothing and rather gentle and calm. I imagine the spirit only wants to make her presence known.

The doctor did not offer any insight or information about the ghostly voice, but I did learn something more about it from a visitor. One day, an older Hispanic gentleman came in, and we began a polite conversation about my artwork. Then he told me he had once been a resident of our gallery–home and that his great-grandmother had died in the very room from which we heard the gentle voice. He said that after his great-grandmother had died, he and his brothers and sisters didn't want to sleep in her room because they could see her spirit materialize and it would try to talk to them. Being children, they pulled the blankets up over their heads and yelled for their parents.

At this point I stopped him and told him about the "voice." He did not seem surprised, but at that moment, we were interrupted by some customers asking about a piece of framed art. He bid me farewell, and I have not seen him since.

I'm convinced that things are not always as they seem when a person dies. I don't believe that death is necessarily the end of a person's existence. There are moments when I feel the close presence of someone in the room with me. Even though I bought, and hold title to, this building, I know that I do not own it. I believe that the original owner still holds a spiritual claim on it and my family and I are simply its current caretakers.

THE LEGAL TENDER

Constructed in 1881, the Legal Tender was originally known as The Annex Saloon, and much later, in the mid 1950s, it was called the Pink Garter Saloon. Over the years it has enjoyed a reputation as a dance hall, vaudeville theatre, general store, and fine restaurant. Sadly, it is now closed.

Various owners contributed much to modifying the building, adding priceless works of art, Victorian period furnishings, and a hand-carved cherrywood bar imported from Germany in 1894. It was renamed The

Legal Tender in 1969, and the American Room—with its distinctive tinned ceiling, train-station windows, and antique decorations—was added.

Throughout the years, ghosts have been observed nonchalantly meandering among the guests. The apparitions include the "Man in Black," reputed to have picked up a stray bullet during a gambling dispute; the "Lady in White," who wears an elegant, white Victorian gown; and a child in a long dress. The origins of the woman and the child are unknown, but the "Lady in White" has been seen by both owners and patrons gliding up the steps toward the balcony, and the child has been observed by several patrons sitting on the steps.

EMMA CORDOVA'S STORY

I have worked at the Legal Tender restaurant for nearly 15 years and have experienced several encounters with what I call ghosts. One night, after a busy day of waiting tables, I was helping Bertha, the bartender, clean up the bar area. As I finished wiping off a table, a strange feeling came over me, causing me to pause and look at the front door. At that moment, I noticed Bertha, staring in the same direction. Simultaneously, we saw the same unexplainable sight.

A short man—a stranger— drifted in from the outside and nonchalantly passed between us, making his way around the bar counter to the soda and water dispensers. Without saying a word, he took a clean glass, drew himself a Coca-Cola, and drank it. Then he placed the empty glass on the bar and walked past us into the dining room where he simply evaporated into the air.

Although Bertha and I were baffled and shaken by the experience, we managed to observe some important details. The man was dressed in the style of a bygone era, wearing a top hat and black suit. However, he had no face! The area where his face should have been was a blur. He was not wearing a bandanna or any theatrical mask; the face area simply had no flesh or bone, as if someone had taken an eraser and rubbed out his nose, mouth, and eyes.

Bertha and I decided not to share this experience with anyone for fear we'd be accused of drinking on the job—or worse.

Throughout the years, I have seen this scenario played out three more times, but every time I was alone. The man entered, took his drink, then disappeared into the atmosphere of the dining room.

On two other occasions, I saw a different ghostly figure. One day, as I was working with several other employees in one of the smaller dining areas in the "Parlor Room," I suddenly caught the scent of a flowery perfume. We all smelled it, and I soon learned that this scent heralded the appearance of the "Woman in White."

Later, when I was alone in the bar, I turned around and faced the stairs that led to the second-floor balcony. There I saw a woman, about 5'5" tall, with a full face, standing on the fourth step. She stared at me for less than a minute, then turned and leisurely ascended the stairs. At the top of the stairs, she changed into a misty fog and disappeared. As with the faceless man, the woman, with waist-length black hair and wearing a long-sleeved white gown, never said a word.

I have experienced one other unexplainable occurrence. One morning, about a week after one of my encounters with the faceless man, my husband and I arrived at the restaurant to do some general cleaning up. As I was mopping on the first floor, my husband, who had gone upstairs, called out, "Emma, come here quick!" I dropped the mop and raced up the short flight of stairs. I found my husband standing beside a small round table. On the table was a dinner plate with a freshly cooked New York steak and a baked potato with melting butter, sour cream, and chives. Steam was still rising from the food. A glass of red wine and a glass of water stood like sentinels beside the plate.

We decided that somehow an intruder had entered and cooked himself a nice meal, so we dashed to the kitchen. As soon as I entered the room, I knew it had not been used recently—the grill and the oven were stone cold and clean. I got goosebumps and a chill ran down my spine. We never learned where the food had come from or who had cooked it.

These experiences puzzled and frightened me. I'm still afraid of what I experienced. I still feel a chilling sensation whenever I recall them.

RAYMOND TAYLOR'S STORIES

I am Raymond Taylor, the current owner of the Legal Tender restaurant in Lamy, New Mexico. I have owned the restaurant for over seven years, and although I have not personally witnessed ghosts or spirits, I have sound reasons to believe they exist and inhabit this building. Perhaps they are waiting for the appropriate moment to appear to me—as they have done to patrons and some of my employees.

I recall the experience of one former employee, Joe, a dishwasher and janitor, which happened in the winter of 1987. One evening at about seven, I began my daily task of closing out the bar cash register. Everyone except for Joe and I had gone home. We were the only "living" beings in the entire building. Joe, who was about 50 years old at the time, was working at the opposite end of the restaurant, in the hall area between the kitchen and the storage section.

As I was working, I suddenly heard the sound of approaching footsteps. I turned to see Joe, mop and bucket in hand, coming towards me. He was pale and unusually jittery.

Haltingly, he asked, "How long have you been in the bar?"

The Legal Tender co-owners, Amy Cort and Raymond Taylor.

I replied, "About five minutes, why?"

He said, "Oh, nothing," and returned to the kitchen. He quickly finished cleaning up and immediately went home.

Joe worked three more nights then quit.

It wasn't until about a week later that I learned of Joe's strange experience. I was talking to a few other employees and found out that that night, as Joe was mopping the hall floor, he felt a shove, as if someone had pushed him out of their way. He assumed it was me and never looked up. But, when he came into the bar and saw me busy at the cash register, he realized I could not have pushed him. Since we were the only people in the building, Joe concluded that a spirit had made contact with him.

Babe, my general manager, told me of another spiritual encounter. One night, while replacing a roll of paper towels in the men's bathroom, he glanced to the side of the room and saw the disembodied head of a woman materialize. He said that the apparition hovered, suspended in the air for about 15 seconds, then slowly disappeared as he stared at it.

I learned of another ghostly meeting when I met and conversed with two regular patrons from the nearby El Dorado community. They told me that they continually chose to sit in a specific section of the dining room because they hoped to see the spirits again. I asked for an explanation.

Apparently, one Sunday evening, as they were having dinner, the woman excused herself to visit the ladies' room. When she returned, she told her husband about the extraordinary couple she had seen as she was coming back to their table. The woman was dressed in a long-sleeved white dress, and had long dark hair hanging loosely down her back. She was accompanied by a Hispanic man with a moustache who wore a dark suit. Because of their unusual dress and stately appearances, the woman who had observed them decided to take a closer look. So as she passed the curious couple, she turned her head in their direction. They were gone. They had disappeared in the time it takes to blink an eye.

CASA REAL

There are presently three senior health-care centers in the city of Santa Fe. Built in 1985, Casa Real, at 501 Galisteo Street, is a 112-bed convalescent center.

As most of the older city residents can attest, the land on which Casa Real stands was originally the location of the State of New Mexico's penitentiary graveyard. Various criminals and "outlaws" of the Old West were incarcerated at the penitentiary. Murderers were executed by hanging, and because they were usually denied burial in consecrated cemeteries, they were buried at the penitentiary graveyard.

DAVID RODRIGUEZ'S STORY

Since the day I began my employment at Casa Real, I was ill at ease and uncomfortable whenever I was inside the building. I felt a strange atmosphere of uneasiness about the place—like there was a heavy pressure on my shoulders or a pair of invisible eyes watching my every move.

David Rodriguez.

Nurses, nurses' aides, patients, visitors, and office staff all have stories to tell about this place. Most of the stories and personal experiences regarding Casa Real have occurred during the night—probably because of the quiet, eerie silence. Some of the nurses have approached me concerning strange, unexplainable, loud clapping noises; at other times, people have reported hearing the moans of a person in great pain coming from an empty room. I've come to regard these numerous experiences of the medical staff as a clear indication that something very strange is going on in this place.

One morning, two night nurses were visibly shaken as they recounted to me their experience of the night before. They said that while walking the corridor between the north and south side of the facility, one of the nurses, Nurse Newport, decided to pay her respects to a deceased patient she had known. The coroner had been called minutes earlier to remove the body. As she entered the room, nothing seemed out of the ordinary: the windows were closed and the curtains were drawn. But as she viewed the lifeless body on the bed, suddenly a crisp, chilling air enveloped her. Although the doors and windows were shut tight, the rosary pinned to the wall above the bed swung from side to side as if moving on its own power. Somewhat hysterical, Nurse Newport ran to the nurses' station, where a fellow nurse tried to calm her down.

When the coroner arrived, the other nurse, Nurse Parra, packed the deceased patient's few personal articles into a small cardboard box for the family. But about two hours later, after the room had been emptied, the nurse call light above the door went on. The nurse who had cleaned the room went to investigate; finding nothing, she reset the call button. About 30 minutes later, the light came on again. Thinking there might be a short in the wiring, the nurse returned to the empty room, unplugged the call button and cord, and placed them on the freshly made bed for the maintenance personnel.

Not more than 10 minutes later, the light above the deceased patient's room came on again. This time, both nurses were very shaken, so several minutes later they went together to the room to unscrew the lightbulb. While one nurse was up on a chair, Nurse Newport suddenly turned and ran to the nurses' station, yelling as she went, "Something grabbed me!"

Before the nurse on the chair could react, she felt a blanket of chilling air envelop her legs. She jumped down and immediately returned to the station where both nurses remained all night.

Two years ago, we admitted an elderly Native American woman from a nearby pueblo. As she was wheeled into the lobby, she asked her family to pause. She looked around, and with the sound of discomfort in her voice, announced that there were "bad spirits in this place." She resolved to get out as soon as possible, and a few days later, she was transferred to another facility.

These strange paranormal experiences are not isolated. For a long time incidents of moaning, strange noises, and other ghostly phenomena have regularly been taking place in empty rooms on the north and south wings.

Recently, one of our patients had a Native American visitor. This woman visitor asked to speak with the administrator about something very important, so I met with her. She informed me that she felt a distinctive atmosphere of unearthly beings seized and held within the walls of Casa Real. "You have a lot of spirits in here," she stated. "I will take care of them if you want."

I told her that I was interested in her assessment and would like to hear more about how she would rid the building of its "spirits." She then said that she would return in a few days with the materials she needed and perform the ritual.

Although I was unsure of what to expect, I agreed, and in the rush of daily work, soon forgot about our brief meeting.

Four days later, the woman returned and met me in my office—ready to perform the ritual. She said that I would have to be still and speak only when she gave me the signal. I nodded my head in agreement. Then she brought out small bundles of herbs from her purse and a leather pouch that she called her "medicine bag."

She burned the herb bundles in an ashtray and, after reciting a prayer and petitions, drew from her bag a collection of small stones of various colors and shapes. Again she chanted a prayer and burned more herbs.

Next, she handed me a candle, a book of matches, and a copper ring. She instructed me to burn the candle and to set the copper ring over and around the lit candle. After I had done this, she blew out the candle and presented me with both the candle and the copper ring. She told me to light the candle again at the next full moon and allow it to burn itself out. Then, at the following full moon, I was to take the copper ring and bury it in the inner courtyard of the facility. I thanked her, and she left.

For days I kept both the candle and the copper ring in my desk, occasionally glancing at them. When the full moon arrived, I did as the woman had requested. I felt it couldn't hurt. So, with the assistant director of nurses at my side, I lit the candle and let it burn itself out. For the following full moon, we located a suitable place and buried the copper ring in the courtyard garden. As of that date neither my staff nor I have experienced any further strange or ghostly phenomena. I hope that whatever is buried deep within the foundations of this building stays quiet and at peace—at least until the day I move on.

THE LADY IN ROOM 222

Although it was a year ago, it is still very difficult for me to think about the experience I had at Casa Real. I do not want to experience anything like that again. Try as I might, I have not been able to erase it from my mind, and I definitely believe there is reason to wonder about the existence of life after death.

When I was the facility director of nurses at Casa Real, I supervised the nurses, verified that the patients were on their proper medications, and ensured that doctors' orders were followed. Due to a shortage of nurses, I often worked the night shift to make sure the facility was properly staffed.

Three days prior to the night of my experience, an elderly woman with terminal cancer was admitted. Although in much pain, the woman was lucid, aware of her surroundings, and had a clear understanding of her prognosis. When dealing with the staff, she attempted to disguise the inevitability of her death. We soon learned that this lady had led an active and social lifestyle before her illness befell her.

The only time she complained was when we had to change her bed linen. The nurses' aides had to gather around her bed and turn or lift her while the sheets were changed. In her dear, sweet manner, she always apologized for her short moans of discomfort.

On the third day of her stay, the woman abruptly refused to take food. When I arrived later that evening, I immediately learned of her grave condition. A few hours before I had come on duty, she had regressed into a comatose state. The woman was now placed on close observation and intravenous therapy in order to keep her hydrated. But our efforts were in vain, and a few hours later she lapsed into a deep coma with no response to outside stimuli. From my many years of experience, I knew that once a terminal cancer patient reaches this stage, death soon follows.

I remember the details of that night vividly and completely. I recall specifically the manner in which her hair was combed, the pattern of her nightgown, and especially her hands—marked with dark blue and purple blotches from the numerous needle pricks.

Not long after she had passed away, the paramedics from St. Vincent Hospital arrived, and I was called on the intercom. I proceeded from my office towards her room, number 222, but I stopped at the end of the hall and watched the paramedics take her draped body out of the room on a stretcher. I just stood there and watched, not wanting to interfere with the process.

As soon as they left her room and turned into the hallway, I noticed the nurse call light above the door to her room came on. There was no reason for the staff to turn the light on in an empty room. I thought in their haste, the paramedics might have dropped the call button on the floor, triggering the light. I waited for someone to reset the button. Strangely enough, no one did.

But stranger still was what happened next. As the stretcher passed each patient's room, the nurse call light above the doors lit up. I could not move a muscle. I stood there, overcome with amazement and fright at the sight of the lights going on as the woman's body passed each door.

As the stretcher reached the nurses' station at the opposite end of the hall, I could watch no longer. I felt the hair on the back of my neck stand on end. I yelled to the paramedics to look at the lights, but they did not grasp my meaning. Their eyes were focused on the exit door ahead of them.

Such a great fear came over me—I think I became hysterical, because I rushed out of the building into the parking lot. There, I gathered my senses, took a deep breath, and watched the ambulance drive away into the darkness. All I could do was look up at the moon and stars. I knew I had just had an experience with ghosts.

FLORENCITA AND EL ZORRILLO

FLORENCITA'S STORY

My experience with the supernatural happened when I was only 14 years of age. My personal experience with evil left me with no doubt that I will carry the aftereffects of my encounter throughout my adult life.

It began innocently enough one warm afternoon, when my brothers and I decided to follow the Santa Fe riverbank from our neighborhood as it made its way through the landscape southward. We wanted to see how far we could travel. It was my idea, but my brothers were elated.

"Sure, we might even find some gold or something," said my brother Vicente.

My brother Fidel located a large tree that had been struck by lightening, and we broke off branches to make walking sticks. Then with Oso, our dog, we set off on our "big adventure."

After following the river's winding curves and valleys for over two hours, we came upon a thicket of cottonwood trees.

When I joined my brothers, who had gathered on the riverbank, I saw a structure on the other side of the river. We decided to investigate. We crossed the river at its narrowest point, using large rock boulders that had been lodged in the debris as stepping-stones.

Once on the other side, I saw that the structure was an old abandoned adobe house. Its earthen walls lay in a large crumbling rubble on the ground, but the half-collapsed chimney and part of the roof were still intact. So we climbed onto the roof and threw pebbles towards the river.

My brother Gregorio said, "I think I know whose house this is. It was the witch's, Diego Blanco, 'El Zorrillo.' Remember the story about him?"

We all knew the story because my father and his friends inevitably brought up the subject whenever they gathered together for a late night song and drink.

EL ZORRILLO

Diego Blanco was a man in his late 50s who had built his home on the outskirts of the city soon after he had arrived from the eastern part of the state. He told the few people he chose to talk to that he was from the Mora Valley area.

He was tall, and had a large streak of light gray hair that started on the left side of his forehead and ended behind his left ear. Another peculiar, and not very welcoming, trait was his strong unpleasant, unwashed body odor. My father always referred to him as El Zorrillo (The Skunk). Because his reputation as a practitioner of witchcraft was well known throughout Santa Fe, he was not welcomed in the city. So he settled further down the river.

Soon after El Zorrillo's arrival, he befriended a young Indian, Eliseo, from the Tesuque Pueblo. Eliseo helped El Zorrillo build his home. Several months later, when Eliseo did not show up for the pueblo corn dance ceremony, the other members of the pueblo decided something had happened to him.

The pueblo members were very concerned, and many people, both Spanish and Indian, rode out on horseback to search the surrounding mountains. They found nothing . . . no evidence of Eliseo.

Then, one morning, many months later, a woman and her two grandchildren climbed to the top of a small mesa near the pueblo looking for herbs. There they found Eliseo's partially decomposed body. My father told us that the body had been painted with some sort of black paint and his hair was covered in an offensive-smelling sap or juice that had hardened. Because the body was missing two fingers on each hand, the pueblo people claimed that Eliseo had been tortured and killed in devotion to the devil. Everyone immediately assumed that El Zorrillo was responsible for the gruesome deed.

Because my father traded with the Tesuque natives, they asked him to join them in confronting El Zorrillo. On horseback, the men followed the river for several miles, eventually coming upon the grove of cottonwoods and the house. Dressed only in trousers, El Zorrillo came to the door and yelled every known obscenity at them.

He looked straight into the eyes of one of Eliseo's uncles and shouted in Spanish, "Sons of the great demon, remove your rotted bodies and filthy animals from my property!"

As he screamed, his face became twisted with rage and large globs of foam appeared at the corners of his beastly mouth. He was so overwhelmed with anger that his words became muffled and indistinguishable. At one point, he began spitting at the men in an animal-like manner. Then he moved to the outside wall of his house and began slapping his hands against the wall, calling out the names of Lucifer, Satan, and other dark angels from hell.

When one of Eliseo's uncles picked up a dead branch and threw it at El Zorrillo, the men gathered their courage and made a dash towards the madman. They were able to overpower him. As they wrestled with him and got a good whiff of his body, the men learned why he was called The Skunk. Although there was no visible evidence of blood, my father had worked in a pork-processing plant, so he immediately recognized the familiar putrid odor of rotted pig's blood. He could also smell the stale stench of urine.

The men managed to bind El Zorrillo securely. Then the men entered the house. In spite of the dimness inside (the windows were covered with gunnysacks), my father found, hanging on the south wall, a wooden crucifix. It was about four feet by four feet and painted black and red, with a human finger nailed to each end of the cross—Eliseo's missing fingers. The putrid smell of the house became so offensive that the men finally had to run outside. Then they discovered that El Zorrillo had escaped—rope and all. The next morning about 20 or 30 people from the pueblo went to the house and burned it, reciting prayers to disperse the evil El Zorrillo had brought with him. That was the last anyone ever saw or heard of El Zorrillo.

Because we knew the story so well, my brothers and I were convinced that we had stumbled upon the ruins of Diego Blanco's home, but the bright sunlight of the afternoon and the cooing of the desert doves made it seem like just another old adobe ruin. We didn't feel threatened by its evil history, and we began rummaging among the rubble. Pushing aside burnt boards and twisted metal, we occasionally disturbed a lizard. Fidel found an old shoe and threw it at me, bopping me on the head. I remember Fidel saying that the old shoe belonged to El Zorrillo and it would follow me home. Then my younger brother yelled that he had found something.

We joined him at a mound of broken blue glass, and he pointed with his walking stick at a small black book. As we examined it, we saw that most of the pages were burned and covered in red mud. About 20 pages, written in longhand, remained intact. Fidel wiped off the mud and examined it carefully. He told us it contained instructions on witchcraft. We took his word for it, and swore not to tell our parents. Fidel took charge of the book and said he would take it to the church and sprinkle holy water on it. With grave authority, he told us that the holy water would conquer any evil left in it. We all agreed and promised not to tell anyone—not even our friends.

I whistled for Oso and we began our trek home. On the return trip, Fidel stopped and read some of the pages to himself. He told us they were instructions for summoning a spirit. My younger brother asked him to stop reading because the sun was beginning to set and he was getting scared. Fidel put the book away and we proceeded home.

The next day, Fidel told me he had taken the book to the St. Francis Cathedral, sprinkled holy water on it, and placed it behind the altar. Later, I learned that he and my younger brother Vicente had taken the book behind some haystacks and read it in secret. Fidel had never gone to the cathedral. But I did not find this out until one terrifying night about a week after we had found the book.

My parents had to go to a wake in the small town of Chamita, north of Santa Fe, and left us in charge of our baby sister. That night, Fidel brought out the book and told us he would entertain us by reading it. At first I was angry, but my curiosity got the better of me.

Fidel read a passage. It instructed that there should be two windows at opposite ends of the room. Since the room we had gathered in had the windows, we decided to follow the instructions. We opened the windows, and Fidel read aloud some strange prayers and the names of archaic angels. Next, my brother Daniel wrote the foreign symbols in salt on the floor. Then we just sat there and waited. When nothing happened, we laughed nervously and joked about the mess on the floor.

I got up to go to the kitchen to give Oso the soup bones my mother had left for him. Just as I was reaching for a kerosene lamp I heard a strange noise outside. I froze. Oso was barking and growling and scratching wildly at the back door. The sound, like a low cracking of thunder, continued, but it was a clear star-filled night without a cloud in the sky. Then, a strong wind billowed the curtains and everything in the room shook. Suddenly, we heard the sound of a man screaming, and the cracking noise got louder.

We were so frightened that we ran under the table. The curtains swayed wildly from side to side, rose to the ceiling and fell. Oso had stopped barking and scratching, but the chilling screams increased, ending in mad laughter. We cried and prayed at the same time. My brother held my baby sister close as we covered our faces with our arms. The screams continued, increasing in intensity. It was awful.

The kerosene lamps flew off the tables and crashed onto the floor. Kerosene oil spilled everywhere; we were bathed in it. But somehow the house did not catch on fire. I peeked over my arms and caught the image of a large shadow of a human being standing in the middle of the room.

I yelled, "It's the devil!"

The image had very long hair flying all around its head, but in the darkness, I could not make out the facial features. Then, this evil-looking figure raised its left hand up over its head and threw its head back, letting out the most awful scream I had ever heard . . . or could imagine. We were all crying loudly and uncontrollably as another blood-curdling scream came from this thing. The windows shattered and slivers of glass flew in all directions.

Suddenly, everything stopped. The wind, the screams—everything came to a complete halt. We were praying, saying the Our Father, the Hail Mary, and any prayer we could make up. Our arms and faces were covered with dirt, tears, and glittering shards of glass. But the stress of the experience had taken its toll, and we soon fell asleep.

I'm not sure how much time elapsed before the sound of our parents' footsteps and voices awakened us. We ran to the door shouting and talking at once. After seeing our tear-stained faces, my mother cried in distress and shook me, asking what had happened.

We regained our composure and described the book, the ritual, and the demon spirit that we had conjured up from hell. My parents could not hide their shock as they entered the house and saw its condition. The strong scent of sulfur overpowered the smell of kerosene.

Then my father lit a lamp and held it up, and we clearly saw the damage. The curtains that my mother had laboriously sewn hung in shreds, and strips of curtain fabric littered the floor. But, most frightening of all, were the large claw marks etched deeply into the walls. It appeared as if a large, cat-like animal had savagely dragged its claws across the walls. Even pieces of glass left in the windows had vicious scratches on them.

That night we all stayed at my uncle Raphael's small two-bedroom adobe. We were cramped, but safe. It was difficult to erase from our minds the image we had seen earlier, and the stench of sulfur lingered on our clothes. My father lit a candle and placed a small *santo* (statue of a saint) of the *Virgen de Dolores* by our bedside. Eventually we were lulled to sleep by our parents' soft voices as they prayed the rosary. I vividly remember the closeness of the family and the yellow glow of the bouncing candlelight in the small room.

The following morning, accompanied by relatives and neighbors, we returned to our home. A priest came along to bless the house and remove the remains of the book. We searched every corner of the house, but never found the book. My mother opened the back door, then rushed back in, crying that the devil had killed our dog.

Slumped against the side of the house, with an expression of terror frozen on its face, was Oso's lifeless body. His mouth was partially open, exposing the teeth on one side of his face. He looked as if he had been growling. The strangest thing about Oso's body was that when he was alive, he had a beautiful red-brown coat, but now, after his brush with terror, his entire coat had turned a light gray.

As I reached out to stroke my dog, my father held me back and said, "It is better for you not to touch him. He suffered a lot, and we cannot be sure that the evil influence is not still on him."

We all cried for our dog.

Later that same day, my uncles built a large bonfire and tossed into the flames every bit of evidence that remained from our experience . . . including the lifeless body of my dog.

Now, as an adult woman, I think back to that time and sadly reflect on the faces gathered around the fire. I will never forget that night as long as I live. Never.

TEN THOUSAND WAVES

Located three-and-a-half miles from downtown Santa Fe, Ten Thousand Waves is a health spa with hot tubs, modeled after the hot springs resorts of Japan. The following story, related to me by the owner, Duke Klauch, gives much food for thought.

★   ★   ★

DUKE'S STORY

Six years ago I bought this property, known as Rancho Elisa. At that time, it was elevated land covered in piñon and juniper trees, and it included a house and horse corral. Because of its isolation and raw beauty, this piece of land would be the perfect setting for my Japanese-style spa. The main road was the only trace of civilization in this verdant mountain spot.

When I purchased the property it was my understanding that it belonged to the Zinn family. The Zinns had constructed the house before the birth of their daughter, Elizabeth. Since its construction, the

Zinns had made a few improvements. When their daughter grew up, she married, and moved away.

Gradually, the mother became ill. She died and was buried somewhere on the mountain. Upon the death of her mother, Elizabeth returned to the property and lived in the house.

Once I purchased the land and buildings and signed all the paperwork, I moved into the house and focused on the new construction, with the goal of eventually turning the home into condominiums. I also focused on major landscaping projects and interior decoration. The many years of habitation and hot-and-cold weather had taken their toll on the property.

However, not long after I moved into the house, I experienced what I call "ghostly events." There were nights when I was awakened by what sounded like iron hitting iron, or chains and metal items being dragged across the hardwood floors. I'd sit up in bed, peer into the darkness, and listen. Eventually, I would get out of bed, walk around the house, and search for a clue to the origin of the noises. After I had made the rounds in the murky darkness, I would return to bed. I did notice the time when I was awakened by sounds—the clock face on top of my dresser marked 3 a.m. Other than that, I discovered nothing unusual.

Once, a woman friend of mine spent several nights at the house. She slept at the opposite end of the house, and one morning she told me of her frightening experience. She said that during the night, she had been awakened from her sleep by unidentified noises. Then, she noticed faint movements in the dark room and immediately felt a strong, heavy pressure on her chest. This pressure was so powerful that she was unable to move. It felt as if her whole body was wrapped in a tight cloth. Unable to move even one finger, she remained in this condition for what seemed like two hours. She was, in her own words, "totally terrified." She described the presence as very strong and overwhelming. She believed it was a man. Needless to say, thereafter she never spent another night at my home.

One evening, Elizabeth, the previous owner, and her husband came over for dinner. I soon learned some very unsettling details about the history of my property.

Towards the end of dinner, Elizabeth, unaware of my experiences, asked, "Have you seen my daughter?"

"I don't know your daughter," I said.

"She's dead," responded Elizabeth.

I was taken aback by her comments. But before I could respond, Elizabeth told me the following.

Her daughter was having a party with some friends late one night at the house. The daughter was distraught about something, and at about 3 a.m. in the evening, she took a handgun from her father's dresser drawer, walked to the horse corral, placed the barrel to her head, and pulled the trigger.

Less than a year later, in utter despair over his daughter's suicide, Elizabeth's first husband looped a rope over one of the *vigas* (beams) in the living room and hanged himself.

Several years before I bought the property from Elizabeth, a local physician was living in the house. One night, as the doctor was strolling by the horse corral (now the lower parking lot), he heard someone call his name. He turned and saw a young girl in a long white dress. He called out sharply, "What are you doing on this property?" She did not respond, and as he stared at her, she slowly disappeared before his eyes.

Needless to say, for the remainder of that evening I was very uncomfortable, and once the Zinns left, I decided to put the whole story out of my head and get on with my life. At first, it appeared that I was going to be successful.

The months flew by and I lost touch with the Zinn family. I began to focus on working on the major project of building Ten Thousand Waves. During the construction, it was necessary to blast and level large portions of the upper hillside to accommodate the various buildings and the road that presently runs from the highway to the upper-level parking lot. Although there are no records describing the exact location of the mother's place of burial, I now suspect that the construction crew may have destroyed, moved, or upset the grave in some way. I do know that Elizabeth's mother died over 60 years ago. However, I had lost touch with the Zinn family and had no way of establishing the location of the burial site.

When I opened the business in 1981, "ghostly events" began to occur almost immediately. A fellow by the name of Ted was in charge of opening the business each morning at 7 a.m. He told me more than once that while he was alone in the dressing rooms, making sure everything was in order, he had heard footsteps on the stairs—coming up from the main entrance, proceeding along the halls, and arriving at his location. But as the footfalls arrived, Ted could see nothing, so he would go to the front lobby and check the main doors. Invariably they were locked, with the dead bolt firmly set.

This series of events happened to Ted almost daily. But soon things progressed. He would hear the main doors open and close with a loud slam, but after investigating, he found nothing. Then, one morning, Ted felt a presence in the room with him. He says that as he turned, he caught sight of the misty, white figure of a woman standing absolutely still. Then, as he watched, the figure slowly disappeared.

At this point, Ted and I decided we were dealing with something weird and that we'd better do something about it. Ted contacted a priest at the St. Francis Cathedral in town about the possibility of conducting an exorcism. After Ted had told our story, the priest said he would see what he could do. A few days later, a car pulled up and three priests got out. I showed them to an office area where they changed into the habits of the Franciscan order. They had brought incense, holy water, a crucifix, and a Bible.

Proceeding throughout the establishment, the three read passages from the Bible and sprinkled holy water. From hot tub to hot tub, dressing rooms to the grounds—the three holy men made their rounds. When they had completed this procedure of cleansing, they approached the front lobby and placed a small wooden crucifix next to the Japanese bell on the wall behind the main counter. The crucifix remains there to this day.

Since the visit from the priests, I have not heard or seen any ghostly activities—except for once. One night, while dusting, a cleaning lady removed the crucifix and placed it on the counter next to the cash register. After she had finished dusting, she forgot to replace the cross, and no one noticed it had been moved.

Soon, members of the staff began complaining that they heard the sound of footsteps and other noises they could not explain. When word finally reached me about these incidents, I immediately questioned the staff and eventually discovered the missing crucifix. I soon found it and restored it to its original resting place, instructing my employees to make certain it was never moved again. We have had no further disturbances.

Given the suicides of the young woman and her father, and the possibility that we disturbed the grandmother's grave, I am convinced that their restless spirits remain on the property. I am grateful that—at least for the moment—all is peaceful at Ten Thousand Waves.

ST. VINCENT HOSPITAL

St. Vincent Hospital, Santa Fe's newest and largest, was completed in July of 1977. The Sisters of Charity founded this three-story Catholic hospital. The hospital, as well as the nearby health-care facility, Casa Real, was built upon the original site of the New Mexico State Penitentiary graveyard. I had the pleasure of interviewing Maryclare Henebry, RN, who works on the third floor in the adult psychiatric unit. People generally expect hauntings to occur in old, timeworn buildings, but her story explodes that myth. When the ghosts of Santa Fe wish to make their presence known, they choose the location with no preference for age—it can be a 300-year-old one-room adobe or a modern 200-bed hospital.

★   ★   ★

MARYCLARE'S STORY

I have worked at St. Vincent's for several years. Presently, I work in the adult psychiatric department, which has two units: one secured, the other nonsecured. The secured unit has a set of double doors that remain locked at all times because of the psychotic behavior of the patients. The doors are heavy, and have a large panel of thick, shatterproof safety glass, providing a clear, but safe, view of the hallways leading to the units.

The nonsecured unit, directly across the hall, has a pair of similar doors—except they are unlocked. As the night charge nurse, I frequently make visits to both units, helping with admissions and other duties.

My encounter with the supernatural occurred one night in the secured unit. At about 2 a.m., after I had finished my usual charting, I gathered my array of books and magazines and made my way towards the locked doors. As soon as I had placed the key into the lock, I felt a presence beside me. Still holding the key, I slowly turned to my right and saw a small Hispanic man withdrawing his hand from me, as if he had been caught attempting to touch my right shoulder.

I quickly turned away from him, and moved up against the side of the door, giving me the opportunity to get a good look at him. I had assumed he was a patient who had managed to sneak by my desk, but he was somehow different. I had never seen him before, and he was dressed in a style of clothing I did not recognize. He wore dark pants, crudely stitched and made of a heavy fabric. His white shirt was buttoned at the neck, and it had a wide, old-fashioned collar. He wore black leather shoes. He was very short—I am 5'3" and I towered over him.

I was startled when I concluded he was from another time. I asked him who he was, but he just stood there looking at me with his dark eyes. Then, to my complete amazement, he slowly disappeared—gradually and simultaneously—from both his head and his feet. I felt a coldness envelop me.

I quickly tried to gather my faculties and make my way out of the unit into the hall. My hands were shaking so badly that I fumbled with the key as I placed it in the lock. Finally, I opened the door, rushed through, and locked it again. I ran to the unit across the hall and sat at my desk. I did not mention the man to my fellow workers in the next room, who were discussing a patient's treatment plans. Somehow, the incident seemed out of place in this medical setting.

Knowing I had to return to the secured unit in one hour, I tried to convince myself I had imagined the man and his clothes. At 4 a.m., somewhat self-assured, I made my way out of the nonsecured unit. The hall was well-lit and seemed safe, so with keys and charts in hand, I trudged steadily forward.

I paused at the doors, waiting for something to happen. All was quiet. I searched the brightly lit hall and looked through the glass window to the secured unit. The silence was both comforting and unsettling.

As I began to slip my key into the lock, I again saw the little man at the east end of the hallway. I froze. As I watched from behind the safety of the locked doors, I lost sight of him. But my curiosity got the better of my fear, and I pressed my face against the window, trying to see him. Then I backed away from the window, and as I did, I caught sight of another figure—a woman.

She passed quickly by me down the hall. She was a bit taller than the man, and wore a white gown. Because she wore a black veil, or *mantilla*, I could not see her face. She ran past me, and I noticed her hair fell long and loose down her back. As she passed by me, I looked down at her feet. There was nothing there. The woman was floating above the floor by two or three inches. I stood absolutely still and watched her glide along the hall, turn a corner, and disappear.

Before I could get over this mentally staggering episode, the small man reappeared. He came racing down the hall, passed me, and disappeared in the same manner as the woman. I got the impression that he was chasing her, and I suddenly realized that this little escapade of "cat and mouse" did not include me. I was simply a witness to some ghostly game.

Reflecting now on all that happened that night, I am drawn to the thought that perhaps I could have helped the couple. When the man first appeared, he reached out to touch me. Perhaps he was making a plea for my help. Maybe he was trying to locate a lost love. Or perhaps the man confused me with the woman in white. It is also possible that the woman was in danger, or that she was trying to escape from the man. Maybe he had killed her. I'll never know the reasons for the apparitions, or why I was chosen to view them, and I've never had another experience like that. Perhaps it's just as well.

LA RESIDENCIA

La Residencia is a seven-year-old nursing facility located on the corner of Paseo de Peralta and Palace Avenue. Prior to October 1983, the building

housed the original St. Vincent Hospital, which provided for the health-care needs of Santa Fe and northern New Mexico.

Many of the city's health-care workers who served there believe it to be haunted. Specifically, those nurses who completed residence work at this facility for their New Mexico nursing licenses. Having to spend many hours at the facility, these students have reported unusual, and very scary, ghostly apparitions, voices, and noises. The following narratives are based upon interviews with three em-

ployees of La Residencia: the nurse coordinator, the charge nurse, and the nursing assistant.

★   ★   ★

80

THE NURSE COORDINATOR'S STORY:
BLOOD IN THE BASEMENT

All the nurses that I now work with, and have worked with in the past, are very much aware of the ghosts that dwell in La Residencia, but the basement holds its own special, grisly power. I personally can attest to this. You couldn't pay me a sack of gold to walk into that basement—day or night.

When staff members ask me to accompany them to the basement, I tell them, "The day I go back into that hell is the day I turn in my resignation!"

The basement has many rooms and hallways, and it's very dark. The State Museum's offices, which are located in the building next to La Residencia, use one large hallway as a storage area for Native American artifacts, such as stone tools, pottery, and grinding stones. I imagine these items, and others stored in large, sealed crates, have been excavated from burial sites. Considering how non–Native Americans treat living Native Americans, it would not surprise me if there were skeletal remains down there in cardboard boxes.

I am convinced that there are a lot of upset spirits in that basement. Other employees have reported hearing loud banging noises and voices coming from the basement at odd hours of the day and night. No one—except for new employees—ever ventures to the elevator and presses the "B" button.

In the past, the "seasoned" staff members used to initiate new employees by escorting them to the basement and leaving them there to find their way back, through the dark maze of hallways, to the stairway—without the aid of a flashlight. The only available light would be the green glow from the "Exit" signs. Eventually, the initiates—pale as ghosts—would reach the upper floor, where we would welcome them.

One evening, I was selected to accompany a new nurse's aide to the basement for this eerie "rite of passage." We rode the elevator down, and arriving at the basement, I sent her off with the usual instructions: "Find the stairs and meet us on the third floor."

She hesitated, then said, "I'll do it."

As the elevator door squeezed shut, I shouted, "Good luck," then went upstairs to wait with the others.

We waited and waited. Nothing happened. The aide did not arrive within the expected time, and we began to worry about her safety. Imagining all sorts of disasters—a broken leg, a hit on the head—another nurse and I decided to investigate.

Once in the basement, we called out the aide's name. No response. While the other nurse held the elevator door open, I shined a flashlight around—spotting dusty chairs, boxes, and crates. Elongated shadows flickered and fluttered against the walls. I definitely wanted to be somewhere else. I called the aide again, and this time I heard a weak response. I followed the sound of her voice—down one hall, then to the left. Finally, I located a room. I called to her again. "I'm here, down here on the floor," she said.

She was in one of the storage rooms, crouched in the corner, in almost total darkness. She told me she had lost her way, then became confused and scared. I hugged her and she took my hand. Then I yelled to the other nurse that I had found our missing aide.

As we turned to make our way out of the room, the beam of my flashlight caught something on one of the walls. I thought it was water, but as we looked closer, we saw that it was blood. It was fresh and it glistened in the light. It covered over half of the concrete wall and seemed to be oozing from the wall itself. I could even smell the unique iron scent of hemoglobin. There was no doubt in my mind—this was blood.

Well, after a scream or two—who's counting—we hightailed it out of the room toward the elevator.

"Press the button! Press the button!" we yelled to the startled nurse.

When we reached the others upstairs, I told them what we had seen. Everyone got so scared that no one even considered the possibility of returning to the basement—ever.

However, on the following day, after much deliberation, two nurses talked me into taking them to the room where we had seen the blood. Down we went with flashlights in hand, along the dark hallway, my stomach in knots.

We found the room, and I said, "Right in there, on the wall by the door."

We aimed our flashlights, but the wall was dry—clean as sun-bleached bones. There was no trace of blood on the wall or on the floor.

I remember saying, "Let's get the hell out of this place!"

Two days later, I asked one of the maintenance men who had worked in the facility when it was St. Vincent's if he was aware of any strange happenings in the basement.

He told me that he had heard stories from other employees, but didn't pay them any mind. When I asked him about the room where I had seen the blood, he told me there used to be a small furnace in that room where the hospital's surgery department cremated amputated limbs and organs. I just about died on the spot.

As you may have already guessed, there have been no more initiations in the basement.

ROOM 311

About six years ago, when I was working as a nurse's aide, I had a weird, ghostly experience during—of all times—the Christmas holiday. I had just finished preparing one of our patients for bed, when I heard the sound of crying coming from one of the rooms at the opposite end of the hall. I waited to see if another aide was investigating, but when I did not hear anyone approaching, I quickly ran down the hallway, concerned that a patient might have slipped and fallen.

As I neared the room from where the crying seemed to be coming, it suddenly stopped. However, I was sure that it had been emanating from room 311, so I opened the door and looked inside. The room was empty.

Then I went from room to room in the general area and checked for the source of the crying. All of the patients were fast asleep in their beds, and there was no one on the floor. I thought perhaps a patient had been experiencing a nightmare. I waited in the hallway a few more minutes to make sure everything was in order, and then made my way towards the nurses' station.

The crying began again. It stopped me in my tracks, and I listened carefully. It was a soft, baby-like crying, and it was coming from room 311, the room I had just investigated and found empty.

Immediately, I returned to room 311, opened the door, and turned on the lights. The room was still empty. I looked under the beds, thinking a kitten might have found its way into the room, but saw nothing. Nothing that lived or breathed was in that room, but something was in there—for sure. I turned off the lights, closed the door, and returned to the nurses' station.

"The crying began again. It stopped me in my tracks . . ."

Later the same night, the crying started again. I jumped up, ran to the room, and yanked the door open. Immediately, the sound stopped. Either I was terribly scared or mad.

On the following day, I described my experience to another nurse.

"Honey," she explained, "everyone who has ever worked that third floor has heard that same crying sound. You're not alone with this one! Just forget about it. You'll get used to it."

Later that night, as I was making my nightly bed check, I heard the crying from room 311 again. My patience was wearing thin, but I listened carefully and identified the painful crying as that of a small child. It sounded to me like a child between the ages of three and five. I had once worked directly with traumatized babies and children in the pediatric unit of another hospital, so I soon realized the crying was very much like that of a child gasping for air.

In the pediatric unit, I would at times cradle and rock babies who had been given a terminal prognosis, so I can never erase from my memory the sounds of a baby's last few breaths of life—that sad, drawn-out, labored cry. The sound coming from room 311 was that very sound. There was no doubt in my mind the cries I was hearing were the gasps of a dying baby.

It was Christmas Eve, and because of the cold, all the windows were shut tight. I just stood there and listened to the gasping cries as they mingled with the muffled singing of Christmas carolers on the sidewalk below.

I was overcome with sadness at the thought of what might have been the cause of this child's suffering. Two days later, I was having dinner with a group of colleagues at the hospital, and I brought up the subject of the crying sounds. I expected to be the butt of several jokes, but when I told the women about my experience, they reacted with sincere empathy.

One woman told us that when she had worked at the facility—years ago—when it was known as St. Vincent Hospital, she had been on duty on the third floor's pediatric unit during the night shift on Christmas Eve.

"It was Christmas Eve," she said, "and we received an emergency radio call from the state police informing us of a fatal accident on I-25. A father and son were in a two-car collision; the father had been killed instantly, but the little boy had sustained internal injuries. He was still alive—in critical condition. I can still recall the child's little body gasping for breath and his long intermittent cries of pain. I felt so sad watching him suffer and gasp for life."

I asked her which room the baby boy had been admitted to.

"Oh, that was on the third floor, room 311."

CLARA VIGIL—THE NURSE ASSISTANT'S STORY: THE CALL LIGHT

My experience happened about three months ago when I was working on the third floor of La Residencia. One of the patients that I had become fond of expired. Even though she had been very demanding, she had the character of a saint, and talking to her was a joy.

But each evening at the same time, she rang the nurse's call bell, and the light above her door turned on. We would always respond and ask what she wanted. Usually, she asked for the drapes to be drawn or opened, for a glass of water, or for some other small favor, but we all knew she just wanted company— someone to ease her mind until she fell asleep.

I often kept her company and tried to ease her loneliness. However, there were busy nights when her calling would stretch our physical and mental limits. Sometimes, one of the nursing assistants would have to sit with this lady—if the supervising nurse felt it was necessary—and sometimes I was chosen. I sat with her until she fell asleep.

One night, the lady suffered a massive stroke in her sleep and died. The staff nurse noted in her file that she must have died between 11 p.m. and midnight, since bed checks were conducted on a set hourly schedule. After the coroner had arrived, had signed the necessary paperwork, and had removed her lifeless body, her bed was changed and the room was made ready for another patient.

We had all come to know her well in the months she was there, and felt quite saddened by the news of her death.

The following evening, while we were accomplishing our various assignments, the nurse's call bell in the lady's room rang, just about midnight. We knew the room was still empty, so we circumspectly looked at each other and at the silently flashing light above her door.

I made the first move to investigate, but was soon joined by another nursing assistant. As we opened the door slowly and turned on the lights, we saw nothing out of the ordinary. I reset the call bell and closed the door behind me.

For about a week after that, the nurse's call bell and light was somehow activated every night at around midnight. We all knew that this was no coincidence, no electrical malfunction. We agreed that it was the lady's spirit trying desperately to communicate with those who had spent the last days of her life with her.

The following night, when the call bell rang and the light came on, we entered her empty room and softly called out the lady's name.

"Everything's all right, dear," we said gently.

I admit I was not sure what would happen next. Nothing did. Since that night, whenever the call bell had been activated, one of us has gone into the room and called out her name to reassure her spirit that everything was okay. Sometime after that, these strange happenings stopped.

Whenever I recall this story, my heart becomes heavy with sadness. I never realized how much I had grown to love this lady until after her death. I guess there is a lot to be said about human compassion and caring.

I thought the strange happenings were over, but last Thursday night, I heard a loud screaming—sort of a crying sound—coming from room 311. I have heard from other employees that the room is haunted, so I stay as far away as possible from that area.

DOLORES TRUJILLO—THE CHARGE NURSE'S STORY: ROOM 311

One of the more frequently haunted areas of La Residencia is room 311, where the disturbances occur so often that administrators try not to rouse any further gossip and stories about the ghost.

Around the year 1987, I was working the graveyard shift on the third floor. I was busy charting away in the patients' files and answering an occasional phone call. It must have been around 1:30 a.m. when I heard what sounded like a baby crying down the hall. I figured it was probably a cat trying to get in, and didn't give it another thought.

But after hearing the crying sound again a few minutes later, I decided to pull myself from the files and investigate. As I got up, I heard the sound again distinctly—the sound of a baby crying. There was no mistake. It was louder and more pronounced. I easily traced the sound down the hall to room 311.

As I approached the room, the sound suddenly stopped. I opened the door cautiously, not knowing what to expect, and reached for the wall-light switch. I turned on the light. The room was empty, the mattress bare, and the windows shut tight.

If there were a cat, I don't know why it would have chosen such a cold, empty room on the third floor. I was at a loss. I closed the door and went back to work.

Two weeks later, I was with a patient and her husband, and she asked me if I had brought my baby to work with me.

"No. Why do you ask?" I said.

"We've both been hearing a baby crying for the past few nights. Poor little thing sounds like it's in an awful lot of pain."

A cold chill went up my spine. Someone else had heard the crying sounds. It wasn't my imagination.

Since that incident, I have not heard the sounds again. I do know several other employees who work the night shift, and we have discussed our experiences with the crying "ghost" baby.

★   ★   ★

FOOTSTEPS IN THE HALL

Charge nurse Dolores Trujillo tells another fascinating story about phantom footsteps heard in the hallways of La Residencia.

One night, three nurses and I were gathered at the nurses' station on the third floor. It was approximately 10:30 p.m., and we were discussing patients' medical conditions and internal departmental issues. All of a sudden, we heard the sound of someone running down the hall. We stopped talking, and turned in the direction of the footsteps. They sounded like those of a woman in high heels, and seemed to be coming from the direction of the west wing. Because I was the closest to the hallway, I went to investigate.

The hall was empty and nothing was out of place. I returned to the nurses' station where everyone was waiting to hear who was the "jogger" in the hall. Just as I was saying I had seen nothing, we heard the footsteps again, and they seemed to be heading straight for us. From the echoing, reverberating, sound, they were traveling at a very fast pace. Just before it sounded as if they would make contact with the desk, they made a sharp turn, and headed left along the south hall.

La Residencia, north view.

We just stood there, with eyes and mouths wide open, frozen in time. Then we all knew at the same moment that we had just experienced a ghost. We instinctively reached for each other's hands, trying to gather our composure. Then, one nurse made the sign of the cross and prayed aloud for the "thing" to go away. For the remainder of the night, everything was quiet and uneventful.

But a month later, things started happening again. One morning, at approximately four o'clock, I was talking to one of the nurses who had heard the ghostly footsteps. We were sitting behind the nurses' station desk when we heard the familiar footsteps running down the hall.

As they rounded the desk and made their way down the south hall, the other nurse whispered, "Let's follow them and see where they go."

Although her words were courageous, I heard a slight tremble in her voice. I nodded in agreement, and as soon as the footsteps had passed us, we followed them down the south hall where we ran into another nurse who was coming out of the elevator. We explained our mission and she joined us, but suddenly, the sound of the footsteps ceased.

As the three of us returned to the safety of the nurses' station, we talked about the ghost footsteps and laughed nervously. We had just settled down when we heard the footsteps again. This time we were ready, and we followed close behind like bloodhounds.

When the footsteps approached the stairwell door leading to the basement, they stopped abruptly. I opened the door and we heard the footsteps clicking down the stairs. "That's it," I said. "I'm not going down there. This is as far as I'm going." The nurse who had joined us at the elevator said, "I'm going. I don't believe in ghosts, so if they don't exist, how can they hurt me!"

She got a flashlight and descended the stairs alone. The other nurse and I, too frightened to follow, remained where we were. A few minutes later, the elevator doors opened, and the investigating nurse stepped out . . . pale, and close to tears.

"My God! What happened to you?" I asked.

"I followed the sound down the stairs, and when I reached the basement, I heard them turn and walk down one of the halls. I followed, and when I reached the end of the hall, I turned to the right and standing there in the darkness, in a doorway, was the figure of a woman with long white hair, wearing a big, dark coat. Although I couldn't see her face clearly, she seemed to be upset. She shook . . . as if she were sobbing. Then she moved towards me, reaching her hands out to me. I was so scared, I turned and ran for the elevator. It was the most awful experience I have ever encountered." Then the nurse broke down and cried and cried.

Immediately, I got on the phone and asked my husband to pick me up as soon as possible.

Other employees have told me they have heard the footsteps, but no one has ever had the courage to follow them to the basement.

About a year ago, a nurse's aide, working on the first floor, was near the cafeteria when she heard the sounds of someone walking by the freezer in the closed kitchen area. Thinking it was an employee sneaking a snack without permission, she tried to open the door. It was locked. Then she peered through the glass window of the door. She saw a woman with long white hair wearing a fur coat. In the dimly lit kitchen, she could make out the woman's face. But as the woman passed one of the serving counters, the aide saw that the woman's feet were not touching the floor. The aide left the area immediately, and the following morning made a full report to the dietary supervisor.

The next morning, when the kitchen crew opened the locked door to the kitchen, at first, everything seemed normal. But then, one of the cooks reached down to the floor and picked up what appeared to be several strands of long white hair.

La Residencia strictly follows New Mexico's regulation demanding that at the end of each working day the kitchen floor be swept and mopped. However, from time to time, the kitchen staff will arrive in the morning and discover strands of long white hair on the floor and the countertops.

POOR MICHAEL

Michael's former home at 934 Lopez Street.

I interviewed Evelina Romero at her home, which is located on the west side of Santa Fe. Evelina is divorced, and lives with her six-year-old daughter, two gray cats, and a canary. Although Evelina was visibly shaken when recounting Michael's story, she steadfastly assured me that her hope was to prevent such an event from ever happening to someone else. Evelina's desire is for the readers of her story to fully comprehend the scope of evil and its all-encompassing nature.

The story of Michael that follows will provide the reader with some insight regarding Evelina's hopes.

★　★　★

EVELINA'S STORY

Michael and I grew up on the south side of Santa Fe. We attended the same schools and worshiped at the same church. Our families got along together well, and were regarded as model citizens by the rest of the community. We were wealthy in spirit and values—if not materially. As we developed into young adults, we began to date. At this time, I was about 18 years old.

After about seven months of dating, I noticed that Michael was acting differently towards his parents and towards me. He had begun to hang around with a new circle of friends who made me feel uncomfortable with their cussing and drinking. They were all from the Cerrillos–Madrid area, about 25 miles south of Santa Fe. It seemed as if every time I ran into these guys, they were high on pot or drunk on booze. Michael didn't seem to mind. In fact, he told me that I was too "uptight," that I should try to be more "social."

Needless to say, Michael and I would eventually end up in an argument, so I decided to put our relationship on hold for a while. I felt that Michael was heading in a direction that I did not want to follow, and soon after our split, he indeed gravitated towards these new friends.

As the months progressed, Michael's appearance changed slowly. He let his hair grow, he grew a short beard, and he began wearing "biker" clothes and jewelry—silver skull rings and necklaces with small iron stars or pentagrams, and black leather boots. His parents told me that Michael would leave on the weekends with his friends and not return for several days. When he returned from these jaunts, he spent all his time sleeping. He had become rude and demanding towards his parents, and one time threatened to strike his father. Consistently, he yelled that he wanted to be left alone, and then he would storm off to his room. Soon he lost weight, and whenever my parents or I visited him, he was hanging onto a can of beer.

One evening, I went to Michael's home to deliver a plate of *biscochos* (cookies) that I had baked. Michael wasn't home, so his mother, grateful for my kindness and aware of our longtime friendship, asked me to speak with Michael and inquire about his strange behavior and long absences. I comforted his mother and told her I would do my best.

At that moment, Michael came in and abruptly said, "I'm going away for a few hours. I'll be back in the morning."

He went into his bedroom for a minute and then raced out the door to a carload of waiting buddies. Both his mother and I watched from the kitchen window as the car sped down the road and vanished into the night. His mother looked at me with despair and said softly, "This goes on all the time."

As she shook her head, I said, "He's changed so much. I only hope he doesn't hurt himself."

Michael's mother sobbed, then wiped her eyes with the back of her shaking hand. "His father has spoken to him, but Michael thinks he's his own boss now and doesn't want anyone telling him what to do. I'm sure he's smoking pot, because I've noticed the smell of something bad burning in his room sometimes."

"Have you been in his room lately?" I asked.

"No. No, I'm afraid of what I'll find."

"Let's go and investigate now that he's gone," I said.

She reluctantly agreed.

We opened the door and peered into the darkened room. As I switched on the light, I immediately smelled the harsh, pungent odor of burnt oil, a sooty aroma. I noticed clothes and shoes tossed haphazardly about the floor, and posters of naked women and one of the "grim reaper" decorating the walls. On Michael's dresser lay a rusted knife, whose handle had been wrapped with a leather strap, numerous colored stones, a partially smoked marijuana joint, and a small statue of Jesus Christ with its head broken off.

His mother said, "Let's leave before he returns."

So we left the room as we had found it.

Several days later, I got a chance to speak with Michael. As usual, he had a beer can in his hand and sipped on it throughout our conversation.

When I casually asked what he'd been up to, he told me, without hesitation, that he and his friends were involved in a new religion. I was caught completely off guard, but asked him to explain. Being a bit drunk, he openly discussed this new cult he had been initiated into. Basically, he described the symbols used in the religion and left the rest up to my imagination. He rattled off words and sentences about the use of certain colored candles, herbs, and prayers and then the importance of using virgin blood. This was not a bit amusing, and my face must have shown it.

Then I said, "Michael, are you a devil worshipper?"

He answered, "I guess you could call me that."

Then he tried to convince me of the "positive virtues" of such a group. We spoke for about an hour; then I tried to show him the negative aspects of the situation he was in, by describing his parents' deep distress and sorrow for their son, and how all of this "devil talk" was counterproductive and against the teachings of the Catholic Church. He would have none of that. He laughed loudly and told me what a fool I was.

He said, "Don't you want the best things in life? Well, the only way to get them is through the 'angel of the morning light.' Don't you see . . . he will listen to whoever calls him!"

For about two weeks, I kept this information to myself. I felt very sad for Michael and his family. And I did not speak to Michael for about two months after that. One day, his mother came to my family home and broke down. She cried and admitted that her son needed help. She told us that Michael had gotten drunk the night before, and when his father had questioned him about the large bruises and cuts on his arms, Michael had revealed that he was involved with a group of people who practiced a new form of religion, but he had said he could not reveal many of the details. However, Michael did admit that he was having doubts about staying with these friends because of what he termed "dangerous practices."

Earlier that evening, Michael had found the courage to confront some of the members of the group, and had attempted to terminate his association with the organization, but things had gotten ugly and he was forced to fight his way out. The members of the group had called him a wimp, and told him they would kill him if he did not "think twice" about his "unreasonable" decision.

According to his mother, Michael then began to cry uncontrollably. His parents hugged him and eventually he calmed down and swore he would break away from the group.

About a week later, I went to pay a visit to Michael's home. After getting no answer at the front door, I went around to try the back. There I found Michael, sitting cross-legged on the ground, staring at a lit black candle. Beside him lay the neighbor's German shepherd—dead. Its heart had been cut out of its chest, and Michael was clasping it and holding it above the candle.

"Michael," I screamed. "My God! What have you done to that dog! What are you doing!"

Michael turned to me and shouted, "Get out of here, bitch!"

I ran home and told my parents what I had seen. My parents were struck with amazement and horror. My mother instructed me not to return to Michael's home and to pray for his salvation. I lit a white candle before the statue of the Virgin Mary, and prayed with all my might that Michael would cease his involvement with his "friends." Later that night, around 11 p.m., Michael's mother called, pleading for help, so my mother and I reluctantly went to their home.

When we arrived, Michael's father explained what had happened. When he had challenged Michael about the dog, Michael had told his father that he had had to kill the dog with a knife and that he "had to kill animals because this was what he was supposed to do if he were to save his soul." Then Michael had gone to his room and locked the door. His parents decided to try to put their thoughts aside for the night, and seek professional help for their son the next day. They had just settled down in the living room when they heard a tremendously loud bang coming from Michael's room. Thinking he may have killed himself, they rushed to the locked door and began pounding on it. From inside the bedroom, they heard Michael's frightened voice pleading, "Don't hit me. Get away from me."

Michael's father pushed, trying unsuccessfully to force the door open. Michael's mother ran and got a clothes iron, which they used to smash the lock. Inside, every piece of furniture had been broken or overturned. Clothes and debris were everywhere, as if a huge whirlwind had taken complete control. Even the light fixture on the ceiling had been torn off. The mattress was shredded, and clumps of foam from the pillows floated in the air or rested on the destruction. Michael lay unconscious on the floor.

This is when my mother and I arrived. Michael was covered in large bruises and blood. I phoned for the hospital emergency team, and in a few minutes, the ambulance arrived and took Michael to St. Vincent Hospital.

That night, recovering in a hospital room, Michael told his parents what had happened. He said after he had gone to his room, he began tossing all the symbols of his new religion—pictures, candles, and other paraphernalia—into his trash can. As he was cleaning his room, he heard a noise at the window, so he looked out and saw what looked like the dark figures of a man and a woman. As he stared at them, the figures, like two huge, winged birds or bats, suddenly entered the room and descended upon him. In raspy voices, they told him that because he wanted to leave the group, he would "pay the price." Before he could call for help, the two beat him unmercifully. The woman hit him first, and then the man hit him. They struck him with hands and wings until he passed out.

On Michael's second day in the hospital, the psychologist placed him on a program of antidepressants and psychoanalysis to monitor his behavior. It was obvious that the psychologist did not believe Michael's story, but thought that Michael was suicidal.

All went well for a few days. Michael seemed to be his old self, and we thought, or hoped, that his problems were over. Then one night, about a month later, we all decided to go out to dinner, but Michael refused, saying he didn't feel up to it and would be fine at home. When we returned that evening, we found the house in darkness. Michael did not respond to our calls. We proceeded through the house, and I went to the kitchen. There I found Michael, as before, sitting cross-legged, staring into a flickering black candle. I called out his name, but he did not answer. Then his parents arrived in the kitchen.

They became extremely upset, but called out to him until he responded. He said he was just sitting on the floor and didn't know how the candle got there. His parents decided to readmit him in the morning. They hugged their son and assured him that everything would be all right. However, they never got the chance. During that September night in 1988, Michael ended his troubles by slitting his own throat. He was 23 years old.

After the funeral, I went with relatives and friends to clean up Michael's room. A priest was called in to bless the entire house. Michael's parents put the house up for sale and, five months later, moved out.

For a while, every time the realtor brought potential buyers, the clients complained of an uncomfortable feeling, and some stated that an invisible hand had slapped them. One realtor claims an arm had locked around her neck and pulled her toward the door. For over a year, the house stood empty, unsold.

Today, the house has changed hands, and the interior has been remodeled. The present renter, an artist, told me personally that he has had no unusual experiences.

EL MOLCAJETE

Sofita's molcajete.

I conducted this interview with Sofita Becera at her home, in her living room, which also served as her bedroom. The simple items of decoration displayed about her home provided clues to Sofita's modest taste. Handcrafted, crocheted doilies and other needlework rested upon Sofita's well-worn furniture. Placed at the foot of her yellow/green sofa was an oblong rug that Sofita's best friend, Belinda Ortiz, had given to her as a wedding present many years before.

What remains dominant in my memory, however, was Sofita's religiosity. On a wooden table her deceased husband had made over 20 years ago, stood a statue of the Virgin Mary. In front of the statue were a small bouquet of plastic flowers and a votive candle that flickered continuously throughout the interview.

Born on August 12, 1899, Sofita was nearing 93 years of age, but had the spunk and vitality of a much younger woman. She wore thick-lensed glasses because of cataract surgery performed eight years earlier.

Sofita's story concerns a molcajete, *a carved stone kitchen tool developed by ancient indigenous peoples several hundred years ago in the valley of Mexico. It is shaped like an average-sized melon, with the center hollowed out. A smaller stone is used inside the hollowed-out portion of the* molcajete *to crush or grind herbs and spices. This stone "mortar and pestle" was so useful that it remains a popular tool with people on both sides of the border dividing the United States and Mexico.*

Unlike a metate—*a long, flat stone used by Native Americans throughout the Southwest to grind corn into a flourlike powder—the* molcajete *is rounded and bowl-shaped.*

★ ★ ★

SOFITA BECERA'S STORY

In 1921, I was 22 and had just married Daniel the previous summer. We had a small house about two miles east of the Santa Fe Plaza. In those days, two to five miles was not considered very far to travel, and those of us without horses would walk, carrying supplies of food or firewood. It was not an easy life, but the good times made up for the bad.

My good friend since childhood, Belinda Ortiz, would join me at midday after I had done the cleaning and fed the chickens and goats. Belinda and I passed the time talking about what was going on in our neighborhood, things like who was romancing who.

During one of these afternoon visits, Belinda and I went outside to rid my yard of a stray dog that was barking and chasing my chickens. Three young neighborhood boys came by, saw our trouble, and started throwing stones at the mongrel.

Once rid of the dog, I asked the boys why they were covered in dirt. They explained that they had been exploring in the nearby hills, and had discovered a small cave behind a grove of trees, against the side of the mountain. They had gathered some sticks to enlarge the opening and peered inside. With the help of the afternoon sun, they had seen several pots and a quiver made out of fox pelts that contained arrows. I told them they must have uncovered a burial site, and should not have touched or taken anything because they must respect the dead. They listened with wide eyes, and then said they did not want to return but were afraid that others might disturb the cave. Belinda suggested they take us to the cave and we could help them cover it up. The boys agreed and off we went.

About six miles into the Sangre de Cristo Mountain Range, on the eastern edge of the city, we crossed a small stream and entered a grove of trees. There we found the cave. The opening was about four feet high and three feet wide. We peered inside and saw the small painted pots, a woven grass mat, and the quiver of arrows—just as the boys had described. In the back of the cave, I saw a large dark mass of fur and I knew this was a burial cave when I saw a bony foot protruding from underneath the fur. I realized that the corpse must have been a man and a hunter, because he was wrapped in a bearskin and had his hunting weapons with him, but I kept this knowledge to myself and made the sign of the cross.

I turned to Belinda and the boys and said, "We will have to seal this up, so go down to the stream and bring mud and stones."

While they were all busy at the stream, I looked inside the cave again. This time I noticed a roughly carved *molcajete*. I knew that taking anything from the dead or a burial is very wrong. I was raised knowing this, but mentally putting this knowledge aside, I nervously reached in and grabbed the *molcajete* and the small grinding stone that lay beside it. At the time it didn't seem wrong to take the stone tool, and I thought this would fit in my kitchen perfectly, so I carried it some distance away and covered it with grass and leaves. I felt it was worthless compared to the pots or the fox quiver.

A modern molcajete.

We diligently worked with our hastily gathered adobe building materials, and soon the sun had caused a thin crust to develop on the surface of the moistened mud. We placed large branches with lots of leaves in front of the sealed entrance. We all agreed that we had done a "good job."

I instructed the boys to return home on their own, but Belinda and I stayed behind. After they had gone, I told Belinda about the *molcajete*. She was not happy about what I had done, but after she had seen it, she agreed that it would do no harm to put it to use once in a while, after all those years lying in the cave.

I retrieved the tool and we went home. I scrubbed the *molcajete* clean of all mud and placed it on the kitchen table to surprise my husband. When Daniel saw it, he admired its beauty, but asked nothing about its origins. Instead, he suggested I grind some chile for the following day's dinner.

So the next day, I did as he had suggested and crushed some dried red chile pods for dinner. The *molcajete* performed very nicely, but later that night, while I was sleeping, I was awakened by a loud banging sound. I shook my husband out of his sleep and told him to listen, but the sound had stopped. The next night, I was again awakened by the same sound, but this time I recognized it as the sound one rock makes as it is hit against another—a "click/click" sound. Immediately, I knew it was the *molcajete*. I got goosebumps on my goosebumps, but I kept still and eventually, after what seemed an eternity, the sound stopped.

A metate.

The next morning, I told Belinda about the sounds in the night. She said it was my own fault for taking what was not mine. I agreed, and asked her to return the *molcajete* to the cave. She refused and insisted I do it myself. But I was too frightened, so I carried the stone to the back of the house and left it there beside the back door.

From time to time, I would hear the familiar sound, but I dared not tell Daniel where the *molcajete* came from. I just endured the night poundings and the guilt that had overcome me. Out of fear I could not bring myself to return the *molcajete* to its rightful resting place.

One November night, as a soft snow dusted everything, I heard the *molcajete* again. It had been several months since the last time I had heard it, but as usual, the clicking sound awakened me from my sleep. I got out of bed, went to the back door, and carefully peered through the window. I saw the freshly fallen snow glistening in the bright light of a full moon. Then I looked down to where the *molcajete* stood and was surprised to see the imprints of a barefooted person in the snow. The footprints slowly moved away from the *molcajete* until they disappeared behind a large cottonwood tree. Although snow covered everything else in the yard, the exposed *molcajete*, which was being used as a doorstop, had been brushed clean, and the fresh human footprints surrounded the *molcajete*.

Since that night, I have heard the clicking sounds of the *molcajete* only twice: on the day that my good friend Belinda died, and on the day that Daniel was laid to rest. But I am no longer afraid. I guess I've come to accept the spirit that dwells in or around the grinding stone as something that I will have to live with. I now consider the *molcajete* as if it were a chair or table, something to be taken for granted, but useful when needed. I believe this "stone friend" will stay with me and provide companionship until I leave this world.

★ ★ ★

Author's Note: *In September of 1991, Sofita suffered a massive heart attack and died at home, surrounded by her son and two neighbors. Later, her son contacted me and informed me that his mother had mentioned to him that she had wanted me to have the* molcajete. *I accepted the gift with nervous apprehension, and assured her son that I would take care of it and that eventually I would place it in a location that befits its history.*

★ ★ ★

ABIQUIU

BEAUTIFUL ABIQUIU

The Abiquiu Valley is an area rich in ancient human history that can be traced back over a 1,000 years. Anasazi is a term generally used to describe the original inhabitants of the valley. Anasazi is a Navajo word, which means "the ancient ones" or "ancient enemies." Although the current Eight Northern Pueblos do not have a common name for their ancestors, the term "ancestral Puebloans" is used to describe them when English is spoken.

The ancestral Puebloans settled and farmed the region between AD 1000 and AD 1300. They produced ornaments, tools, pottery, and extraordinarily fine baskets.

These ancestral Puebloans were rich in spirituality, and maintained an ingenuity of herbology and knowledge of their environment. Their ability to exist in an area of extreme weather changes and unfriendly raiding neighbors cannot be overestimated. Their achievements included an elaborate trade network with other pueblo regions throughout the Southwest, which spanned the modern states

Canadian artist Doris McCarthy capturing the Abiquiu landscape on canvas.

of New Mexico, Arizona, and Colorado. Of great historical importance, which can be seen in the Abiquiu Valley today, are their cliff dwellings and pueblos (apartment-style villages).

In addition to these ancient ruins, the Abiquiu Valley also contains the modern monastery of "Christ in the Desert," which was founded in 1964 by Father Aelred Wall and two other monks from Mount Saviour Monastery in New York. The Benedictine monastery is nestled in the stunningly beautiful Chama River Canyon and, with prior notification, welcomes visitors.

With the opening of the new Georgia O'Keeffe Museum in Santa Fe, the reputation of Abiquiu's beautiful terrain is captivating artists far and wide, and drawing many visitors to the valley. One such artist who visited the valley is Doris McCarthy. McCarthy, like many others, was drawn to paint the landscape that similarly enchanted Georgia O'Keeffe. McCarthy is considered by many to be one of Canada's predominant landscape painters, and is a member of the Royal Canadian Academy of Arts.

As the history and culture of this enchanted valley becomes ever more popular with the outside world, one thing is certain: Abiquiu will always remain an extraordinary retreat for the human soul. As one older Hispanic resident stated to me, "*No necesito nada mas. Cuando Dios me puso en esta tierra, me dio el cielo.*" ("I have no need to desire anything in life. When God placed me in Abiquiu, he gave me heaven.")

THE PENETENTE AND THE WITCH

My interview with Napoleon took place on the porch of his home, which is located directly across the street from the old Abiquiu village church—St. Thomas Apostle.

The village of Abiquiu is where Napoleon was raised. Located just walking distance from Napoleon's house is Georgia O'Keeffe's home. Napoleon was eager to share local lore and bits of information of his childhood, including stories of ghosts! Napoleon is also well known throughout the Abiquiu Valley for being a man who can direct the visitor to points of interest in and around Abiquiu. Various carved crucifixes and pueblo ladders that Napoleon carved out of native Aspen wood decorate his home. Some are available for purchase.

Among other topics, Napoleon is proud to state that his family helped with the construction of the nearby Benedictine monastery—Christ in the Desert. My impression of Napoleon is that there are many more interesting facets to his life. Presently, he is content living in Abiquiu and assisting the many tourists that wander upon his humble village and home. The visitor, however, would be well cautioned to keep questions about Napoleon's life with O'Keeffe to a minimum. You see, Napoleon is currently compiling his own memoirs for a future book on this very subject.

★ ★ ★

NAPOLEON "PAUL" GARCIA'S STORY

I am a native of Abiquiu and have lived in the village of Abiquiu all my life. I currently offer information to tourists such as maps and points of interest, which only a native of this area, like myself, is most qualified to give. I offer this information service directly out of my home. I frequently get asked questions about Georgia O'Keeffe. I am very happy to share my personal information with anyone who asks, since I knew her very well. I also try to inform tourists about my village of Abiquiu and the surrounding country, because there is a lot of history here that is just as important as the stories I can tell about Georgia O'Keeffe.

As you might know, I personally knew Georgia. She and I began our acquaintance when I was just a child. As the years progressed and I entered adulthood, I was hired by her to help in the restoration of her home here at the village. I also planted many of the trees that decorate her home's gardens and property. I took care of any repair work that was needed in her home; repairing walls that needed plastering, electrical work, etc. I also was hired as her personal chauffeur, driving her to and from appointments between Taos, Santa Fe, and Albuquerque.

Now, as far as ghosts are concerned . . . well, I don't know if you're going to believe me, but my wife, my sons, and myself have all experienced strange happenings here in our home. I would say that we definitely have a spirit or ghost that dwells among us. When we are in our beds, sometimes we will get the feeling that someone is in the room with us. Although we can see that no one is actually in the room, there is a strong sensation of a "presence." Very soon after we have this feeling, the spirit will make its presence known to us in the guise of loud footsteps walking up and down the stairs. The sound of the footsteps will enter our bedrooms, and our mattresses will actually show the indentation of a body that has sat at the foot of the bed! We all hear these footsteps that walk from room to room. We believe that the ghost is the spirit of a man, because of the heavy, loud footsteps.

This ghost also moves such items as my personal wood-carving tools, and coffee cups that are filled with freshly poured hot coffee! I will look all about the house for these items and they are nowhere to be found. I think that the ghost is a friendly spirit, because if it wanted to do us any harm, he would have done so a long time ago. I think he just wants to play and visit with us.

The people of the village also tell of a woman who can be heard screaming or crying. The sound comes from the cemetery that is located up above the village, just west of the *morada* or penetente chapel. This woman is dressed in dark clothing, and she allows people to view her from a distance. When anyone attempts to get close to her, she disappears. I have heard about this woman for many years. For lack of a better word to describe her, we all just refer to her as La Llorona (The Weeping Woman).

I can remember, as a young boy, I would see balls of light that would bounce off the roofs of houses in the village. My friends and I would sit on a *banco* (bench) on the plaza at night and we would witness these strange lights, which would make us quite scared. Our parents would tell us that the lights were witches, so we were very cautious around these lights. Things used to be different many years ago in Abiquiu; for instance, when a person would die, the *velorio* (wake) would be in the family's living room. The coffin and body would be displayed for the mourners to view in the house. This might seem odd, but at that time we had no morticians or methods of embalming. The deceased would be given the *velorio* usually the same evening of their death, and then buried the following day.

There is a story that people tell in the village that I have heard since I was just a small boy. The story is about a member of the religious penetente brotherhood. Years ago, the penetentes used to walk the dirt streets of the village on special religious holidays. They would wear a large *paño* (handkerchief) over their heads to disguise their identities. As they walked the streets, some would carry a whip of knotted cords that they used for self-flagellation. They would do this to show their devotion and reverence to their spirituality and their Catholic faith.

There was one penetente that was different from the rest. This penetente would conduct his walk by himself at night. As he would make his way through the village, the people would show him respect by making the sign of the cross as he passed. The people did not recognize this strange devotee, but nonetheless, because of his strong self-sacrifice, they gave him respect. This penetente also had the unusual habit of walking down roads that led away from the *morada*. When some individuals followed him at a distance, to their surprise, they discovered that he would simply disappear! Of course, the village people knew immediately that this was no ordinary penetente, but a spiritual being.

As the story goes, there was one individual who decided to follow the penetente the next time he walked through the village. This young man was wanting to prove to everyone that he was not afraid and was braver than the rest. He wanted to find out who this penetente was. The next time the penetente walked through the village, he was ready.

The night was very dark, and sure enough the penetente walked by with the young man following behind. Nearing the edge of the village, the penetente noticed that he was being followed and extended his arm, gesturing for the young man to "stop!" He did not say anything, he just made it clear to him that he was not welcome to follow the penetente any further. The young man chose to disregard the warning and continued to follow.

The penetente continued his walk, but this time he took a new route that led up to the cemetery. With the young man following close behind, they both entered the cemetery grounds. Well into the cemetery the penetente slowed his pace, allowing the young man to get fairly close to him. When he got close enough to the penetente, the penetente stopped and turned to face the man. The man walked right up to the penetente and asked him, "Who are you?" Slowly the penetente raised one arm to his head and took hold of the handkerchief, then quickly pulled it off to reveal a white skull!

Another quite well-known story is that of a witch that lived in the village many years ago. This witch was left alone by the people, and because of her powers was known to have the ability to turn herself into animal forms. This ability allowed her to sneak up to houses and peer into windows without drawing the attention of the occupants. She used the information she gathered to use against the people.

One evening, there was an unusually large black owl that kept flying around the village. The people had their suspicions that it was the witch who had transformed herself into an owl. Because the people believed her to be something evil, they encouraged one of the men in the village to kill her. The man brought out his rifle and inserted a bullet into the chamber. Before he placed the bullet in the gun, he took out his pocketknife and carved a cross on the tip of the bullet. This was done to insure that the bullet would reach its mark.

The man went out to where the owl was spotted, took aim, and fired. The bullet hit the owl, and in a cloud of black feathers, the owl flew away into the nearby hills. The following day, the woman who the people suspected to be the witch was seen in her yard with a large, bloodied bandage wrapped around her shoulder!

There are other stories of the valley, and one in particular takes place just north of Abiquiu, in Ghost Ranch. Years ago, it was called *Rancho de los Brujos* (Ranch of the Witches). Long ago the cattle rustlers used to steal cattle from the local ranchers and take them to the box canyon— Rancho de los Brujos. If anyone dared to be so brave as to follow these phantom rustlers into the canyon, they would never be seen again! The stories told are of ghostly sounds of horses, gunfights, and of balls of fire that bounce off the canyon's walls.

Today the local people of the village find lots of Native American artifacts that are buried on private land in the village. I know people who, having dug holes for their fence posts, have found large *metates* (grinding stones), bowls, and skeletons. We are very respectful when we find a skeleton. We will take the bones to other locations in the hills and rebury them. I also know that some people have taken them to our cemetery and buried them there. We never display the bones out of respect. Native American ruins and ancient sites surround the whole village of Abiquiu.

GHOST RANCH

On February 12, 1766, 10 years before the signing of the Declaration of Independence, the King of Spain granted 50,000 acres of land to Pedro Serrano. Ghost Ranch is a part of this land grant; originally known as *Piedra Alumbre* (Alum Rock) the name has evolved into *Piedra Lumbre* (Fire Rock).

Succeeding years saw the grant gradually divided, largely by the Spanish pattern of inheritance. Small tracts in large numbers were traded back and forth. Several elaborate partition suits were filed in order to establish simple title to the northerly third of the grant. In 1929, the A. B. Renehan Estate presented all conflicting claims for a little more than $20,000. A man named Arthur Pack purchased 21,000 acres of this land, which included the Ghost Ranch homestead. Title can be traced directly to the Board of Christian Education of the Presbyterian Church.

It was called Rancho de los Brujos (Ranch of the Witches, freely translated as Ghost Ranch) because of the local belief that the canyon was inhabited by ghosts. For 25 years the Packs operated Rancho de los

Brujos as a working dude ranch. This land that inspired the creativity of artist Georgia O'Keeffe, was for Arthur and Phoebe Pack "a treasure of the spirit." The Packs felt the need to share the treasure of this land. In 1955 they offered their ranch to the United Presbyterian Church to use as a study center. It was their dream that this sprawling piece of sand, butte, and mesa, with breathtaking views from every turn of the trail, would one day become a magic place of physical and spiritual renewal for many thousands of people. The church accepted the gift of Ghost Ranch, and the challenge to make this remote ranch into an educational facility.

Arthur Pack died in 1975. His ashes rest on the hill above Ghost House. The simple marker reads, "Phoebe and I believe that we have found the real treasure—an understanding of the love of God and an overwhelming sense of His living presence here." Phoebe Pack now makes her home in Tucson, Arizona.

THE GHOST RANCH LOGO

Rancho de los Brujos it was called; Ranch of the Witches, haunted by evil spirits. It is not surprising that today's name for this land is Ghost Ranch, and the logo is a cow's skull.

For many years, only a narrow dirt road led up the twisting Chama River Valley northwest from Abiquiu. The turnoff to Ghost Ranch was marked by an animal skull long before Arthur Pack bought the ranch in 1933.

There were many bones to be seen in this high desert country, and they entranced O'Keeffe, who painted them, displayed them, and shipped a barrelful back to New York. One of her Ghost Ranch neighbors, a Navajo named Juan de Dios, had a pet steer that he was very fond of. When it died, he gave the animal's skull to O'Keeffe for her collection. O'Keeffe made a drawing of this cow skull and presented it to Arthur Pack as a gift. He promptly adopted the artwork as the logo for Ghost Ranch.

When the Presbyterian Church first acquired Ghost Ranch, they used a sketch of Chimney Rock as the logo. By 1971, partly at O'Keeffe's suggestion, her familiar skull design was firmly established as the official Ghost Ranch logo.

★ ★ ★

I interviewed Nola in the bookstore of the Ghost Ranch visitor center. Nola has completed several tasks while working at the ranch, notably the design and layout of the ranch's annual calendar.

Nola's long-term employment at Ghost Ranch has provided her with many interesting experiences, and the opportunity to meet notable personalities—such as Georgia O'Keeffe.

Nola enjoys her work, and based on the positive comments from her co-workers, Ghost Ranch equally enjoys Nola.

NOLA SCOTT'S STORY

It has now been more than 20 years since I began working at Ghost Ranch. Currently, I am the manager and book buyer of the Ghost Ranch trading post. All types of souvenirs are sold at the store, including books, jewelry, and personal supplies that our guests might need. When I first started working at the ranch I was a volunteer, and then was hired as the receptionist. I've done about every job, from registration to payroll. Working for the ranch is not so much a job, to me, as a way of life only a few people have the privilege to experience.

Regarding ghosts, well I can tell you that there are definitely people who have seen some very strange things on the ranch. I personally have not had a ghost experience, but guests have come up to the staff and informed us that they have "unseen" visitors in their rooms. For instance, we had a guest who was staying in a room named "Juniper." She came to us and stated, "Has anyone ever died in my room? There is a presence in that room."

Other guests have claimed to have seen shadows moving about in their rooms, and we even have had guests state that furniture in their rooms has moved on its own! From time to time, guests have told us that doors will open and close by themselves. Now as I said, I have not experienced any ghosts at Ghost Ranch, but there are lots of folks who say that they definitely have.

I'll now tell you about my own personal experiences with Georgia O'Keeffe at Ghost Ranch.

Years ago, I recall having had numerous one-on-one conversations with Georgia O'Keeffe. Many times I remember watching her from a window as she would drive up our gravel road and turn into our parking area. She was just a lovely person who reminded me of my own grandmother. They were both about the same age. Of course, people do speak about how stern Georgia could be, but she was always friendly towards me.

I recall one day when Georgia and I were discussing the very first time she had visited Ghost Ranch. I was a new employee at the time, and because of this, Georgia felt comfortable going on and on with personal stories about how lovely her first impression was of the ranch. She also spoke about how daily life was conducted at the ranch those many years ago. When she spoke about these times, she would laugh and find a lot of humor in her memories.

At the time, I owned a small Honda Civic, and during one of Georgia's visits to the ranch with her friend Juan Hamilton, she turned to him and said, "That's what I want. I want a little car just like that!" Juan responded, "Oh, no, no, Georgia, you don't want that, you need to get a Mercedes!"

During her visits, the ranch staff made it a point to never get in Georgia's way. If she needed anything she would politely be allowed to make first contact with us. She was a special visitor to the ranch and we never forgot that.

Georgia became very friendly with our former director of the ranch, Jim Hall, and especially close to Jim's secretary, Joanne. Georgia thought very highly of Joanne because Joanne was unimpressed with Georgia as an artist. In fact, when they both first met, Joanne did not even know who the famous Georgia O'Keeffe was. Georgia apparently valued that indifference in a person. I think it would be quite tiring for a celebrated artist like Georgia to be constantly doted upon. People always seemed to be in awe of her. Perhaps that's one reason why Georgia enjoyed being in the open, isolated space of this country.

Joanne eventually was hired to do secretarial work for Georgia and once, when the two of them were together, as Joanne was going through Georgia's papers she asked her, "Who is this person Alfred Steiglitz whose name I keep seeing?" Georgia got a big kick out of her question and just laughed and laughed. She then responded, "Oh, that's just my husband." Georgia and Joanne enjoyed each other a lot, and in time, Joanne really grew to respect Georgia's art and, more importantly, Georgia as a person.

GEORGIA O'KEEFFE AND GHOST RANCH

"When I got to New Mexico, that was mine. As soon as I saw it, that was my country."

—*Georgia O'Keeffe*—

Although both Native Americans and Hispanics might find strong disagreement with her statement on historical and cultural grounds, it was in this way that Georgia O'Keeffe described her instant love for northern New Mexico, a love that would last for the rest of her life.

The time was 1917; the event was a trip O'Keeffe and her sister, Claudia, took to New Mexico and Colorado from their home in Canyon, Texas. Yet it would be 12 years before O'Keeffe would return to New Mexico, and even longer before she would find her way into the beautiful valley that would eventually become her summer home.

In 1929, O'Keeffe went to Taos at the invitation of friends, Dorothy Brett and Mabel Dodge Luhan. There she heard of Ghost Ranch, and once even caught a tantalizing glimpse of it from a high plain. In 1934, she finally found the ranch, but was dismayed to learn that it was a dude ranch owned by Arthur Pack. However, a place was available for her that night in Ghost House, and she spent the entire summer at the ranch.

That summer established a pattern O'Keeffe would follow for years. Summers were spent exploring the area on foot, and on canvas the beauty of Ghost Ranch; and winters were spent in New York. Because she was basically a "loner," she soon sought Ghost Ranch housing that was somewhat isolated from the headquarters area. Pack offered to rent O'Keeffe his own residence called Rancho de los Burros (Ranch of the Donkeys); this suited her very well. One spring, she arrived unexpectedly and found someone else in the house. She demanded to know what these people were doing in her house. When Pack pointed out that it wasn't her house, she insisted that he sell it to her. Thus, she became the owner of a very small piece of Ghost Ranch land: a house and seven acres. (In latter years she told a ranch employee who was doing roadwork near her home, "I wanted enough land to keep a horse—all Arthur would sell me was enough for my sewer!"

But Rancho de los Burros was a summer place and also a desert. O'Keeffe wanted a garden and a winter home. Eventually, she bought three acres in the village of Abiquiu. She spent three years remodeling and rebuilding the crumbling adobes before the place was fit for human habitation. After her husband, Alfred Stieglitz, died, O'Keeffe left New York to make Abiquiu her permanent home.

One of Georgia's favorite subjects: Pedernal—the flat-topped mountain to the south.

When Arthur and Phoebe Pack gave Ghost Ranch to the Presbyterian Church in 1955, O'Keeffe was aghast. The Packs should have sold her the ranch, she thought, and besides, she never cared much for Presbyterians anyway. Her precious privacy would be gone. However, from the very beginning of this new relationship the Presbyterians respected and tried to preserve the privacy of their famous neighbor. Visitors were told, as they are today, that Rancho de los Burros was on private land with no public access. Gradually, her fears were allayed and the relationship grew warmer. Office personnel sometimes did secretarial work for her, and Ghost Ranch folks replaced the pump on her well. O'Keeffe became friendly enough with longtime ranch director, Jim Hall, and his wife, Ruth, to have Christmas dinner with them.

She made a monetary gift towards construction of the Halls' retirement home on the ranch. When fire destroyed the headquarters building in 1983, O'Keeffe immediately made a gift of $50,000 and lent her name to a Challenge Fund for the Phoenix campaign, which resulted in the headquarters building being replaced and the addition of a Social Center and the Ruth Hall Museum.

During the last few years of her life, O'Keeffe was unable to come to Ghost Ranch from Abiquiu. Eventually, she moved to Santa Fe where she died in her 99th year, reclusive to the end. "I find people very difficult," she once said.

Ghost Ranch gave her the freedom to paint what she saw and felt. Knowledgeable visitors can look around the ranch and identify many of the scenes she painted. Red-and-gray hills, like those across from the roadside park south of the ranch headquarters, were frequent subjects. Kitchen Mesa, at the upper end of the valley, is an example of the red-and-yellow cliffs she painted many times. Pedernal, the flat-topped mountain to the south, was probably her favorite subject. "It's my private mountain," she frequently said. "God told me if I painted it often enough I could have it." And of course, the Ghost Ranch logo, used on everything from stationery to T-shirts, was adapted from an O'Keeffe drawing.

There are no O'Keeffe paintings on the ranch, and there is no public access to her Ghost Ranch home. Instead, there are the stunning vistas captured by this remarkable lady.

A CENTURY OF O'KEEFFE

1887	Born November 15 near Sun Prairie, Wisconsin.
1902	Family moved to Williamsburg, Virginia.
1905	Entered Art Institute of Chicago.
1907	Enrolled in Art Students League of New York.
1912–18	Artist in New York: Exhibitions, flower paintings, city painting; marriage to Stieglitz.
1929	First summer in New Mexico (Taos).
1934	First summer at Ghost Ranch.
1940	Bought Rancho de los Burros from Arthur Pack at Ghost Ranch.
1945	Bought house in Abiquiu.
1946	Stieglitz died.
1949	Moved permanent residence to Abiquiu.
1953	Extensive world travel; recipient of awards and honors; continued exhibitions.
1971	Eyesight deterioration began.
1976	O'Keeffe's autobiographical picture book, *Georgia O'Keeffe*, published.
1984	Moved from Abiquiu to Santa Fe.
1984	Died March 6 in Santa Fe.
1997	Museum dedicated to Georgia O'Keeffe opens in Santa Fe.

★　★　★

TAOS

TAOS

Population 3,369 · Elevation 6,983

The Spanish community of Taos developed two miles southwest of Taos Pueblo. It later served as a supply base for the "Mountain Men", and was the home of Kit Carson, who is buried here. Governor Charles Bent was killed here in the anti-U.S. insurrection of 1847. In the early 1900s, Taos developed as a colony for artists and writers.

HISTORIC TAOS

There is evidence that man has lived in the Taos area as far back as 3000 BC. Prehistoric ruins dating from AD 900 can be seen throughout the Taos Valley. The Pueblo of Taos remains the link from these early inhabitants of the valley to the still-living native culture.

The first Europeans to appear in Taos Valley were led by Captain Alvarado, who was exploring the area for the Coronado expedition of 1540. Don Juan de Oñate, official colonizer of the province of Nuevo Mexico, came to Taos in July 1598. In September of that year he assigned Fray Francisco de Zamora to serve the Taos and Picuris Pueblos.

Long-established trading networks at Taos Pueblo, plus its mission and the abundant water and timber of the valley, attracted early Spanish settlers. Life was not easy for the newcomers, and there were several conflicts with Taos Pueblo before the Pueblo revolt of 1680 in which all Spaniards and their priests were either killed or driven from the province. In 1692, Don Diego de Vargas made a successful military reconquest of New Mexico and in 1693, he returned to recolonize the province. In 1694, he raided Taos Pueblo when its people refused to provide corn for his starving settlers in Santa Fe.

The people of Taos Pueblo revolted again in 1696, and De Vargas came for the third time to crush the rebellion by force of arms. Thereafter, Taos and most of the other Rio Grande Pueblos remained allies of Spain and later of Mexico when it won its independence in 1821. During this long period, the famous Taos Trade Fairs grew in importance so that even the annual caravan to Chihuahua delayed its departure until after the Taos Fair, held in July or August. The first French traders, led by the Mallette brothers, attended the Taos Fair in 1739.

By 1760, the population of Taos Valley had decreased because of the fierce attacks by plains Native Americans. Many times the Spanish settlers had to move into houses at Taos Pueblo for protection from these raiders. In 1779, Colonel de Anza returned through Taos from Colorado, where he had decisively defeated the Comanches led by Cuerno Verde. De Anza named the Sangre de Cristo Pass, northeast of present Fort Garland, and also named the road south from Taos to Santa Fe through Miranda Canyon as part of "El Camino Real." In the period between 1796–97, the Don Fernando de Taos grant was given to 63 Spanish families.

By the early 1800s, Taos had become the headquarters for many of the famous mountain men who trapped beaver in the neighboring mountains. Among them was Kit Carson, who made his home in Taos from 1826–68. In July 1826, Padre Antonio Jose Martinez began serving the Taos Catholic population. In 1834, he opened a church school in Taos and published religious textbooks. He printed *El Crepusculo*, a weekly newspaper, in 1835, and was prominent in territorial matters during the Mexican and early periods in New Mexico.

After Mexico had gained independence from Spain in 1821, the Santa Fe Trail became the important route for trade between the United States and Mexico. A branch of the trail came through Taos to supply the town's trading needs.

From 1821–46, the Mexican government made numerous land grants to help settle new sections of New Mexico. During the war with Mexico in 1846, General Stephen Kearney and his U.S. troops occupied the province of New Mexico. Taos rebelled against the new wave of invaders, and in 1847 killed the newly appointed Governor Charles Bent in his Taos home. In 1850, the province, which then included Arizona, officially became the territory of New Mexico of the United States.

During the Civil War, the Confederate army flew its flag for six weeks over Santa Fe. It was just prior to this time that Kit Carson, Smith Simpson, Ceran St. Vrain, and others put up the American flag over Taos Plaza and guarded it. Since then, Taos has had the honor of flying the flag day and night.

The discovery of gold in the Moreno Valley in 1866, and later in the mountains near Taos, brought many new people to the area. Twining and Red River, once mining towns, are now prominent ski resorts.

The Carson National Forest contains forested lands in the Sangre de Cristo and Jemez Mountain Ranges. It was created from the Pecos River Forest Reserve of 1892, the Taos Forest Reserve of 1906, and part of the Jemez National Forest of 1905.

A narrow gauge railroad—the Denver and Rio Grande Western—was built in 1880 from Alamosa, Colorado, and ran for 25 miles southwest of Taos. In later years, it was nicknamed the Chili Line, and eventually connected with Santa Fe. A surrey and four horses joggled passengers from the station to Taos. During World War II, the train was discontinued; Embudo Station on the Rio Grande is all that is left of it today.

The next invasion began in 1898, when two eastern artists came to Taos and depicted on canvas the dramatic mountains and unique peoples. By 1912, the Taos Society of Artists was formed by these and other artists who had been attracted to the area. Also in 1912, New Mexico became a state.

World Wars I and II came and went, and members of the three cultures of Taos—Native Americans, Spanish, and Anglo—fought and died together for their country.

In 1965, a steel arch bridge was built west of Taos to span the gorge 650 feet above the Rio Grande, thus opening up the northwestern part of New Mexico for easy access from Taos.

THE MABEL DODGE LUHAN HOUSE

HISTORY

Mabel Dodge was born Mabel Ganson in 1879, into a wealthy and conservative banking family in the city of Buffalo, New York. She was widowed at age 25 when her husband, Karl Evans, died. Left with a son, John, she married a Bostonian architect, Edwin Dodge, very soon after. They all eventually left the United States to live in Florence, Italy. Bored with Italy, Mabel decided to return to New York,  and bored with her second marriage, she and Edwin divorced. She then married for a third time, to the artist Maurice Sterne. Maurice soon left alone for Taos, New Mexico, to "paint Indians." At his urging, Mabel joined him in Taos in 1916. This marriage also did not go well for Mabel, and Maurice returned to New York while Mabel remained in Taos.

In 1918, Mabel bought 12 acres on the edge of Taos. The building site location was brought to her attention by a local Taos Pueblo Native American, Tony Luhan, whom she later married. Mabel paid $1,500

129

to Manuel de Jesus Trujillo for the land. Existing on the property was a three- to four-room adobe house. With Tony Luhan's supervision, Mabel built several additions on the small house. Eventually, the house grew to 450 feet in length. When the building was completed, the house had a square footage of 8,440 feet, which included 17 rooms.

Mabel was known to entertain her visitors from back East, and friends with Native Americans of the Taos Pueblo. She had them perform their dances and songs in the dining room.

Mabel's death occurred in 1962. Her son, John, inherited the house and was unsuccessful in selling it. Mabel's granddaughter, Bonne Bell, lived in the house for about a year, and then moved out. Actor-producer Dennis Hopper bought the house in 1969. For reasons known only to him, he chose not to live in the larger house but, instead, lived in a smaller home owned by the Taos Pueblo. In 1977, the house was bought again and used as a learning center for workshops, seminars, etc. Presently, the house is being used as a well-known and popular bed-and-breakfast.

MARIA E. FORTIN'S STORY

I've been working at the house since October of 1991. The house is now a bed-and-breakfast, for which I am the receptionist and assistant house manager. It's a pleasant place to work because it's quiet, and, aside from the occasional ghost, I enjoy it here very much.

I recall an experience that happened to me about two years ago. It was a nice spring day. At around 3 p.m., I was sitting in my usual chair behind a desk in the reception room. The reception room currently doubles as the bed-and-breakfast's gift shop but was, in years past, Mabel's library. Located in the reception room is a stairway that leads up to the second floor. There have been several guests who have told me that they have seen the ghostly figure of a woman standing on the stairs. These guests, unknown to each other, have commented that the woman wears a white dress. I knew, from speaking with locals and reading some material on Mabel, that she was fond of wearing white dresses. Some locals at the time nicknamed her "The Bride," because of her strange but cute custom.

Sitting that afternoon in the reception room, I was thinking about what past guests had said about the sightings, and was staring at the stairway directly in front of me. Soon, I turned my attention to the paperwork on my desk and opened the reservation book. I was busy checking the informa-tion regarding check-ins and such, when I suddenly noticed the faint scent of cinnamon in the air. I turned my attention away from the book and deter-mined that, sure enough, there was a cinnamon smell coming into the room. It quickly envel-oped the small reception room. I

Maria Fortin.

rose from my chair and walked over to the rear door. There was no hint of anyone, or of an opened spice jar. I decided to take a look in the kitchen, which was two rooms removed from the reception room, at the north end of the house. Perhaps someone had gone into the kitchen without my noticing them and had decided to bake. Entering the kitchen, I noticed that there was no one around and, strangely, that the scent of cinnamon was not to be found. I thought this was queer. I de-cided to return to the reception room. As soon as I entered the room, it hit me again. The scent of the spice was so overwhelming that it made my head spin. Unexpectedly, at that same moment, a woman who con-ducts tours for visitors to Taos entered the front door and walked over to the reception room. As soon as she entered, her eyes and face lit up with excitement. She took a deep breath and then said, "Mabel is here. Do you smell her presence? She's here right in this room!" I didn't know what this woman was talking about, so I asked her to explain why she was saying these things. She told me that when Mabel Dodge was alive, she enjoyed the smell of cinnamon so much that she always had it around her. She placed small saucers of crushed cinnamon in each room of the house, and hung handmade potpourris of flowers and cinnamon in the closets and on the doorknobs. Apparently, it was an obsession with Mabel. Because of this trait, it was not uncommon for the scent of cinnamon to precede the ghostly apparition of Mabel Dodge.

I was unaware of this information, but then I recalled one of the times a guest had told me about seeing the image of the ghostly figure on the stairs. She had said that at the time of the apparition, she had noticed the strong spicy scent of cinnamon in the room. I got quiet and contemplative. Was I about to witness a ghost? Was the ghost of Mabel Dodge in the room with me? The thought of seeing a ghost overwhelmed me with fear. I got goosebumps on my arms, and the hair on the back of my neck stood on end. All the while, the strong scent of cinnamon lingered in the room.

Minutes later, the tour woman left the house. Not wishing to see the ghost, I decided to take a short walk outside, taking comfort in the

bright, reassuring light of the afternoon sun. I never got to witness the ghost, but I came pretty close that day.

Since then, I've had guests come up to me and tell me that they have been awakened in the middle of the night by an unknown source, and have seen a woman's figure standing before them in their bedroom. She is dressed in a white fabric and slowly disappears into thin air. There also have been guests who have commented to me that they have been awakened by the song of a Native American. They have gotten out of bed to locate the source of the singing. After a few minutes the singing stops. To say the least, these guests were alarmed by what they had experienced. I can't say I blame them. You have to be pretty strong emotionally to see these things. As for me, I just wish every one of the ghosts well, and hope they keep their distance, at least while I'm on duty.

THE GARDEN RESTAURANT

LARRY C. TIBBETT'S STORY

The Garden Restaurant began in this building 13 years ago. Before that, it was an indoor flea market, and before that it was a grocery store. I've personally been associated with the restaurant since it began. Currently, The Garden Restaurant serves breakfast, lunch, and dinner and we have a bakery. We're located on the Taos Plaza, so it's easy to find and it's often a resting point while people are window-shopping or strolling through the many stores and galleries. It's also a popular gathering spot for locals and tourists alike.

It was either the first or second day after purchasing the property that I decided to take the stairs down to the basement and look around. I found the usual items that would be found in such an old building (e.g., cardboard boxes and trash). However, in one corner of the basement there was a cardboard box, which, surprisingly, contained a complete human skeleton. Pulling back the cardboard flaps, I could see the rib, hand, spine, leg, and arm bones, a disorderly mass of bony framework including the skull. The bones were amazingly clean, although dusty. Apparently, one of the past owners of the building was into archaeology. Soon afterward, when the basement has been cleaned and all the trash had been removed, the box that contained the bones was moved to the

Larry C. Tibbetts, co-owner.

rear of the basement and forgotten. Two years later, the restaurant changed hands. The new owners, who were devout Catholics, took notice of the box with the skeleton and decided to have a local priest perform a blessing over the bones and bless the building. An archaeologist from the local museum was also called in and revealed the origin of the bones. We were told that they were of a Native American woman. For their own reasons, the new owners named the skeleton "Snowflake." After the priest was done with his blessings, the box of bones was taken somewhere in town and reburied.

I've never had anything spiritual or unusual happen to me here in the building, but employees have. I've been told about strange noises, cold chills, and other ghost-like things that have happened to workers, like seeing dark figures walking about the building. Our two bakers, Anna and Earl, who spend most of their time in the basement where the bakery is now located, have experienced such strange things.

"SNOWFLAKE"
ANNA M. JOHNSON'S STORY

I have been one of the bakers at The Garden Restaurant now for about seven months. The ghost, or Snowflake, as the employees call her, has made her presence known to me in very strange ways. Although I have been scared by her, I want to think she'll never do me any harm. I hope she is a kind and friendly spirit, at least to me. I try to do nice little gestures to show her that I would like to be her friend. For instance, whenever I have any leftover dough, I will bake her own miniature loaf, and place it away from the other employees' view. I usually place it on top of a shelf and in the back, away from view. Strangely, when I have looked for it in a few days, it would be gone. I'll then ask the others about the "missing" bread and they won't have a clue. I make these personal offerings of goodwill to Snowflake because I don't want her to do anything mean or evil to me. I admit that when I'm alone in the basement, the last thing I want is to have a nasty ghost watching my every move. Of course I get scared. Who wouldn't? So my little bread loaves for Snowflake are my guarantee that she will leave me alone.

Former employees, Earl P. White and Anna M. Johnson.

NEW MEXICO GHOST STORIES, VOL. I

The restaurant's bakery is located in the basement. I know when Snowflake is around because I'll hear strange footsteps on the ceiling above me. When I'm alone down there in the wee hours of the morning, sometimes I'll hear these footsteps. The temperature in the basement reaches between 90 and 100 degrees because of the ovens. Strangely, I'll feel the presence of someone in the basement with me. It's a freaky feeling. Then suddenly, I'll feel this bone-chilling cold wind. I'll become motionless, because I already know this is the sign that the ghost is about. Suddenly, this cold wind will pass right through me! The cold air will last about 30 seconds, then slowly it passes. I experience this about once or twice a week between the hours of 9 p.m. and 5 a.m. If someone speaks about the ghost, or mentions her name, it's almost a guarantee that she will give you a dose of cold air. Because I've been talking to you about her during this interview, I know she will become excited and make her presence known to me tonight. I just know it! I'm not the only person who has experienced this. There is another baker named Earl who has heard the noises and felt the cold wind.

A couple of months ago, two other bakers and I were working in the basement when suddenly we all heard the sounds of footsteps coming from above. We stopped what we were doing, and, when the sounds continued, we looked at each other. Then, without any further notice we heard a large metal object hit the floor above us. Boy, we were scared! The footsteps continued, only this time we heard a larger metal object being dragged as well. We all thought it was a burglar in the restaurant above us. Then we heard the footsteps become louder and louder. I grabbed a large knife that was on the table, and with the other two employees following behind, we made our way slowly but cautiously up the stairs. We turned on the lights, but saw no one. We looked under every table and in each bathroom. Nothing was out of place. The doors were all locked from the inside. Immediately, we knew that the source of the noise was not due to any living person. It had to be Snowflake!

There are other times when I'll be in the basement and I'll hear the pots and pans making all sorts of noise. I'll go into the next room where they are kept on the shelves and hanging on hooks. I'll find several pots

136

thrown haphazardly about the basement. It's crazy. Sometimes, I'll be busy at work listening to the radio, and then I'll hear a noise, look up, and see two, three, or more pans just fly off the rack onto the floor, slide across the room, and end up at the opposite wall!

I know there are such things as ghosts. If I didn't know before, I sure do now. I get scared sometimes when I'm alone in the restaurant. Although Snowflake has scared me, I know she is just upset because of all the years her bones were kept unceremoniously in a cardboard box. Her spirit must be trapped within the walls of the restaurant. I just hope she finds rest and peace someday.

EARL P. WHITE'S STORY

I've baked for The Garden Restaurant now for over a year and a half. There have been mornings when I've been in the basement between 1 and 3 a.m., baking cookies and such, when I've heard thuds and footsteps on the floor above me. At first, I was just annoyed, but soon I became more and more frightened due to the history of the skeleton in the basement.

I've felt the cold wind that Anna has spoken about. The bakery has no windows, so when this cold wind approaches, you can feel it for sure! It's been my experience that when the footsteps have begun upstairs, the cold wind has surely followed down in the basement. It's difficult to regard this stuff as normal. I sometimes work alone, so I don't want to encourage the ghost to visit me. The whole subject makes me uncomfortable.

THE HACIENDA MARTINEZ

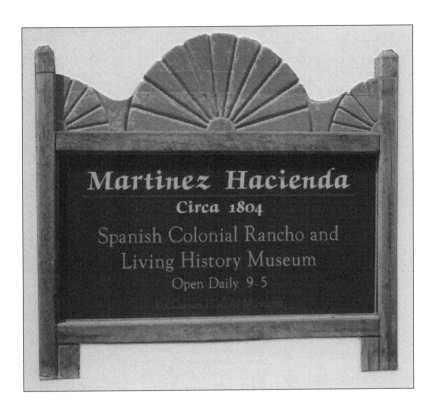

HISTORY

In October of 1983, over 250 descendants of Antonio Severino and
Maria del Carmel (Santistevan) Martinez gathered at the hacienda to

celebrate the opening of their ancestral home as a museum. Members of the family had continuously occupied the hacienda until 1931. The house represents not only the cultural heritage of the Martinez family, but it's a living expression of the continuity and vitality of the Spanish-colonial pioneering frontier spirit of northern New Mexico.

The term "hacienda" may be a misnomer for the structure, as the designation in New Mexico is more appropriately applied to the large, early colonial period constructions of the 17th century that were built by, and dependent on, for the most part, forced Native American labor. After the reconquest the primary form or unit of settlement became the *rancho*, a term common in northern New Mexico for a more modest, self-sufficient establishment of one or more households. The designation, hacienda, does not seem to have been customarily used in this area again until the arrival of the Americans in the first quarter of the last century. At the time of Severino's death in 1827, his sons, Padre Antonio Jose and Santiago Martinez, referred to the home in written documents as a *casa mayor*, or great house (could be old house as well). Regardless, locally the Martinez family's *casa mayor* has come to be known as the Martinez Hacienda, although, to be more correct, in Spanish it should be *Hacienda Martinez* or *La Hacienda de los Martinez*.

Other terms that have come down to us from the Spanish colonial period that could also be appropriate include "restricted plaza" and "casa-corral." The restricted plaza identifies a single extended family-occupied fortified compound containing a small plaza or *placita*. "Casa-corral" is perhaps an even better designation, as it is defined as a *placita* surrounded by living quarters, storage areas, and rooms for entertaining. This is all attached to a second *placita*, or walled corral area, that may or may not have had additional rooms for servants or slaves and enclosures for animals, supplies, and tack. There are no indications in the historic record to determine if the second *placita* was constructed in Severino's time, or added later by one of his heirs. However, based on the fortress-like construction of the first *placita*, it seems reasonable that Severino would have built a walled corral for the protection of his animals as well.

RESTORATION OF THE HACIENDA

From 1804 until 1931, members of the Martinez family owned the hacienda. With the death of Severino Martinez in 1827, the hacienda passed to his wife and children, and when Maria del Carmel died two years later, the entire estate transferred to the children and their spouses. The youngest son, Pascual Bailon Martinez, eventually acquired sole possession of the hacienda. Pascual continued to increase the family's landholdings, while maintaining extensive ranch and trade operations that extended to Chihuahua in the south and St. Louis to the east. Pascual died in 1882, and the hacienda remained with his heirs until 1931.

Each generation of the Martinez family has made untold changes to the building by adding and enlarging windows and doors, and altering interior and exterior spaces to meet the needs of the new families and the changing times. In the early years of the 20th century, Taos Society of Artists member Eanger Irving Couse rented a portion of the hacienda from the Martinez family and had a huge north-facing window installed for his studio.

The hacienda began to fall into disrepair around the time of World War II, and was little more than an abandoned ruin in 1964 when Jerome and Anne Milord purchased it and started a major restoration project of the structure. The Milords were unable to complete the work, and in 1972 sold the hacienda to the Kit Carson Memorial Foundation, now known as the Kit Carson Historic Museum.

With the assistance of historians, archaeologists, historic preservation architects, and the descendants of Severino and Maria del Carmel Martinez, the Foundation, under the leadership of Director Jack Boyer, began the extraordinarily ambitious project of restoring and furnishing the hacienda to reflect the 1820s period, when it had been occupied by Severino and his family. One of the most important contributions to the restoration was a historic document, the "Last Will and Testament of Don Severino Martinez." The will and associated probate documents provided a detailed accounting of virtually all of Severino's belongings and their relative value, as well as the number and size of many of the rooms within the great house. Through these documents we are able to view the material culture and to appreciate the lifeways of the late Spanish colonial and early Mexican Republic periods of Taos.

Today, the Hacienda Martinez is a restoration. Sincere attempts have been made from the beginning of the project to recreate the atmosphere and character of the early part of the 19th century. As future research and scholarship reveal new information about this special place, the museum will continue the interpretation-and-restoration process. Additional alterations will be made to reflect the new findings in an effort to more accurately represent the site and times. This ongoing process of interpreting and authenticating will give visitors a better understanding and appreciation of the historical and cultural developments of northern New Mexico.

ELMA TORRES'S STORY

I've been working at the Hacienda Martinez now for seven years. When I began, I was the receptionist, and now I'm currently the head receptionist.

I'm not the kind of person who welcomes ghostly experiences or expects any unusual happenings or apparitions. That's why I was left with such a feeling of shock when I had my experiences at the hacienda. I'm hoping that the spirits I encountered at the hacienda continue to be friendly to me. After all, I'm still working at the house and I don't want to upset anyone living, or especially anyone who's dead. I'm hoping that if I ever have another encounter, I'll be able to deal with it—but who knows?

My first experience at the hacienda took place during one October evening. It was around 5 p.m. I remember that I had been employed for three years and, until then, had never had any unusual ghostly encounters. I had heard from other employees and groundskeepers that strange things did go on at the old adobe compound, but I didn't pay their stories too much attention.

Well, that evening it was quite cold, and all the tourists had left the property hours before. I was seated in the bookstore/entrance area browsing through one of the many books that are sold at the hacienda. I was just passing the time until 5 p.m. when I could go home. I began to hear some noises directly outside the front door. I placed the book I was reading down on the desk, and waited for the knob to turn and for a tourist or two to enter. I heard the sounds of someone moving about and the shuffling of feet. I waited for the door to open, but no one came in. Thinking whoever it was had changed their mind about entering, I glanced at the clock and picked up my book and began to read. About 15 minutes later, once again I heard someone outside the entrance door. I could clearly hear the shuffling of shoes and other sounds that indicated to me that there was someone on the other side. I placed the book on the desk, rose from my chair, and made my way to the door. I placed my ear to the door in an attempt to hear a voice, but I heard nothing. I took hold of the knob, gave it a strong pull, and opened it wide. Expecting to see someone, I was quite surprised to see I was alone. There was no wind, just the stillness and cold of the fall evening. I took a few steps, looked around the building, but saw no one. Who could it have been? I

"I heard footsteps on the gravel . . ."

didn't have a clue, but I know that I heard someone. I just know it! Was it a ghost? You tell me. What else could it have been?

The following year, also in October, I was closing up the hacienda. All the tourists had left, and I was making my usual rounds and checking to make sure all the doors and windows were locked. I made my way through each room. I then went outside and proceeded to the breezeway that connects the first courtyard to the second. As I walked through the breezeway, I immediately felt the presence of a person close to me. I naturally stopped and turned to face the person. There was no one visible to me. Then I thought to myself, how odd that I would sense such a thing. I tried to disregard this strange feeling, and once again took a few steps in the direction of the second courtyard. I found that the overwhelming feeling of someone standing next to me was too strong to ignore anymore. At this point, I heard the footsteps on the gravel of someone rushing up to my right side. I froze, and then suddenly I heard the deep, hard breathing sounds that someone makes as they inhale, then exhale, a breath of air. I actually felt the breath on my neck! I don't know what snapped inside me, but at that point I quickly turned around and dashed to the front office. I didn't care if the remainder of the building was not secured and locked. I had just one thing in mind: to get the heck out of there! I managed to turn off the main light switch, lock the front door, and get into my car. I'll never forget this experience. I was told sometime after this that several people have seen and have heard a woman crying in one of the rooms. We've even had a medium, or psychic, walk through the room who has told us that the woman is definitely very sad about something. Some employees have reported seeing this ghostly woman walk by the windows as they watch from the outside. I get goosebumps just hearing their stories. Although I've not seen this woman's spirit, there have been times that I have been leisurely walking through the hacienda and I have seen shadows. It can be day or night. I've noticed the silhouette, or shadowlike

"I immediately felt the presence of a person . . ."

143

presence, of someone either looking at me from a window or walking past a door. I know what I've seen is real. I even saw the outline of a person's head facing me from a window.

All these things have given me, over time, the emotional toughness and energy I need to simply deal with the ghosts. They haven't hurt me, so, since I don't talk bad about them, I hope they keep their distance.

Another employee had an experience when she was also alone at the hacienda one night. Her name is Dolores. She really got scared at the time. It seems that strange things happen to us when we are alone, and towards the end of the day. That's just the way it is, I guess.

DOLORES I. STRUCK'S STORY

I began working at the hacienda in February 1993. My present position is receptionist/clerk. I was born and raised in Rancho de Taos.

It was a cold October evening, and the time was 5:30 p.m. I was at the hacienda and was alone. I was counting the money and totaling up the day's receipts from the admissions and book sales. Suddenly, I heard a man's voice singing or humming outside the front door. The sound he was making made me think he was very happy about something. It was loud and joyous. I stopped what I was doing, and went to see if there was a tourist that had lingered too long and was locked out. I opened the door, looked around, and didn't see anyone. I'm not sure why this affected me so negatively, but I got scared. I wanted to get out of there fast. I was very sure that what I had heard was not my imagination. I knew it wasn't. I hadn't heard this singing before, so I was scared.

Another experience that I've had at the hacienda is the feeling that someone is staring at me. I feel someone's eyes just watching me. This always happens unexpectedly. Just out of the blue, I feel someone's glaring eyes watching me. I turn around, and there is no one; I am all alone in the room.

People have told me about the ghost of a woman crying in one of the rooms. I haven't seen her, but people have heard her crying.

There are other incidents that have happened to me in the first courtyard area. When I've gone from room to room, closing and locking up the windows and doors for the evening, I've returned to discover three of the windows wide open. Could it be the wind? Maybe. I don't want to talk about this anymore . . . I just hope it's a friendly ghost.

THE STABLES ART CENTER

The Stables Art Center was once the home of Arthur Rochford Manby, an Englishman who came to New Mexico in 1883 to seek his fortune. It was in this house that his headless body was found on July 3, 1929.

In April 1898, Manby bought seven parcels of land (about 23 acres) just north of Kit Carson's home and the old wall of Taos, and east of the public road to the Taos Pueblo.

Manby had been trained as an architect in Belfast, Ireland, and promptly set about designing and building his enormous Spanish-style hacienda of 19 rooms set in a square with three wings, stables, and outer walls. The adobes were made in the back pasture (Kit Carson Park), and timber and *vigas* were cut and hauled from the nearby mountains. In 1907, the house interior was described by visitors as having rough plank floors, spruce rafters, and walls plastered with *tierra blanca*.

The house was furnished in 1907 with English furniture of walnut and mahogany, old Spanish chests, and fine oil paintings, one of which secured the future of the house. A 1904 photograph shows Manby seated in a wicker chair in front of the kitchen fireplace, where an iron teakettle hangs over the fire.

When heiress Mabel Dodge Sterne arrived in Taos in December 1916, before building her own house, she immediately rented Manby's new house, the "largest and most attractive house in town." She agreed to pay Manby $75 a month and Manby moved into the west wing of the house. Manby's house was large enough to fit both their needs, and thus, they both benefited from this arrangement.

Soon Mabel moved out of the home, and not long after Manby died in 1929. His death created "the greatest unsolved mystery of the West."

The property then was bought by Dr. Victor Thorne, a wealthy New York art collector, who had purchased one of Manby's paintings, a Van Dyck. In 1936, he sent an employee of his, Helen Williams, to Taos to discover the condition of the house. She arrived to find the roof fallen in, squatters in some of the rooms, the front porch fallen down, and the windows all broken out. She wrote to Dr. Thorne that the place was beyond repair, "absolutely ridiculous," but he sent instructions to go ahead with remodeling the home at any cost.

Dr. Thorne never did get to Taos. When he died suddenly without leaving a will, Williams continued to respect his wishes, renamed the home Thorne House, and opened it as a community center. Religious groups met in Thorne House, brides held their receptions there, and music lovers gathered in the gardens to listen to each other's records.

Inevitably, with the passing years, Helen Williams aged. Hoping to see Thorne House continue to serve the public, she found an appropriate solution in Emil Bisttram's dream of a museum and gallery for the artists of Taos—and the Taos Artists Association, now known as the Taos Art Association, was founded. In 1952, they purchased the Thorne property—house, lilac garden, stables, and three acres to the east—for $45,000, at one-half of 1-percent interest.

The house was quickly turned into a museum, and then the artists tackled the stables. They tore down the stalls, cemented the floors, and plastered inside and out. The outside doors were left in place, huge doors that could be opened in good weather.

The museum proved to be too difficult for amateurs to manage; all of the borrowed treasures were returned to their owners. For a decade, Thorne House held the newly founded Millicent Rogers Museum, until it could expand into a home of its own seven miles north of Taos. Then came Del Sol, a weaving cooperative, whose members were reviving the old weaving traditions of northern New Mexico.

Finally, in 1972, the president of the Taos Art Association made the decision to move the gallery from the stables into the front house.

People always asked the docents, "In which room was Manby's body found?" There were two adjacent bedrooms in the front of the house. His head was found in one and his body was located in the other.

As we recognize it today, Arthur Rochford Manby's house became the Stables Art Center.

VIKKI E. MADDEN'S STORY

I began working at the Stables Art Center in February 1994. I'm a jeweler, and my present position is gift shop manager.

Prior to my employment here, no one mentioned anything about the place being haunted. However, after three months of working at the gallery, people became more comfortable with speaking of strange and unusual occurrences. I didn't even know the history of the building or about Mr. Manby.

On July 1994, at 6:30 p.m., I was closing the shop and had made sure that everyone was out of the gallery and gift shop. I heard some sounds coming from the back office, and I thought that was strange because the place was empty. The sounds I heard were of someone walking on the floorboards. You know, heavy footsteps. This is an old building, and the floors are original. It's difficult for anyone to sneak up on someone simply because

"On the floor were fresh dog-paw prints!"

the old floors are so noisy. I suspected that someone was in the back office and was walking about. I decided to investigate. I looked about the rear of the gallery where the offices are located and, not finding anyone, I decided to leave. I turned, and as I approached the front door, I heard the unmistakable sound of footsteps once again. I had to satisfy my curiosity, so I returned to the rear office area. I thought that perhaps someone was hiding and playing a trick on me. I turned on all the lights, and inspected behind every door and under every desk. I have to admit that soon after I was feeling pretty creepy. Again, I decided to leave and, just as before, when I reached the front of the gallery, I heard the footsteps once again. At this point I did feel scared. Slowly, I made my way to the rear of the gallery, turning on the lights as I went. I noticed on the floor of one of the rear rooms there were fresh dog-paw prints! I got down on one knee to take a closer look. Yes, indeed, I thought, these prints were definitely not here before. Using one of my fingers, I reached out to touch one of the prints. The print, made out of dirt, was that of a medium-size dog—and it was fresh!

I got up, looked about the room, and rubbed my arms. They were covered in goosebumps. I quickly turned off the lights and swiftly made my way to the front of the gallery and locked the door behind me.

When I returned the following morning, I decided not to mention my previous night's experience for fear that I would be seen as a "wacko." The morning's bright light gave me the courage I needed to once again visit the floor where the prints were. They were gone! Since I was the last person to leave, and the first one to enter in the morning, I was upset by the whole experience. People have told me that Mr. Manby owned a dog that went everywhere with him.

I definitely get an eerie feeling that comes over me when I'm alone here at the gallery. I mean, the owner's headless body was found in this very room years ago. This is reason enough for me to believe that some negativity is still around, wouldn't you agree?

ARTHUR R. MANBY HOUSE'S CHRONOLOGY

1898   In April, Arthur Manby bought the land and began to build his hacienda.

1907   Manby furnished his house with English pieces in walnut and mahogany, old Spanish chests, and fine oil paintings.

1916   In December, Mabel Dodge Sterne agreed to rent the "largest and most attractive house in town" from Manby for $75 a month.

1921   Mabel Dodge Luhan moved into her own home.

1929   On July 3, Manby's headless body was found in the house.

1936   Helen Williams arrived to refurbish the Manby house for Dr. Thorne.

1938   First central heating in Taos installed in Thorne House.

1940   Thorne House opened as a community center.

1952   Thorne House and three acres of land to the east purchased by Taos Art Association.

1953–57 TAA Museum period rooms furnished from local collections.

1958–68 Millicent Rogers's museum collection displayed in Thorne House. Del Sol weaving cooperative in the building.

1972   The Stables Art Gallery moved from the stables into the house.

1980   The structure of the TAA changed, making this the Stables Art Center.

"GRAMPS"

BOBBIE A. GONZALES'S STORY

I'm a firm believer that life goes on after our physical bodies have been laid to rest. I know this to be a fact. As you hear my personal story, you too may come to believe this as well.

My story is not scary or morbid. It is, instead, a personal story of the love I had, and still hold, for my grandfather, Jesse Parra.

Jesse Parra, "Gramps."

Bobbie A. Gonzales.

Gramps was born in 1905. As a child, I always sought attention from Gramps. I loved his warm hugs and caring face. I know now how fortunate I was to know the warmth of my grandfather's love. I respected and honored him for simply being Gramps.

As an adult, I always made it a point to make contact with him each day. Gramps lived in his own place with his little dog, Señor. I would either pay

151

Gramps a daily visit or give him a phone call just to let him know I had not forgotten him. Many evenings I would walk with Gramps and Señior, taking in the fresh air and beautiful sunsets for which Taos is famous. When I would arrive at Gramp's townhouse, he would proudly bring out a fresh bowl of his homemade salsa, which we both quickly finished off.

One day, I convinced Gramps to take a short vacation to visit my brother and sister in San Francisco. While Gramps was off in California, I decided to shampoo the rugs in my home. Since the rugs were wet, I thought it would be best to spend a couple of days at Gramps's place until they had dried out. At the same time, I could watch over Gramps's little companion, Señior. I phoned and spoke to Gramps, who described in detail all the fun he was having in Northern California. One portion of the conversation I clearly recall was his enjoyment in describing how much he loved walking on the seashore, collecting sand dollars and shells. He also spoke about attending a football game and eating ice cream with his nephew. The following day everyone, including Gramps, was to rise early and go deep-sea fishing. His voice was filled with excitement, and I was so very happy to know that things were going well. We ended our conversation with "I love you."

That evening, as I slept soundly in Gramps's bed with Señior by my side, I was awakened. I slowly opened my eyes and turned to see what time it was. The clock marked the hour at 4 a.m. I sluggishly sat up in bed, and without any clear thought gazed towards the hallway. There, in the dim

"There, in the dim light, I saw the image . . ."

light, I saw the image of my grandfather. Without pausing to make sense of the moment, I accepted what I was seeing. He was dressed in his usual flannel shirt, a white T-shirt, and brown pants. I was not alarmed, I just absorbed the moment, so to speak, and peace came over me. I saw Gramps's little dog, Señor, by the bed viewing everything, but not making a whimper. He just seemed to take everything in his stride. When I returned my eyes to Gramps's image, I saw Gramps extend his arm, and turn his hand palm up, and then slowly raise it to the level of his waist. For some unknown reason, I understood the message that Gramps had successfully conveyed to me. Gramps had died, and he had come back to say good-bye. At that moment, as I understood the purpose of his visit, his spirit must have known I understood, because the image of my grandfather then slowly began to fade away. I was left feeling a serene peace. The world was a beautiful place at that moment. A smile came over my face. The silence was broken when, after only four minutes had passed, the phone by the bed rang. When I placed the receiver to my ear, I heard my mother's voice. Before she could say another word, I stated, "Grampa died, didn't he?" She said yes, and that he had died of a stroke in his sleep.

Gramps was laid to rest in Santa Fe. Whenever I think back to the days we shared together, I feel sad and long for his company. But my grief doesn't last very long because I know that even though death is a powerful force, it can't conquer love.

WINDSONG GALLERY

WENDY WYSONG'S STORY

When I moved into the building in July 1994, I could clearly see that the place needed major work and a loving touch. Apparently, a lot of rainwater had destroyed most of the wooden floor planks, so I proceeded to make the floor my first priority when I remodeled. I removed the rotted planks and replaced them with new wood. During this process, I also reapplied mud to the old scruffy adobe walls, which were water damaged, too. I have to say that I turned the building into something I'm proud of. Currently, I'm leasing, and using, the building as a business. One portion of the building is a gallery, where I sell local religious art—santos, retablos, etc. I also try to feature local jewelers' work and Native American art. Directly above the gallery, on the second floor, are my personal living quarters. Outside the gallery building is my other business—an espresso bar named Teo's, where I sell various fresh pastries and coffees.

From what I've been told, the structure, which is over 300 years old, was part of a fortress that predates the St. Francis Church, which is located just a few yards away. I was surprised to learn that the building I'm in used to be a part of a long, massive wall that connected all the buildings that surround the present-day church. The wall formed a large rectangular shape surrounding the outside of the property, one

Wendy Wysong.

side facing the present highway to the west. Apparently, men used the top of the wall as a lookout for Comanches and Utes, who made raids on the compound day or night.

The original owners of the compound were the Arragon family. A more recent descendant of the Arragon family was a man named Timoteo. After Timoteo's death, a Texas couple bought the property and soon sold it in 1994 to the present owners. Timoteo's brother, Pedro, or Pete, lived with him. Pete had a small adobe building behind the house, which he used as a barbershop. Before her death, these two brothers' mother had requested that her older son, Timoteo, look after his younger brother, Pete. Both brothers lived in the portion of the building that's presently the gallery, until Pete's death. Pete died upstairs in the second floor above the gallery showroom in 1986. Sometime later, when Timoteo was 85 years old, he himself became very ill and was taken by his nephew to live with his family in Denver, Colorado. Sadly, while in his care, Timoteo died. In Mr. Timoteo Arragon's honor, I decided to name my espresso bar Teo's.

Well, early one evening after closing up the gallery for the night, I went upstairs to prepare dinner and settle in for the evening. Trying to decide what to prepare for dinner, I opened the pantry doors and walked inside. I stood there, and after determining what I wanted, I reached for a can on the shelf. Suddenly, the door behind me closed with such a force that I was pushed into the shelves of cans and dry goods. I immediately assumed there was someone who had walked into the gallery and come upstairs. Perhaps a friend was attempting to play a strange joke on me. I turned, and moved away from the pantry, looked around the room, and then quickly went outside. I saw no one. There was nothing available that would explain what I had just experienced in the kitchen. I heard no footsteps running away. I was left feeling bewildered. I soon realized that there was something more to this experience. I didn't feel that it was a negative force, mean or evil, despite what it had done to me; rather it was more like a wake-up call. I took it to mean that a spirit was responsible, possibly Pete or Timoteo. I believe that the spirit wanted to make itself known to me; in other words, I felt as if this entity wanted me to know that it had not left. He was still the caretaker of the building.

Señor Timoteo Arragon.

I have two cats that I brought to live with me in the building. These cats have noticeably become very nervous and strange in their habits. They used to simply lay about the house in an easygoing, cat-like manner. But now they appear nervous, and stay up all night. Also, at the sound of any small, insignificant noise, they'll jump away, turn their heads sharply towards the direction of its source, and loudly hiss. It's weird to witness their reactions. I don't see or hear anything at all, but apparently they see something very important to them. I've found them both looking up at the ceiling for several minutes at a time. They just stare and stare.

My ghostly experiences here in the building have definitely made me more aware of my surroundings and of the unique quality of this area in Taos. I'm now tuned into the sensibility that I've developed in the short time I've lived here. I'm aware of a presence, which is looking out at me, hopefully as a protective force. I can sometimes feel the eyes of someone's stare, or the physical presence of someone standing close to me. It's not a negative feeling; I just get the impression that "it" wants me to know it's here in the building with me. I guess because of the positive manner in which I've gone about remodeling the property, keeping the original owners in mind, the spirits are thankful for my sensitivity. There are a lot of new buildings being constructed all around the property. My opinion is that with all this new construction, the ghosts are feeling threatened for their beloved property. I'm sure the ancestors who took pride in their land and traditional way of life are very upset. I'm not much surprised to think that the ancestral spirits may not be happy at all to learn how we, the living, go about making changes to the area.

TAOS PUEBLO

HISTORY

Taos Pueblo, home of the Native American Taos-Tiwa, is the site of one of the oldest continually inhabited communities in the United States. Taos Pueblo is the most northern of New Mexico's 19 pueblos; it is located 70 miles north of Santa Fe, the state capital, two miles north of the world famous art colony of Taos, and some 15 miles from the internationally renowned Taos Ski Valley. The pueblo is at an elevation of 7,000 feet.

The origin of the pueblo in its present form goes back many hundreds of years before the Spanish arrived in 1540. It goes back some 300 years before Marco Polo traveled to China in the 13th century. Had Columbus "stumbled" upon the "new" world even 500 years before he did, back when Europe as we know it was young and "America" was not even a vision, and had he proceeded immediately to the great Southwest after stepping ashore on a remote island off the Atlantic Coast, he would have found in place in Taos a vibrant and established culture. The pueblo was here long before Europe emerged from the Dark Ages and made the transition from medieval to modern history.

A regiment of Spanish conquistadors from Coronado's 1540 expedition were the first Europeans to see Taos Pueblo. The Spaniards reportedly were on a quest for the Seven Cities of Cibola (the fabled cities of gold), and they believed they had finally found one of the cities of gold when they saw Taos Pueblo from afar, perhaps with the sun shining upon it. What the Spaniards saw was not a city of gold, but two massive, multistoried structures made of mud and straw and with soft, flowing lines. This came to be the distinctive architectural style of the entire Southwest. Taos Pueblo then looked very similar to the way it does now, with houses to the north and south divided by the westerly flowing Rio Pueblo de Taos.

In 1680, a massive revolt against the Spanish was conceived in Taos and launched successfully by the united effort of all the pueblos. The Spanish were driven back into Mexico and all of the territory of New Mexico, including the Spanish capital of Santa Fe, was again in Native American hands. This was an event truly distinctive in the annals of Native American resistance to the spread of the "New World." It remains today the only instance where extensive territory was recovered and retained by Native Americans through force of arms.

Taos, the seat of the rebellion, returned to its traditional, full independence for a period of almost two decades. The Spanish returned in 1693 with a large army, but Taos itself remained the center of open rebellion for some five years after the southern pueblos were once again subjected to foreign control. This distinctive military success is especially noteworthy in light of the fact that it was achieved by the traditionally

peaceful, agrarian-based pueblos, a tranquil society that initially
welcomed the foreigners with open arms.

The pueblo's native religion and culture survived not only the turmoil of the last decade of the 17th century—a hundred years before the
birth of the United States of America—but also the 1847 rebellion of
the pueblo against the new American government that had replaced the
Mexican, and other centuries of Spanish, Mexican, and American dom-
inance. Taos Pueblo has retained its old ways to a remarkable degree.

The rich cultural heritage of the pueblo is exemplified not only in the
exquisite architecture, but also in the annual seasonal dances. Visitors to
the pueblo are welcomed to observe the dances, but are not allowed to
take photographs of them.

The current reservation economy is primarily supported through
the provision of government services, tourism, arts and crafts, ranching,
and farming. In 1980, the tribal council established a Department of
Economic Development to generate tribal revenue and job opportunities and to assist local Native American businesses. Many opportunities
for development are available to the pueblo, some of which include increased capitalization of tourism, labor-intensive clean-industry plants,
and office rentals.

ALFRED J. MONTOYA'S STORY

I was born on the Taos Pueblo Reservation in 1950. The beautiful mountains that surround the pueblo are the Sangre de Cristos (Blood of Christ). The Spanish gave them this name because, during some sunsets, the light that reflects from the sky onto these mountains colors the mountains red. These mountains are sacred to the pueblo people and are always honored in a very special way. I always enjoy hiking in the mountains and being at peace with our Mother Earth. I do some deer, elk, and bear hunting and a lot of fishing. As a member of the pueblo, I don't need a hunting license to hunt these animals; however, outside of the pueblo land it's required. I prefer to stay here in our mountains where I feel free to do as I wish without restrictions. It was in these sacred mountains where I had my first experience with spirits.

In the fall of 1974, I was employed by the forest service. My job was to clean up areas where irresponsible hikers and campers had tossed papers, bottles, cans, and other trash in the forest. The crew of guys I was with used horses to travel around the area. One day, we were instructed by our supervisor to ride up to Blue Lake, which lay deep within the mountains, and clean up the area. I was busy with some other work at the time and was excused from heading out early. The others in my crew, including my supervisor, left in the morning. I was to meet up with them later in the afternoon.

At about 3:30 p.m. that afternoon, I eventually reached the lake. I scouted the area and spotted horse tracks and footprints all about the ground. I knew that the crew had done their job of cleaning up the area, so I decided to head out in the direction the crew might be in order to meet up with them. I had been instructed by my supervisor earlier that day to locate and follow an old, crude barbed-wire fence. By following the fence, I would travel in the direction the men would be going. This was a shortcut. I gazed above the mountaintops and noticed that the clouds were traveling fast. The cold night would soon come, so I attempted to hurry as best I could. Luckily, I had packed a few food supplies and a bedroll on my horse before leaving for the mountains. All I knew was that my destination, where I would meet the others, was what we called in our pueblo language, "place of the onion grass."

Ultimately, I did locate the barbed-wire fence. It branched out in two directions; one went East, the other, West. I sat on my horse for a few minutes, trying to decide which way to go. Trying to make sense of everything was difficult, especially since the forest was pretty thick with growth. I decided the best option was to follow my instincts and go in what I thought was North. I began to notice that things were not right. I knew I was getting lost because, after about five miles of riding, I began to travel down a ridge that was unfamiliar to me. To make matters worse, the sun would soon be giving way to the night, so I needed to locate my friends.

Before long, I reached an area that I recognized from other previous visits. Immediately I knew I had gone too far and had missed the trail. I reached a stream and followed it north; I needed to hurry, because the sun was now behind a ridge and a cool breeze was blowing. Suddenly, I turned to my right and I saw a beautiful big buck, 10 points to his antlers! The buck had his head lowered and was drinking from the stream. My horse made a noise, and the buck raised his head. He faced my direction and I could see his big, dark eyes gazing at me. I always carried a pistol with me, so when I saw this buck out in the open, I knew the opportunity for fresh deer meat was just a few feet away from me. I slowly reached for my gun, brought it into my line of sight, and had the buck in my view. Something inside me made me lower the pistol. I decided not to shoot. I put my pistol away and then looking right at those big black eyes, I held up my hand and in the Indian way said, "Good-bye, my brother. We will meet again someday." As I rode my horse away, I glanced behind me and noticed the buck just staring at me as I rode away. I soon reached the meadow area known as "the place of the onion grass." Since it was already dark, I thought it would be best to make camp for the night. I could join up with my buddies in the morning. It didn't take long for me to make a fire and roll out my sleeping bag. I led my horse a little way to a grassy area of the meadow and left him to graze for the night.

It was definitely a dark night. As I ate some of the food I had brought with me, I gazed up at the stars and felt at peace. I asked the Creator and Mother Earth to protect and watch over me. I threw more wood on the fire and listened to the cracking and snapping noises it produced as the wood was consumed. I rose from where I was seated, and went to get my horse. I returned to the camp and tied my horse close to where I could keep an eye on him. Throwing more wood onto the fire, I decided to make some coffee. There I was in the cold darkness, with both hands wrapped around my coffee mug. Everything was peaceful, and soon I felt sleepy enough to climb into my sleeping bag for the night. I watched the fire dance before me and very soon my eyelids became heavy. Before I closed my eyes, I heard some noise to my right. I sat up within the sleeping bag and turned my head in the direction of the noise.

The flickering light of the fire illuminated the area I was looking at. There, from the forest came into view a man dressed in old, traditional-style Indian garments. He was dancing, but had his back towards me. He came closer and I kept still. He had an odd manner of dancing that I was not familiar with. Soon, he was opposite the fire from me. Although I heard no music, no drumming sound, he danced and sang with a rhythm all his own. He danced in a backward motion. I was unable to make out his facial features because his head movements were so quick and sudden. I just saw a blur. It was very difficult to focus on his face. The song he sang was unrecognizable to me. Even the words he sang were strange. I was interested in knowing who this man was, but at the same time I was scared.

It was very odd to see this man out there in the forest before me. I knew he was from another time because of his clothes. As he danced, he raised his arms and soon began to motion towards the darkness. He motioned as if calling someone to join him in his dance. It was strange to see this faceless man dancing and motioning as he did. Then, from the direction he was facing, came another figure, a woman. She slowly entered the lit area and began to dance with the man. Unlike the man who sang throughout his dance, the woman remained silent. She danced in a forward direction, taking steps left then right, left then right. I was frozen with fear and amazement. I was as still as I could be. She was also dressed in old-style clothes. She wore traditional leggings and moccasins, and her hair was in the traditional pueblo woman manner. Over her back she wore a manta (a shawl worn over the shoulders and back). Although I was able to make out all the details of her outfit, her face was a blur also, and she was not someone I recognized. I kept quiet as they both danced in unison. I was mesmerized.

Suddenly, they made their way away from my camp and fire and moved towards the stream. It was at this point that I heard them both laughing. They soon disappeared by the stream and into the darkness of the night. During this "spiritual performance," I was unable to move

my arms, legs, or other parts of my body. My eyes saw the vision and my ears heard the sounds. My focus was centered in simply observing and nothing more.

After they had left me, I was alone with my thoughts. I knew what I had just witnessed was a spiritual sign. I was left mentally numb. I just sat there in a void.

Then again, I heard some sound coming from the north. I turned and saw what appeared to be flashlights coming my way through the forest. Great! I thought, my buddies had seen my fire and had located my whereabouts! There were three lights and they moved around in the darkness, coming closer and closer towards me. I was so relieved and happy that they had found me. After what I had just seen, they couldn't have come at a better time. As the lights came closer, they suddenly stopped about 100 yards away. I threw more wood onto the fire and waited. Expecting to see my friends' faces any second, I sat back in my sleeping bag.

Out of the forest came three male figures, three men whom I did not recognize! As they got closer I saw that they had three horses with them. When they got to about 50 yards from me, I saw that they were Indians and were dressed in white man's clothes: Levi's jackets, jeans, etc. Once they were close enough for me to hear their voices, I heard them speaking in mumbling tones. I was unable to make out what they were saying. As soon as they spotted me, they stood still. I don't know why or how, but immediately I knew I was being visited by more spirits once again. As soon as this thought came over me, I closed my eyes and prayed. When I opened my eyes, the men were opposite the campfire.

Then suddenly, in an instant, they had moved to another area of my camp, horses and all! Then, in a blink of an eye, they were back where they were before, all seated and gazing in my direction.

Together, they extended their fingers towards me, and pointed in a way that made me think I was something funny to them. They spoke, but all I could make out were mumbling sounds. At one point, one of the men bent forward to get a closer look at me. I looked at their horses and then at the fire that separated us. The man who had his eyes focused on me then let out a big laugh. I was scared. I must have passed out because when I came to, I found myself out of my sleeping bag, on the ground, several feet away from where I had been by the fire. I was on the cold ground, shivering. The last thing I remembered was being in my sleeping bag, and now here I was freezing on the open ground several feet away. I got up and walked over to where the fire was. It was out, but there were still some hot glowing coals in the pit. I threw in more wood on top of the coals and soon I had a fire going again. I took my loaded pistol in one hand and a flashlight in the other and walked around the area where I had seen the three men. There was no sign that the ground or grass had been disturbed. I noticed that the sun was lighting up the sky, before it made itself known above the mountains. As the light made the ground around me more visible, the only tracks I could find were the ones I had made coming into the meadow. There were no others. The grass was wet with dew and undisturbed.

I soon packed up my horse, cleaned camp, and rode up the ridge away from the meadow. I couldn't erase from my memory what had happened to me just a few hours before. I was comforted by the morning sunlight that warmed my face and by the songs of the birds flying in and out of the trees.

Up in the distance I spotted my friends riding down the ridge. I heard them let out a yell and call out my name. I knew immediately these people were not spirits, but living human beings! As we met up with each other, my buddies had a shocked expression on each of their faces. "Hey, Alfred, you look pretty pale," one guy said. "What happened to you?" I began to describe the night before to them. They freaked out! They were quiet throughout my story and when I was through, they began to tell me a story of their own.

They said that at about the same time that the spirits had appeared to me, they had all seen two Indian spirits! At first, they had heard the sound of footsteps running over the forest ground among the trees. Then, a strange sense of someone watching them from the darkness overwhelmed them all. As they all sat quietly before their campfire, looking at each other, suddenly two Indian men dressed in traditional-style warrior outfits came out of the forest, running at full speed right by them. Of course, they all knew something unusual and spiritual was taking place. The two warriors just raced by and disappeared into the forest, from where they had come. After discussing among ourselves the possible reasons for what we had all experienced, we were left with no answers and feeling perplexed. I was apparently the most puzzled of all. I guess my friends saw this and decided that I needed to have a spiritual cleansing. My friends had me face North, and in the afternoon sunlight I was prayed over in the Indian way, in order to remove the bad forces I might have been exposed to. We all headed back home and did not speak about what had happened anymore.

That evening, at my house, I did mention my experience to my grandmother. She looked at me and listened to each word as if I was telling her something very important, something sacred. Then, after I was through, she held my hands and informed me that she had some sad news for me. I was told that my other grandmother had died the same night I had had my vision. My grandmother also told me that what I had experienced was my other grandmother's way of showing me that she was all right and was now passing into the other world, the spirit world. Grandmother further informed me that the dancing man and woman had headed in a southerly direction and disappeared because, "That's the spirits' way; they travel south. Where you were is where our Sacred Blue Lake is located. It's the spirits' way."

Grandmother then told me that the three men who had showed themselves to me, after the two dancing spirits had left, were very different from the man and woman. "You know, those three spirits were very powerful. It was a good thing you did not speak to them. Keeping quiet was the best thing for you to do. Otherwise, those spirits would have taken you away with them. You would have been left dead in the forest, your spirit would have been lifted away, and all we would have found would have been your body. We would not have known what was the cause of your mysterious death. What saved you was the campfire that kept burning between where you were and where the spirits were. It was good that you asked the Creator for a blessing and for Mother Earth to protect you that night."

The story I have just told you is the truth. It is what I saw with my own eyes. There are people who do not believe in these things, but some do. I'm happy to know that my grandmother, who passed away, chose to let me know how she was and that she was heading to the spirit world. Because of the darkness that night, I could not recognize her. The dancing spirits were presented to me for a purpose; they were not bad or evil. But the other spirits, the three men . . . Well, I knew something was not right when I saw them.

You know, there are many other stories and incidents that have taken place in and around the pueblo. I have experienced some very strange things. There are such things as witches and evildoers, but I would rather not talk about them. To talk about them would only give them more strength and increase their power for doing bad things.

The mountains above Taos Pueblo.

There are areas of power up here in the mountains, areas that feel negative to the soul. Indian people whom I've spoken to have told me that, as they travel through the forest, they can sometimes feel the presence of eyes gazing at them from between the trees. Some have even told me that they feel the presence of someone following them, something that moves from behind the trees, and hides among the shadows.

There are a lot of things that have happened to people around here. Most people prefer not to talk about them. Perhaps it's best not to. We'll leave it at that.

★　★　★

ALBUQUERQUE

ALBUQUERQUE, THE "DUKE CITY"

Albuquerque, New Mexico's largest city (current population approximately 480,000), actually was named in honor of an authentic Spanish duke, the tenth Duke of Alburquerque. Colonial Governor Don Francisco Cuervo y Valdez selected the name, but the first "r" was subsequently dropped.

In 1706, Albuquerque was founded by a group of colonists who had been granted permission by King Philip of Spain to establish a new villa on the banks of the Rio Grande (which means big or great river).

Two or three Native American pueblos were already in the vicinity, and the colonists chose a place along a wide curve in the river, which would provide good irrigation for crops, and be a source for wood from the bosque (cottonwoods, willows, and olive trees) and from the nearby mountains. The site was also convenient for aid, protection, and trade with the Native Americans.

The early Spanish settlers were religious people, and the first building erected was a small adobe chapel. Its plaza was surrounded by small adobe homes, clustered close together for mutual protection against any threats posed by hostile forces in this vast and dangerous country.

The church, San Felipe de Neri, still stands on this spot. The building itself has been enlarged several times and remodeled, but its thick original walls are still intact. The church is the hub of Old Town, the historic and sentimental heart of Albuquerque, with activity revolving around shopping and dining. To this day, special holidays and feast days are still commemorated as part of the year-round attractions of this "original" Albuquerque.

Two changes contributed to the early development of Albuquerque. First, the Rio Grande changed its course to run a little further west, causing a slight shift in the population. Second, the railroad came to Albuquerque in 1880, and "New Town" grew along the tracks two miles east of Old Town.

From the beginning, Albuquerque was a trade and transportation center. It was an important station on the Old Chihuahua Trail, an extension of the Santa Fe Trail winding down into Mexico.

Between 1850 and 1875, many forts were established in the Southwest to protect the westward migration. Albuquerque was a major supply center for these forts. During this same period, merchandising companies that had first shipped goods by wagon across the Santa Fe Trail, then by rail after 1880, established warehouses and stores in Albuquerque. Manufactured goods from the East were brought in. Hides, pelts, livestock, lumber, and minerals were shipped out.

Albuquerque never went through the lawless days of the raw frontier as did other Western towns. When those times came (the last quarter of the 19th century), there was already an established culture, a century-and-a-half old.

Much of Albuquerque's appeal today can be attributed to the subtle blending of the many cultures that comprise its fabric—Native American, Spanish, Anglo American, African-American, and Asian. Each has left its mark in food, music, religion, art, customs, architecture, traditions, and attitudes.

Albuquerque is a "spread-out" horizontal city. Because it covers so much geography, it includes a surprising diversity of terrain. Along the river, in the north and south valleys, elevations hover at around 4,800 feet. To the east, land rises over *mesas* (flat tabletop land) to the foothills of the Sandia Mountains at an elevation of 6,500 feet.

West of the Rio Grande, where much of Albuquerque's growth is now taking place, the mesa rises more abruptly than it does to the east—with a difference of 1,700 feet in the lowlands and highlands of Albuquerque. There is a variance in temperatures, often as much as 10 degrees. Just as elevations and temperatures vary, so does the weather. It has been known to snow or rain in one section of the city with nary a flake or a drop in other areas of town!

Dancers at the Pueblo Indian Cultural Center.

NEW MEXICO GHOST STORIES, VOL. I

The Sandia Mountains visually dominate the city and exert a great influence on its climate. They are a bulwark against the cold winds and storms that sweep across the plains of the Midwest. In summer, great thunderheads build up above the mountains, spilling brief, dramatic showers over the city.

The Sandias rank among Albuquerque's greatest recreational assets . . . a mountain playground at the very edge of the city. On the west side, facing Albuquerque, is a rugged, rocky escarpment rising almost vertically for a mile above the city. Sandia Peak Tram, the longest clear span tramway (2.7 miles) and most spectacular tram ride in the world, rises up the mountains' west face.

There are picnic areas, horseback and hiking trails, canyons, streams, and ski runs on the east side of the mountains. Skiers can take the tram up to the top within 15 minutes and ski down the east side, or they can drive up the east side and be at the base of the runs in half an hour.

The highest point of the Sandia Mountains is Sandia Crest at 10,678 feet. Sandia Crest is the officially determined summit of the Sandia Mountains. The Crest is located within Cibola National Forest, officially designated as a National Forest Recreation Area.

The drive, an easy 30 miles from downtown Albuquerque, takes you through breathtaking vistas, from piñon and juniper vegetation at 6,300 feet through stands of stately ponderosa pine and mixed conifer, spruce, and fir forests at higher elevations. The view from Sandia Crest is awesome, with a 360-degree panorama encompassing 11,000 square miles!

Because of the mild winters, comfortable summers, and invigorating elevations, it is possible for people to be outdoors much of the time. All sorts of spectator and participation sports are available here or within an afternoon's drive.

Albuquerque's year-round calendar of events includes two major arts and crafts fairs: MAGNIFICO! Albuquerque Festival of the Arts (held every summer), and the annual New Mexico State Fair (one of the top ten in the nation). There's also hot-air balloon events including the Albuquerque International Balloon Fiesta, and a prominent Hispanic arts and crafts exhibition, the Fiesta Artistica de Colores, which is held every August.

Luminarias are lit in the Old Town Plaza in Albuquerque during the Christmas season.

If you are interested in Native American culture, there are a number of events at the Indian Pueblo Cultural Center, offering displays and working exhibitions by members of the 19 New Mexico pueblos. Pueblo is the Spanish word for a town or village. The Pueblo Indians had already been living in multistoried "apartment"-type dwellings for 1,000 years when the Spanish arrived, and had a highly developed culture. The Indian Pueblo Cultural Center tells the story of the Pueblo people from past to the present. The center also houses an excellent gift shop and a restaurant specializing in Native American-style cooking. Native American dances are held on weekends from Mother's Day through early October in the center's open-air dance plaza, and photography is allowed.

Christmas festivities in Albuquerque feature special "luminaria" tours. For centuries, Hispanic villages along the Rio Grande have lit luminarias (popularly defined as "little lights") as a sign of rejoicing. Originally, luminarias were small bonfires. With the arrival of brown wrapping paper, people began making paper lanterns to enclose their festival lights. On Christmas Eve, entire neighborhoods light luminarias to guide the faithful to midnight mass as a symbol of their joy.

Adding to the cultural arts and entertainment mix are touring road shows, the University of New Mexico's programs and sporting events, and the emergence of many theater and musical groups.

THE KIMO THEATER

The KiMo Theater opened in September 19, 1927, as a Pueblo Deco picture palace during a period when Art Deco was in and picture palaces were the rage.

The style of Pueblo Deco was a flamboyant, short-lived architectural style that fused the spirit of the Native American cultures of the Southwest with the exuberance of America during the roaring 1920s.

It emerged at a time when movie-mad communities were constructing film palaces, loosely based on such exotic foreign models as Moorish mosques and Chinese pavilions. Native American motifs appeared in only a handful of movie theaters. Of those few, the KiMo was the undisputed king.

Nearly every town worthy of its name boasted its own movie palace, designed in Moorish or Gothic or Oriental flamboyance equaled only by the splendors of the film world. Not to be outdone, Albuquerque and the Bachechis planned to have their dream house. The KiMo was highly representative of its time. It would be unique, without Moorish or Chinese motifs and decorated instead in its own Southwestern style.

Oreste Bachechi, one of the founding members of the Albuquerque Italian-American community, came to the United States in 1885, and set up a bar in a tent near the railroad tracks. Bachechi's fortunes expanded with the city's growth; he became a liquor dealer and proprietor of a grocery store, while his wife, Maria, ran a dry-goods store in the Elms Hotel.

Bachechi first became involved with the movies around 1919, when the Bachechi Amusement Association operated the Pastime Theater with Joe Barnett. By 1925, he had decided to achieve "an ambition, a dream that had long been in realization" by building his own theater, one that would stand out among the Greek temples and Chinese pavilions of contemporary movie mania.

Bachechi chose Carl Boller of the Boller Brothers, whose firm had acquired a considerable reputation for catering to the fantasies of movie patrons. The Bollers had already designed the Wild West–Rococo-style theater in San Antonio and a Spanish cathedral-cum-Greco-Babylonian interior in St. Joseph, Missouri.

Carl Boller traveled extensively throughout New Mexico, visiting the pueblos of Acoma, Isleta, Cibola, and the Navajo Nation. After months of research, Boller submitted a watercolor rendering of the interior. Oreste was pleased with the design.

The interior included plaster-ceiling beams textured to look like logs and painted with dance and hunt scenes, air vents disguised as Navajo rugs, panoramic murals depicting the Seven Cities of Cibola, chandeliers shaped like war drums and Native American death canoes, wrought-iron birds descending the stairs, and rows of garlanded longhorn steer skulls with eerie, glowing amber eyes.

Carlo Bachechi was 18 when his parents built the KiMo. "There were plans all over the house," he remembers. Decisions had to be made about materials, colors, labor, and contracts for out-of-town work. "One difficulty was getting people to make the medallions for the walls," Carlo says. Like the terra-cotta, which had to be fired elsewhere because of a lack of local kilns, the medallions had to be shipped from the West Coast.

"None of the designs were chosen at random. Each had historical significance," he says of the myriad of rain clouds, birds, and swastikas, which are Navajo symbols for life, freedom, and happiness.

Colors took months to choose. Like abstract symbols, color, too, was part of the Native American vocabulary. Red represents the life-giving sun, white the approaching morning, yellow the setting sun of the west, and black the darkening clouds from the north.

The crowning touch was the seven murals painted by Carl von Hassler. Some of the work he painted himself; the rest was traced from heavy butcher-paper cutouts, which were taped to the walls and filled in with paint by workmen.

Speaking fondly of Von Hassler, Carlo Bachechi says he and the "proud Prussian" were very close. "He was quite a drinker and a playboy, but he also was quite a painter. You couldn't take that away from him."

Working from a platform hung from the ceiling, Von Hassler reportedly worked for months on his creations. "He would hang up there for hours at a time," said Bachechi, who bought the last 12 paintings Von Hassler did in Albuquerque before his death.

The theater was completed in less than a year. It cost $150,000, plus $18,000 for the elaborate Wurlitzer organ that accompanied the silent films of the day.

On opening night, the crowd watched performances by representatives from nearby Native American pueblos and reservations. The performers, reported the *New Mexico State Tribune* in an advance story, included "numerous prominent tribesmen of the Southwest who will perform for the audience mystic rites never before seen on the stage."

Isleta Pueblo Governor Pablo Abeita won a prize of $500—a magnificent sum for the time—for naming the new theater. Reflecting the optimism of the time, the "KiMo" (a combination of two words, literally meaning "mountain lion," but more liberally interpreted as "King of Its Kind") could not have been more appropriate.

With the theater at more than its capacity at the grand opening, the Bachechis kept an anxious eye on the balcony. Carlo explained, "The structure of the balcony was always a big worry, because it spanned from the east to west wall without support. When the house was packed we could see it drop four to eight inches in the middle. When people jumped up and down, it really moved." Bachechi laughed, and then explained that it was purposely designed to give and sway.

"We had Bingo. Every Friday we gave away a Model T or a Chevrolet (you could buy a car in those days for 700 dollars), and we gave away tons of dishes. Anything to attract audiences," Bachechi said.

The first movie shown in the KiMo was *Painting the Town Red* and the first talking movie was *Melody of Broadway*. Frances Farney played the Wurlitzer organ during each performance.

The KiMo was also an important employer for young people just getting started. Vivian Vance, who went on to achieve fame as Lucille Ball's sidekick in the *I Love Lucy* series, started working at the KiMo. The theater also hosted such Hollywood stars as Sally Rand, Gloria Swanson, Tom Mix, and Ginger Rogers.

A year after the realization of his dream, Oreste Bachechi died, leaving the management of the KiMo to his sons, who combined vaudeville and out-of-town road shows with movies. Extra revenue came in from the luncheonette and curio shop on either side of the entrance. In later years, the Kiva-Hi, a second-floor restaurant, and KGGM radio, housed on the second and third floors, were major tenants.

When management of the theater passed out of the Bachechis' hands in the mid-1930s, the KiMo was altered several times, partially to keep up with current theater trends. More drastic changes resulted from two disasters: a 1951 boiler explosion that killed a small boy and demolished part of the lobby area, and a 1961 fire in the stage area that destroyed the original proscenium.

In 1968, after shopping centers and modern theaters had made serious inroads in the downtown's attraction to moviegoers, the KiMo closed as a picture palace. Over the next 10 years it was used as offices for Commonwealth Theaters, and occasionally opened for local performing arts groups.

★　★　★

I interviewed Jewel Sanchez at her home and found her to be a sincere and friendly individual. Enthusiastic about her strange experiences at the KiMo Theater, she became excited and animated during the interview, using her hands when describing what she saw.

The theater's receptionist, Jewel, is very approachable for a quick chat. Her amicable personality welcomes both friends and strangers, be they living or . . . .

JEWEL SANCHEZ'S STORY

I've worked at the KiMo Theater since November 1979. I've done various tasks while employed at the KiMo, but presently I work as the receptionist and do clerical work. There currently exists a tradition at the theater that involves, of all things, donuts. I know it sounds a bit strange or funny, but believe me, there is a reason.

Several years ago a little boy was accidentally killed when a hot-water pipe burst. Apparently, this young boy had happened to be backstage one evening next to the pipe, which carried the theater's hot water supply. Although I don't know all the circumstances of what happened, I do know there was an explosion and the child was killed. Apparently, this little boy's ghost decided to linger in the theater. Maybe his ghost needs the reassurance of familiar surroundings. There have been many persons who have witnessed his spirit within the theater. Many years ago a tradition of offering the child's spirit donuts and candy was started to appease his mischievous nature.

"The stage crew began to leave uneaten donuts for the dead boy's spirit . . ."

It's customary to have a box of sweets, usually donuts, backstage for the stage crew and performers on the opening night of every performance. Eventually, someone decided to tie a donut to an exposed water pipe. As you can imagine, throughout the years the string grew longer and the assortment of donuts grew also. At this very minute, if you take a look backstage, you'll notice several very old, dusty, hard donuts hanging on that water pipe. It might seem strange, but there they are for all to see.

One Christmas Day in 1974 there was a performance of some sort, and a member of the crew, who was unaware of the donut tradition, saw the collection of sweets hanging on the water pipe and, apparently disgusted with the sight, removed them and placed them in the trash. I was told that as soon as they had been removed, all sorts of weird and negative stuff began to happen. Anything that could go wrong, did go wrong. Props that had been well anchored to the floor toppled over, as if intentionally pushed by invisible hands. Electrical cables blew up in a storm of sparks and flashes. The most obvious of the strange occurrences involved the onstage actors themselves. While performing they tripped and fell over an invisible object. Some actors stated that it had felt as if a pair of invisible hands had caused them to fall—that they had been quickly but firmly pushed to the floor. Well, very soon someone decided that the cause of all this might be related to the removal of the donuts. As soon as this connection had been made, the donut tradition was started up again. Immediately, the strange and negative occurrences ceased.

My first personal experience with ghosts at the KiMo Theater happened one day around 3:30 in the afternoon. I was sitting at my desk, at the front of the theater, and decided to use the bathroom. I had to walk a long distance to where it was located in the hallway of the theater. I was thinking about something at the time, and I made my way with my head bowed. As I neared the bathroom, I noticed the ceiling lightbulb had burned out, because the only available light for the hallway came from the exit sign above the door at the end of the hall. Suddenly, I saw a woman leaning against the bathroom door. I stopped dead in my tracks.

She was about 25 feet away from me, and I didn't recognize her as a member of our employee staff. Though the dimly lit hallway made it difficult for my eyes to focus clearly, there was no doubt in my mind that I was seeing a woman. I can recall her dress, made of a gingham pattern, with a bustle. She stood about five feet high and sported a bonnet on her head. To describe her in common terms would be to say that she looked as if she had walked out of an Old West pioneer movie. Her face was turned away from me, so I am unable to describe her facial features. In fact, my overall impression was that she seemed to be a shadow with an aura of gray. Then she disappeared into thin air. I was unsure what I had witnessed, so I decided to go into the bathroom. It was only after some minutes I understood that what I had seen was a ghost! Strangely, I was not afraid. I took the experience as being normal. I was intrigued by it all, and when I returned to my work area, I asked my co-workers if they had ever experienced such an apparition. No one said they had. Of course, I tried to explain that what I had seen had been caused by the dimly lit hallway, or my imagination, but my attempts to do so never fully convinced me that it was all in my mind. No, I could not explain away what I had seen as being my imagination. What I had seen was a ghost. Since that time, I've not seen her again.

"The only light came from the exit sign above the door."

My second ghostly encounter at the KiMo happened one evening at around 5 p.m. I was busy making my way up the stairs from the theater's lobby. There is a staircase on the opposite side of the lobby, and as I made my way up the stairs, I happened to glance over towards something on the other staircase. A little boy was scampering up the

stairs. He seemed to be playing, making a game of running up and down the stairs. He was wearing a striped shirt and jeans. He had light-brown hair, and was so involved in his activity that he took no notice of me. As he scampered up the stairs for the last time, he disappeared! He was there one second and was gone before my very eyes

"As he scampered up the stairs for the last time, he disappeared!"

the next. Seeing him convinced me that there are ghosts in this theater who are very active.

I'm convinced that the little boy I saw on the stairs has to be the child who was killed by the exploding water pipe years ago. I'm so sincerely convinced that since that evening I've made my own little offering to the boy, and have placed a bit of candy at the corner of my desk—just for him.

THE OUIJA BOARD

REBECCA VILLA'S STORY

I've lived in the city of Albuquerque for a little more than four years. When my mother moved my younger sister and me from California to New Mexico, I was 16 and my sister Anita was 14. My mother, who is originally from Albuquerque, had to separate from my father because of his drinking and the severe abuse he inflicted upon his family. My father physically and verbally abused my mother in what seemed to be a daily occurrence. After years of this treatment, my mother had had enough and decided one day that the only salvation for her and her two daughters was to pack up her things and to return to her parents' home in Albuquerque. My mother saved her money until she had the amount necessary for the trip. I remember one morning, when my father had left for work, she gathered four suitcases and some cardboard boxes she had stored in our backyard, placed all our belongings inside, and bound up the boxes with tape and string. At 12:30 that afternoon a friend of hers came by and we all jumped into her car. After a short and sad drive to the train station, we got out, and boarded Amtrak to our new home: New Mexico!

It didn't take long to settle into Albuquerque and we adjusted eagerly to the clear blue skies and vistas of the surrounding Sandia Mountains. What a change from the big city of Los Angeles! Although we missed our school friends, we knew things would be better for us away from my father.

My father did track us down eventually, and called to speak with my mother. We lived with my grandparents, my mother's parents. Although my father knew where we were, he did not make any attempt to visit us. Whenever he did call on the phone, both my sister and I would talk with him. We always hung up with tears in our eyes. Somehow I knew I would never see him again.

Eight months had passed since we left California, and one Tuesday morning we received a phone call from a friend of my father, who informed my mother that my father had been killed in a work-related accident. Although we were sad to hear this news, my father had been prepared for such a possibility. He had life insurance. My mother received a sizable check from an insurance company. She used this to purchase a modest home on the west side of the city.

My sister, Anita, and I began attending the same school and soon developed friendships with classmates. One Saturday morning, I was preoccupied reading a teen magazine on our front porch when I heard someone approaching. It was my sister and two of her girlfriends. I recognized one of the girls, Gloria, who was carrying a long, flat box. As they neared, Gloria spoke. "Hey, Becky, why don't you come to the backyard with us? Look what we have." I answered, "What's in there?" She answered, "It's a fortune-telling Ouija Board." I said I did not know what a Ouija Board was, and that I was busy reading. Then Gloria said, "Oh well, you're going to miss out. We're going to contact some spirits with it and have lots of fun, so go ahead and read your dumb magazine." I picked up my magazine once again and watched the girls as they walked to the backyard. After a few minutes, I decided to see what they were doing. I heard laughter coming from our garage and curiosity got the better of me. I opened the side door to the garage and saw the three of them seated on the garage floor. They all encouraged me to "come in, and shut the door." I stood above them as they were seated in a tight circle. My sister and her friend, Gloria, had the Ouija Board balanced on their laps. They both had their fingers resting on a white, teardrop-shaped pointer. They explained that after they asked a question aloud, a "spirit" helped them move the pointer. The pointer answered a "Yes" or "No" question by pointing to either of these two words printed on the board. The board also had the alphabet printed in large black letters, which the pointer used to spell out other words and sentences.

My sister asked a question about a boy she liked at school: "Does he care about me like I care about him?" After just a few moments of stillness the pointer "came to life" and began to move over each printed letter until, pausing at certain ones, it spelled out, "More than you think." This answer made the girls laugh. This went on for several minutes, and I must admit that I also became caught up in their game. I soon took my place among the girls and placed the board on my lap. With my fingers on the white pointer I began to ask a question or two of my own.

We were really "into it," and after a couple of hours we became exhausted. Gloria asked if she could leave the board in our garage, because her mother did not want such things in her home since it scared her. I said, "Sure, why not. Just leave it here in the garage so my mother won't get the same idea." We put the board away in its box and placed it on top of some boxes, out of view.

A couple of days later my mother, my sister, and I were having dinner. There was a knock at the door and Rosie, a friend of mine, came in to visit. Rosie was a girl I had recently met at school, and because of our common interest in music and boys, we had started to hang out together. I must admit that Rosie was a bit "wild." She smoked, and had little regard for authority. My mother considered her to be a bad influence on me, and warned me about spending too much time after school with her. I was fully aware of Rosie's nature, and I took care not to be overly influenced by her. Though she had some faults, she was always fun to be with.

After dinner that night, Rosie and I walked outside and sat on the porch to talk. Knowing Rosie would be very interested in something new and different, I told her about the Ouija Board, and the fun I had had with it. Instantly Rosie said, "Let's find out if it will talk to me. Come on, let's try it." I agreed, and we both headed for the garage. We sat cross-legged on the garage floor and placed the Ouija Board on our laps. I explained how the Ouija Board worked. She asked questions, and then I asked a couple. Soon Rosie became very excited and eager to ask more and more questions. Her questions also started to take on erotic overtones. Rosie asked, "Am I wearing any underpants?" or "Should I go all the way with Henry," etc. I was becoming uncomfortable with these questions and wanted to change the subject matter, but Rosie just got more "into it." Pretty soon she changed her focus, and was centering her questions on the spirit. She began by asking, "Do you think I'm sexy?" The pointer then moved to the word "Yes." Then she asked, "Would you make love to me if I let you?" Once again, the pointer moved to the word "Yes." I tried to tell Rosie that her questions were bothering me, but she would not pay attention to me. She continued asking her nasty questions. Her last question was, "Will you make love to me tonight?" The pointer moved to the word "Yes." Then it moved in her direction and pointed at her. This was enough for me. I removed my fingers from the board and told Rosie I did not want to continue. She just laughed at me and said, "This is all make-believe. There ain't any spirits." I answered, "Maybe so, but I'm scared, I want to stop." Rosie said, "This is all a bunch of shit. There's no such thing. This spirit can go to hell!" I placed the Ouija Board back in the box and once again placed it out of sight. We walked back to the porch and soon after Rosie left for her home.

Around 10 p.m., everyone in our house went to bed. I couldn't get Rosie's questions out of my memory. Soon I drifted off to sleep. At

11:30 p.m. our phone rang. My mother came into my room to say that Rosie wanted to talk to me and that it sounded urgent. I grabbed the phone and could hear Rosie crying hysterically, "Becky, come over now! Please, please help me. The thing is inside me!" I said, "God, what happened?" She exclaimed, "The spirit, it's inside me!" I said I would be at her home in a few minutes. I asked my mother to drive me to her home. On the way to Rosie's house, I explained everything to my mother. She was very upset with what we had done and began to pray. We didn't know what we would encounter once we arrived at Rosie's house.

Nearing her home, we noticed many lights on in the house. I walked up to her house and Rosie's mother welcomed us. Her mother was confused and uncertain about what had happened to her daughter. Before I could explain, I noticed Rosie sitting on their couch, crying and rocking back and forth. She was covered in perspiration. I put my arms around her. "Rosie," I asked, "what happened?"

After taking a few moments to compose herself, she began her story. "I was asleep in my bed. Then something woke me up. I felt like opening my eyes, and when I did, I saw this man standing at the foot of my bed. I had never seen him before. I asked him, 'Who are you? Don't get any closer to me.' He took a few quick steps and before I knew it, he had his body on top of me! I tried to move and to scream, but I was unable to move or make a noise. I could feel him over me, but he was weightless. I felt his beard and his breath, and when I looked at his eyes, they had no whites. They were just big black circles! I was able to breathe, but I couldn't talk. I closed my own eyes, knowing then this was something evil. I was so terrified. I felt him having sex with me, and even though there were blankets between us, I still felt everything. It felt like over an hour had passed. Then slowly he started to fade away and the sensation of him on top of me left. I immediately began to cry, and my mother came into my room. I told her what had happened, and she took all the blankets and sheets off my bed and threw them outside. That's when I called you to come over. I'm so sorry about what I said. I didn't mean anything. I'm so sorry."

I hugged Rosie, and told her everything would be all right now. She looked at my mother and me and said, "I have to show you this." Rosie extended her arms and we could clearly see the dark blue bruises of a man's handprint on her upper arms. Rosie's mother slumped into my mother's arms and cried. We were all stunned by what we had seen. The evidence was undeniable. Something or someone had been in the room with Rosie. Then I noticed that Rosie had scrape marks on her left cheek and throat. She raised her hand to her neck and said, "His beard was rubbing against me here." I can't describe the fear that came over me when I heard her say those words. I was terrified. I began to cry and asked my mother to do something. My mother asked Rosie's mother to bring a rosary. When Rosie held the rosary, my mother asked her to kiss the crucifix. After she had done so, my mother draped the beads over Rosie's head and we all began to pray. We stayed with Rosie and her family until the next day.

Later that afternoon, a priest was called to her house. He burned incense and blessed the house, chasing away any evil that might have lingered in Rosie's bedroom. New sheets were purchased for her bed, and Rosie has since kept a white candle burning before a statue of the Virgin in her bedroom since that night.

When my mother and I arrived home, we immediately went to the garage, found the Ouija Board, and took it into the backyard. My mother started a small fire with some newspapers and cardboard and tossed the flat box containing the Ouija Board into the fire. We both watched as the fire consumed it. With a shovel, my mother turned over the remains, making sure nothing was left untouched.

Since then, Rosie has gone to church and her mother and mine have become close friends. Whenever I hear people talk about ghosts, I make sure to tell them that they should not make fun of the spirits. I don't go into any detail; I just say that the dead should be respected.

THE LUNA MANSION

THE LUNA-OTERO FAMILY HISTORY

In 1692, Domingo de Luna came to New Mexico on a land grant from the King of Spain. A few years later, Don Pedro Otero came to Valencia

County under similar circumstances. These two families grew, acquired fortunes in land and livestock, and became extremely powerful in politics and prominent in territorial society. The family heads became friends and business associates. The marriages of Solomon Luna to Adelaida Otero and Manuel A. Otero to Eloisa Luna in the late 1800s united these two families into what became known as the Luna-Otero Dynasty. In 1880, the Santa Fe Railroad Company wanted right of way through the Luna-Otero property. In return for this favor, and because the proposed railroad tracks went squarely through the existing Luna-Otero hacienda, the railroad company agreed to build a new home to the specifications of Don Antonio Jose Luna and his family. Legend has it that numerous trips throughout the South by the Luna family had inspired the architectural design of the mansion. Whether or not this is true, the building is unique in that, while it is Southern colonial in style, its basic construction material is adobe. The mansion was built in 1881.

Because Don Antonio Jose died in 1881, the first family to occupy the mansion was that of his oldest son, Tranquilino. After Don Tranquilino's death in Washington while serving in the legislature, younger brother, Solomon, took the reins of the family. Although Solomon was probably the most famous of the Lunas, he was not prolific. With no children in his family, control passed to his nephew, Eduardo Otero, in the early 1900s. It was during this time, specifically in the 1920s, that the mansion truly became the outstanding building that now exists. During this period, the solarium was constructed, the front portico was added, and the ironwork was erected to surround about five times as much property as it now does. Responsible for these and other improvements was a talented and creative woman, Josefita Manderfield Otero, the wife of Don Eduardo. Josefita, or Pepe as she is affectionately remembered, was a daughter of William R. Manderfield, founder of the *Santa Fe New Mexican*. This fine lady ruled the mansion with a gentle and loving hand, and spent her days caring for her magnificent gardens and applying paint to canvas. There are those in this area who still remember, and speak highly of, her.

The Luna-Otero Mansion is an important monument to a time now past. The heirs of these families are scattered far and wide in new and different walks of life. The economic viability of the mansion as a headquarters for a livestock dynasty is forever gone. Such monuments as this building usually have one of three fates: they can be torn down and forgotten, to be replaced by new construction; philanthropists can convert them into museums; or someone can inhabit the old structure and put it to a new use. By reopening the Luna–Otero Mansion as a fine restaurant, now known as the Luna Mansion, the current owners have sought to preserve and display an important part of New Mexico's history.

The Luna Mansion is as perfect as a house can get for a ghost story. Its antebellum, Southern-colonial style gives the visitor a feeling of being in the states of Georgia, Mississippi, or Louisiana. Strolling the large expansive veranda, with its four large columns, I expected to see tattered ribbons of Spanish moss hanging listlessly from ancient magnolia trees. Instead, the grounds are surrounded by the impressive, massive dignity of native cottonwoods.

★ ★ ★

I interviewed both the owner, David Scoville, and the head chef, Kyle Lamb, at the restaurant's office, deep within the house. Following these interviews, I was given free rein to wander about the mansion. The midday light, which came through the beveled, antique windows, gave me no cause for concern. But to return to this home late at night, with only the light of a simple flickering candle lighting its rooms and halls can test the courage of any man or woman.

The following two interviews give testimony to an experience that might await a visitor to the Luna Mansion and its restaurant. Do remember, however, that when your waiter or waitress brings you your cocktail, be sure to make a toast to your host, Ms. Josefita Otero. She will appreciate the gesture, as you will soon see.

DAVID SCOVILLE'S STORY

I came to work at the Luna Mansion in 1979, and worked as a kitchen manager until 1983. I left and eventually returned after a three-year absence. My present position is general manager/owner.

I know a lot about the history of the mansion and of stories of the ghosts that inhabit it. The mansion was built by the railroad company for the Luna-Otero families between 1878 and 1881 at a cost of $47,000. It's a two-story adobe in the Victorian-Southern style.

Josefita "Pepe" Manderfield Otero.

My first experience I can recall with the ghost took place in 1980, late at night between the hours of midnight and 1 a.m. At the time, I was up on the second floor of the mansion finishing my bartending shift. All the patrons had left and I was checking the adjacent rooms and ashtrays for lit cigarettes, tossed wrappers, etc. The mansion is furnished with beautiful antique chairs, sofas, and tables, so at the end of every shift the staff checks for any damage,

195

such as cigarette burns, which might have occurred throughout the day. More importantly, we check for smoldering butts. The danger of fire is significant in a house as old as this.

I was making my rounds in the northeast room. There is a nicely decorated Art Deco lamp, which sits on a table there. The lamp has a ribbon of fringe around the base of its shade. Out of the corner of my eye I noticed the fringe move. I thought that an employee had failed to turn off the air conditioner, so I left to check the switch. It was in the "off" position. I returned to the room with the lamp to resume my task, when to my amazement I spotted the fringe beginning to move again. I moved up to the lamp to investigate further. I saw a pattern develop. The fringe moved as if a finger was passing around the face of the lamp. I took a few quick steps back, and all of a sudden there appeared the image of Josefita, the original owner of the house! Josefita was the person who had painted the murals and the paintings, which you can see throughout the house. Josefita was running her finger around the base of the lamp. She was dressed in white clothes. There is only one way that I can describe my reaction to this—I freaked! Not only did I immediately leave the upstairs, I left the building! I didn't bother to shut off the lights; I just let my feet do their job. Others have told me there had been reports of individuals witnessing the ghost of Josefita, but I had not given much credence to such stories, until that night in 1980. I was scared and out of breath. My hair was standing on end. It felt as if I had been hit with a hard blow to the stomach. I can tell you what I remember about her—she wore no jewelry, her hair was in a bun, and she was dressed in a long white skirt of some kind, something that I imagine women wore during the 1920s. She was not translucent as most people imagine a ghost to be. Josefita appeared as a real person, solid and not vaporous at all. Because of my fear, I didn't even notice her facial expression—I don't know whether she was smiling or frowning.

I've since discovered that where I saw Josefita's apparition, is her favorite place to appear. The upstairs barroom was Josefita's master bedroom years ago. Employees and patrons in the barroom have suddenly experienced various things, such as goosebumps, cold chills, loss of breath, sensing her presence, or actually seeing her as I did. After reading the history of the Luna Mansion, I know Josefita's bedroom was originally located at the northwest corner of the house. After her husband had died, she had moved her bedroom there. Another area where she has been known to make her presence felt, or to appear, is at the top of the stairs, which lead to the second-floor barroom. She had her fatal heart attack in this area.

My second experience took place at about 10 a.m. in that very spot. I was carrying two cases of beer up to the second floor. At the very top of the staircase is a door to the right, which leads into the attic. The attic is used as a storeroom for the bar. As I approached the attic door, I noticed a woman walking from the old bathroom in the upstairs area, which has since been renovated to become the bar's cocktail station. This woman walked from the cocktail station into the northeast Cronowitter Room. I was busy carrying the cases of beer up the stairs and thought that the woman was Susie, our housekeeper. I said, "Hi, Susie." I entered the attic/storeroom and knew that Susie was ahead of me. I looked directly ahead of me and saw not Susie, but Josefita dressed exactly as I had previously seen her. Needless to say, she caught me totally by surprise. I dropped the two cases of beer I had struggled to carry up the stairs. I ran—rather, I flew out the room and down the stairs. Since my second encounter with Josefita's ghost, I've spoken to her descendants and described my experience. They informed me that, yes indeed, it was Josefita because every detail of her dress, and the way she wore her hair in a bun, was actually the way she was in life.

Since my second encounter, I've been very sensitive to any unusual changes, such as cold spots, in supposedly empty rooms. These sensations cause the skin on my arms to have goosebumps and the hair at the nape of my neck to stand on end for no visible, apparent reason. Also, I may suddenly lose my breath when I enter what I think is an empty room.

Another time, I was walking on the grounds late at night and had made my way to the front of the house. I felt the eyes of someone staring at me. I didn't pay it any mind, until the sense of these eyes on me became overwhelming. I glanced towards the mansion and my eyes focused on the second-floor windows. There I spotted the image of Josefita, dressed in her white dress, gazing down at me. After the incident, a customer asked to see the manager of the restaurant. She introduced herself to me as a person who is very sensitive to ghosts. And further, she stated that she felt the strong presence of a woman on the second floor of the mansion, one who sits by the window gazing out towards the front lawn. This woman's comments left me with a numb feeling deep inside my stomach. I knew that when I had been outside that night on the front lawn I was being watched. The sensation of ghostly eyes gazing at my every move has left me with a truly uneasy feeling.

There are other odd, unexplainable occurrences that take place at the mansion. For instance, there are light fixtures with bulbs that un-explainably come unscrewed. I can actually count on certain lightbulbs becoming unscrewed almost on a nightly basis. I can walk through the mansion and simply point to light fixtures in the main dining room that I know will have bulbs unscrewed from their sockets by morning. The dining room has beautiful large chandeliers and these chandeliers, for some unknown reason, have attracted the ghost. There are other light fixtures throughout the house with similar unscrewed bulbs, but the chandeliers in the main dining room remain the most common.

I recall an incident that took place about seven years ago. During the month of December, a woman guest was having an evening meal together with a male friend, her sister, and three children. Our host seated them in the main dining room. The gentleman, who sported a ponytail, was seated by the entrance to the dining room. He and his companions were served their meals, and all was going well until I was asked by the host to visit their table. It is my duty as restaurant owner and general manager to respond to clients' problems and concerns.

As I approached the table, I took notice that the man and his companions were quite still. The man stated in a nervous voice that someone had pulled and flipped his ponytail. But as he turned his head to look, there was no one visible in the area. The rest of the diners noticed the action of his hair being pulled, but that was all. No one saw anyone doing the actual pulling. As I heard him tell his story, suddenly the lightbulbs in the chandeliers above our heads began to explode one by one, all in succession as if they were being shot out by a BB gun. Glass rained down upon the diners and their food. We all covered our eyes from the falling glass with our hands and napkins. After just a few seconds, everything stopped. I quickly apologized and told them that we would replace their dinners. To my surprise, the diners remained for the rest of the evening. The staff quickly brought ladders and replaced the exploded bulbs with new ones.

There have been other incidents that have taken place on the main floor of the mansion. Towards the rear of the kitchen, separated by a wall, is my office. This office was once the water-pump room for the mansion. At the time of one occurrence, I was in the kitchen with the cook, Kyle Lamb. My bookkeeper was in the office at the time going over the books. While in the kitchen, I heard a woman's voice call out my name three times, "David, David, David!" Both Kyle and I were jolted by the loud voice. We both assumed some terrible accident had happened to the bookkeeper. We dropped what we were doing, rushed to the office, and quickly opened the door. The bookkeeper was sitting at her chair, startled by our visit. I asked her what she wanted. She answered, "What are you talking about? What do you mean?" I told her I had heard her yell out my name. "No, I didn't call you," she said. Both Kyle and I glanced at each other, and without saying another word, excused ourselves and walked back into the kitchen. No voice called me again, but I was uneasy for the rest of the day.

Another incident I recall involved an antique table. This table belonged to the Manderfield family, the original owners of the mansion. The table, I'm told, is nearly 300 years old. It's a large table and can easily seat 15 people. The table is stored in a locked storage room outside the main house, and is brought out of storage and used in the mansion only on special occasions, such as private parties, etc. For all its beauty and grandeur, this table is not without its own eerie secrets. I've personally arranged flatware and the usual restaurant table decorations upon the table without any problems. But as soon as the glasses were in place, they began to explode and shattered bits of glass flew throughout the dining room. After this happened, I noticed other strange things taking place. The large double doors, which swing on pivots and open into the kitchen, would open wide all by themselves. Then the water faucets would turn on. Now, we can expect unusual things to happen whenever we bring the Manderfield table into the mansion. We know that Josefita's presence will be made known to us without a doubt.

"Lifting herself off the chair was the ghost of Josefita!"

In 1980, I hired a bartender, Birdie Tapia, who actually saw the ghost of Josefita face to face! Walking up the stairs to the second-floor attic, which we now use as a storeroom, Birdie went inside to get supplies. As the little room was flooded with light, Birdie's eyes were drawn towards an old rocking chair stored in the room. Lifting herself off the chair was the ghost of Josefita! As Birdie tells it, she promptly turned and ran to the door, nevermore to enter the attic/supply room. Birdie was terrified by the encounter and, I'm sure, will not forget it. The rocker has since been removed from the storage room and placed on the second-floor stair landing.

Another ex-employee, Vickie Shook, was in the second-floor bar area one evening, after we had closed the restaurant for the night. She was wiping the tables and emptying the ashtrays. She was by herself at the time. Vickie happened to be facing a large mirror that hangs on one of the walls. As she was wiping off a table, she looked up at the mirror and spotted a woman with her body turned away from view. Vickie automatically asked the woman, "Yes, ma'am, may I help you?" The woman didn't respond, so Vickie turned to face her. But as she turned around, the woman vanished.

We have had doors in several rooms of the mansion open and slam shut with a loud bang. One day, I had had enough of this, so with the help of employees, we removed the doors and placed them outside in the storage unit. This didn't seem to help the situation much, since now we hear the ghostly opening of an invisible door followed by a loud slam.

There is also a couch on the second floor that seems to make those who sit on it extremely uneasy. I once saw a male customer, who was sitting on the couch, rise up off it, with his face pale. I asked if he was feeling all right. He answered, "I'll be back." He left the mansion, and returned after a few minutes to tell me that he had had a strange sensation, which caused him to fear being on the couch. He just had to get up and go outside for a while.

Another thing that happens to me even now is that I sometimes notice the shadow of a woman walking past me and making her way into an adjacent room. It doesn't matter what time of day it is. I'll be doing something, carrying boxes, wiping a table, not even remotely thinking of ghosts, and I'll spot this shadow walking right by me.

Except for the feeling that someone is always watching me, I've not experienced any more ghostly encounters. I know the ghost is Josefita's. I don't think she is attempting to harm anyone. Since the house was hers during her lifetime, I believe she is simply caring for it in her own way. Somehow, I don't think it is right for me to chase her away from the home she obviously loves so much. That's why I've not called in a priest to exorcise the mansion. Josefita is a playful ghost, and enjoys surprising people if given the chance. Perhaps one of these nights, if she decides to reappear to me, she'll speak some words. Who knows, she and I might even have a conversation. That would be something.

KYLE LAMB'S STORY

I've worked at the Luna Mansion now for over four years. During these years, I've always had the feeling that something unusual is at work here. A person can feel the history of the house just by walking through its front door.

Currently, my position is the restaurant's cook and head broiler. I've had about three experiences with ghosts at the mansion that I can recall. These experiences totally "freaked me out." If you ask me why these things have happened to me, I won't be able to tell you, but I know I'm not the only one who's witnessed them. That's for sure.

My first experience happened about two years ago. One morning, I was in the kitchen that's located on the first floor of the mansion. I was busy cutting the meat for the day's menu. It was about 9 a.m. Steve, our vegetable prep person, was occupied with his work across the table from me. We were alone in the house. I know, because I had the house key and had opened the door for us, and no one else.

An hour of nonstop work had exhausted us both, so we decided to take a short break. We decided to relax in the bar on the second floor of the mansion. We climbed the stairs, and settled down on the comfortable furniture. As we took advantage of the situation by joking and mentally unwinding, we both stopped our conversation when we heard what sounded like the side door on the first floor open. Time stood still for us. We looked at each other with shocked faces. Immediately, we thought that our supervisor had entered the house and, since we didn't want to be caught doing nothing by the boss, we raced down to the kitchen and took our places at the table, with knives in hand.

Steve and I both heard the voices of a man and a woman coming from the room next to the kitchen where we were working. Try as we might, we were unable to make out what the conversation was about between the two. Steve asked me to investigate who the visitors might be. I followed the voices down the short hallway, which led to the water-pump room, which had been converted into the restaurant's business office. As I arrived at the door, I knocked on it, reached for the doorknob, and turned it. It was locked. Again, I knocked and asked, "Hello? Anyone in there?" Silence. Oh, boy . . . I knew something was up. I took big, quick strides back to the kitchen. Steve anxiously asked who the people were. I told him the door was locked and the room was empty. We decided then and there to check the house for possible intruders. We each took different routes, and after a thorough search, found all the doors and windows locked as we had expected. We knew what we had heard was not the movement of wind. We had heard human voices, but no one else was there.

My second encounter with the ghosts of the mansion took place in the kitchen once again. I was helping the chef clean up the kitchen for the night by putting the cooking utensils in their places above the table on a rack. For reasons that I can't remember, we began to have a conversation about the ghosts that inhabit the mansion. He asked about any stories I had heard and I told him about my one and only experience with Steve and the voices. Some minutes had passed, and I wiped dry the last roasting pan. I then put it on the pan rack. We were done for the night. We turned off the lights and locked the door. We walked into the adjacent room where we met the remaining night staff and just sat around talking.

Suddenly, a loud crashing noise came from the kitchen, startling us all. We ran to the kitchen door. The chef quickly unlocked the door. As the lights came on, to our amazement, we saw all the pots, pans, and utensils that we had just washed and carefully put on the racks were now strewn about the kitchen floor like beads from a broken necklace! Every one of us was visually shaken, especially the chef and I. Who had done this? we wondered. We were left with our mouths open. It appeared as if someone had come into the kitchen and with a purposeful rage had decided to go wild, but who? And why? It was quite obvious to us that no one was in the kitchen. We looked all about and found no other sign of disturbance. The chef decided to shut off the lights, not touch a thing, and lock the door once again. We needed no prodding, but quickly decided to head to our homes for the night. When we returned the following morning, I unlocked the kitchen doors, and discovered, to my astonishment, that all the fallen pots and pans from the night before had been replaced upon the shelves! I spoke to everyone who I thought might have access to the kitchen. Everyone I spoke to denied ever entering the kitchen. There truly would have been no reason for anyone other than the chef or me to do so. I'm not altogether content with the event I experienced that night. If it happened once, it surely can happen again. I am not looking forward to the possibility of witnessing a second rampage in the kitchen, that's for damn sure!

There are other incidents I've witnessed that involve the lights in the dining room. There are times when the lights in the chandeliers will turn on or off by themselves. Sometimes, they just grow dim, and then abruptly light up to full wattage. It's a very strange thing, to be working in a room, and then to have this kind of stuff go on. It kind of puts me on edge.

The last incident that really shook me up took place in a room full of people. I was busing a table at the time in one of the dining rooms on the first floor. Another guy was helping me. After a while, he went to the adjacent dining room to begin busing tables in that room. After a few minutes, he came over from the other room and excitedly exclaimed, "Hey, come quickly. There's something strange going on over here!" I dropped what I was doing and followed him into the next dining room. As we entered, I saw that there were several guests who were seated at the dining table. Everyone was quiet and had their eyes focused on a chair at the end of the table. Slowly the chair, on its own, moved away from the table. It moved far enough away to suggest that someone or something was preparing to sit down at the table. The only noise in the room must have been that of our hearts pounding in our chests from amazement. Then someone yelled, "Did you see that?" I just stood there, for what seemed like an eternity. I gathered my courage and just made my way silently out of that room, not worrying about what the patrons themselves were thinking.

I haven't really spoken much about these things. I've chosen to just let things be. I'm easily freaked out, so if there is a spirit or ghost trying to make contact with me, I would prefer that it leave me alone.

THE DARK FIGURE

When we met, Erlinda hesitated to go into much detail about her experience. She was nervous, and paused from time to time during the interview to make sure what she had said was not going to cause me to doubt her. I assured her that this would not be the case. After two cups of coffee, she felt confident enough to proceed. Erlinda's story provides a new look at how ghosts "travel," be it between the physical/spiritual realms or the Mexican/U.S. border. In this story, the legacy of evil continues, beginning two generations earlier and ending, hopefully, in the present.

★   ★   ★

ERLINDA FLORES'S STORY

My story originates in Old Mexico with my father. When we were young girls, my father sat both my sister and me down, and recounted a terrible story that had beset his family. He told us that when he was a young boy he had lived with his family in Durango, Mexico. His parents had an unstable marriage because of his father's infidelity. In Mexico, which is by and large a Catholic country, divorce is not looked upon favorably, so his parents chose to live under the same roof as two single people. They slept in separate beds, but to all appearances they lived together as a couple. The community knew nothing of this arrangement.

One day, a local fellow appeared who kept following my grandmother around town. He became so obvious in his pursuit that she confronted him, and he disclosed his intentions to her. He told her he was infatuated with her and wanted to marry her. My grandmother was quite upset, and confused. She told this man she had no intention of marrying him and wished to be left alone. Although she was very lonely, given her difficult marriage, she was not ready to pursue another relationship. She clearly informed this man she was not interested in his advances. He, on the other hand, was not easily convinced and slapped her. Then he told her, "You will be mine. If not, you and your family will pay." My grandmother ran away and, during the days that followed, took care not to encounter this man in public. She did notice that there was a strange woman who followed her from time to time. A neighbor friend informed my grandmother that the woman was supposedly a witch, and was the sister of the man who had slapped her!

This news shook my grandmother. Because witchcraft was a power people feared, she began to stay inside her house and went outdoors only when it was absolutely necessary. But there were times during the day or night when my grandmother would be compelled to look out her front window. A strange feeling drew her to pull aside the curtains and look out to the street. There, she would see the witch's brother staring back, the man who had slapped her.

She watched him as he made his way across the street towards the fenced yard. Once at the gate, he reached into a small bag and brought out a handful of dirt, which he sprinkled about her yard very quickly, then just as quickly he departed. She saw this several times, and one day confided to her neighbor this peculiar act. The neighbor responded sadly, "Don't you know what that sorcerer is doing? He's sprinkling cemetery dirt on your yard. He's hexing you!" Unaccustomed to any of this, my grandmother just cried. Incredibly, my grandfather did not know of any of these goings-on. My grandmother made sure she kept quiet about everything.

As my father continued to tell us his story, he said that a few nights later, his mother was drawn to the window once again with the urge to look at the man who, this time, was inside the fenced yard. In the moonlight my grandmother noticed he was carrying a short stick, which he shook at my grandmother and said, "Remember my words.

No one refuses me and lives." At that point my grandmother didn't care any longer and called out to my grandfather. He ran to the window and saw the sorcerer jump over the fence like a cat and disappear. That night, my grandmother decided to sleep in the same bed with my grandfather.

My grandfather woke up during the night with the feeling that someone was in the room. He opened his eyes and turned to look at my grandmother. She was lying in bed facing the ceiling. Suddenly, she began to move slightly, and, amazingly, to rise above the bed. It was as if invisible strings were lifting her straight up, blankets and all. My grandfather panicked and threw his arms about her. He managed to pull her back down to the bed, but as soon as he let go of her, she began to rise above the bed once more. Again he pulled her down, and once more she began to rise, only this time she half sat up. He removed the blankets and, as she floated several inches above the bed, he noticed a red-soaked bloody area below her feet on the mattress. The blood was oozing from a wound in the shape of the letter X on the bottom of her foot. This all was too much for my grandfather. My grandmother then descended back down on the bed. She was unaware of what was going on because her eyes were "glazed over," and she did not respond when my grandfather called out her name. Then she stood up and began to walk towards the door. My grandfather, try as he might, was unable to move her away. His strength was gone. Suddenly, the front door opened by itself and she proceeded outside into the night. There in the yard stood the dark figure of the sorcerer's sister, dressed in a long black lace dress. She had a long black lace veil that covered her head and face. As my grandmother stood motionless in the yard, the witch approached her and reached out her arms to hold her. My grandfather was unable to move. He was being held back by the power of evil this witch had cast over him. The only thing he was able to do was to yell out, "Our holy Mother Guadalupe, help me!" At that moment my grandmother collapsed to the ground. The witch immediately took off running down the street. The sound she made as she escaped was the sound of a hoofed animal, such as a horse or goat.

Soon after, my grandmother died from this terrible experience. My grandfather was left to raise my father and two other sons. As the years passed, my father moved to the United States and eventually married again and settled in the city of Albuquerque. I myself was born and raised in Albuquerque, and also married here. Here is where my own story begins.

One night, about 12 years ago, my son, who was two years old, was fast asleep in his crib next to my bed. I had just turned off the bedroom light, and was drifting off to sleep myself. As my eyes were closing, I immediately began to feel someone in the room with us. Because of his job, my husband was away in Colorado, and my sister was staying with me at the time. She was sleeping in the adjacent room. Instantly, I sat up in bed and expected to see my sister. Instead, at the foot of my bed was the dark figure of a woman in a black veil. I was overcome with fear. I just sat there in bed, gazing at this woman. I tried to speak. I turned to my son's crib. He was already standing on his mattress, holding tight to the crib rails. He, too, was looking in the direction of the woman in black. It was then that I noticed she was extending her hands towards my young son. Something inside my soul gave me the strength to speak. I yelled out my sister's name! As soon as I spoke, the figure disappeared.

My sister entered the room, turned on the light, and hugged me. I explained what had just happened and then I began to cry. I realized that, at the exact moment I called out my sister's name, this evil thing lost all of its power and had to retreat. It was the power in my sister's name, which proved too much for evil to overcome. My sister's name is Guadalupe.

The following day, my sister and I decided to speak to my father about the dark visitor. As soon as we began to recount what had happened, my father placed his face in his hands and began to cry. He said, "*Santanas, por que me persigas! Deja a mi y a mi familia solos!*" ("Satan, why must you continue to follow me! Leave me and my family alone!") Neither my sister nor I were able to console him. Then he cried out, "*Mis hijas estan envueltas en hielo negro!*" ("My daughters are enveloped in a dark ice!") We all held hands and prayed for a long time. Eventually we composed ourselves. My father then sadly reminded us about the story of the Mexican sorceress, which he had told us years before. We were all silent. The silence was broken when I cried out to God for protection. Again we prayed. It has been my practice since that time to have a small statue of the Virgin of Guadalupe in my bedroom. And since the rose is her symbol, I've always made sure to have a fresh rose in a glass of water by her image. Happily, I've not experienced the dark figure since.

Two years ago, my sister Guadalupe came to me and said she was having bad dreams. As she discussed the dreams with me, she said, "You know, I don't think these are dreams at all. They are so real that they couldn't be dreams." I urged her on and she explained that in her house there are stairs that are located directly in front of her bedroom door. Both she and her husband are accustomed to sleeping with the bedroom door closed. At first, she awoke and noticed the door open wide. At her side was her husband, sound asleep. Fully awake, she got out of bed and closed the door. This happened several times and she still thought nothing was strange. Her husband informed her in the morning that he had not gotten up in the night. Still she didn't worry. A few nights later she again awakened and noticed the open door, but this time, at the top of the stairs was the image of a dark figure. As she stared at it, it slowly disappeared into the darkness. She thought she had imagined it and, because it had disappeared, fell asleep. The next time she awakened, the dark figure appeared to her, but this time it was at the door. She woke up her husband and they both searched the house. They discovered no one, and since the doors were all locked, they decided to go back to bed. The following night, this figure once again woke her up and now was at the foot of her bed! Scared stiff, she was not able to move a finger. She said the figure moved from the foot of her bed to the side on which she slept. It came around and paused at her side, raised one arm, and began to make a move as if to touch her. This was too much to bear. She let out a scream and her husband awoke. Although he did not see anything, my sister's emotional distress was so bad that he did not doubt her.

I told my sister that what she was telling me was giving me goosebumps. I told her that her experience was the same as mine: an uncomfortable feeling was causing me to wake up. It was the sensation of an intruder in the room. We decided that she should pray the rosary each night, and, before getting into bed, she should hang the rosary above her bedroom door with a thumbtack so that the crucifix would block the entrance. Since that time, the "visitor" has not come back to me or my sister.

I'm not sure what to make of all this. Both my sister and I had no part in what happened to my grandparents in Old Mexico. Why then would this "curse" reach us, and why would it follow us to the city of Albuquerque? Why? Why? Why?

Recently, my nine-year-old daughter spoke to me about not being able to sleep because of something in her room. I did not want to take any chances, so immediately I bought a small statue of an angel and placed it next to her bed and told her to look at it each night and pray to God. Most parents worry about protecting their children from normal day-to-day hazards. I have an extra worry.

★   ★   ★

THE VIRGIN OF GUADALUPE

It was 10 years after the murderous conquest of Mexico by the Spanish that Mary, the mother of the Christian God, appeared to Juan Diego, an Aztec woodworker. Mary appeared to the native population as an Aztec female deity known as Tonantzin. She spoke Nahuatl, the language of the Aztecs, and would appear on the outskirts of Mexico City. At the time of the conquest, Mexico City had become the locality of Spanish power. Guadalupe, the name she soon became known as, insisted that a shrine be built in her honor. This shrine, she firmly demanded, was to be built on a hill, which was to be located among her beloved conquered people. Guadalupe instructed Juan Diego to return to the "pretentiously dignified" clergy of Mexico City and to "evangelize" them. In these ways our Mother restored hope, dignity, and pride to the Native American people, a people who had been stripped of their dignity and high culture by the oppression of the Spanish.

As she had instructed, the shrine was built on the hilltop where she had appeared. The remaining 17 years of Juan Diego's life was spent at the shrine. He preached her message of liberation and hope to anyone who would listen.

The miracle that is the Virgin of Guadalupe has taught the world a lesson, which the Church must remember. The very things that the Church alienates, be they people, cultures, or lifestyles, are precisely the pillars of strength or gifts the Church needs so desperately in order to thrive and be reformed.

THE ALBUQUERQUE PRESS CLUB

This structure was designed by architect Charles Whittlesey, and built as his family residence in 1903 on the western edge of the high land east of Albuquerque. The house is a three-story frame structure designed after a Norwegian villa. It is characterized by low-pitched roofs with exposed log framing, rough log-cut facades, and a wide porch that circumvents its eastern rooms.

For the Whittlesey family, this rustic and rough-texture structure was, no doubt, a change in lifestyle from their previous Chicago residence.

It stood, at the time, virtually alone on the high land—the town not having grown in that direction. There was no vegetation or trees in the area. The views east to the Sandia Mountains and west to the town, river, and volcanoes were unobstructed. In 1908, the Whittleseys sold the house to Theodore S. Woolsey Jr., who owned the house for the next 12 years.

Albuquerque was known nationwide at this time for its good climate, conducive to the treatment of certain diseases. Located on high land near the house were two sanitariums. Indications are that Woolsey leased the house, with its wide porches and open areas, to many people who came to this city to convalesce. A particular female nurse by the name of "Clifford Emma," who came West with a patient and stayed on to become head nurse at the Albuquerque Sanitarium, passed the house each day on her way to work. She informed a suitor that if he bought the "log" house she would marry him. Arthur B. Hall bought the house from Woolsey in 1920 and she married him. Clifford Emma Hall, A. B.'s wife, lived in and eventually owned the house for the next 40 years. She brought the house through periods of extensive remodeling and interior-style changes.

During the 1920s, the Halls were owners and proprietors of Hall's Royal Pharmacy, on the corner of Gold and Second. They kept the interior of the house in a predominantly Native American motif—much as Wittlesey had done. Navajo rugs covered the rough wood floors; Maria, Tonita, and Santa lined the shelves in pottery; Mexican furniture was common and wrought-iron light fixtures were used when gas was added. Early New Mexican artists, such as Hogner, Redin, and Van Helser, were welcomed to the house, often painting and working on the wide porch. The Halls also collected Chinese furniture, some pieces having been left in the house by earlier lessees who had died there. Of these Chinese and Native American furnishings, many are still in the family today.

In 1930, Clifford Emma was divorced from A. B. Hall. By 1935 she was remarried to Herbert McCallum, but this too would end in divorce in 1938. For a source of income during these years, she rented out portions of the house. The south porch was framed, and part of the first level was sealed off to make a separate apartment. The original stable was renovated and added to, making it an apartment complex. Another apartment was built adjacent to it. As new building materials were introduced, Clifford Emma resurfaced the interior walls of the house. Whittlesey's rough wood and burlap surfaces were covered with celutex, plaster, and wood planking.

By the middle of the 1940s, Clifford McCallum was working for Vanlandingham Studios, first as a seamstress and eventually as owner. During these years, the rough wood floors were resurfaced with oak strip flooring. Knotty pine siding was introduced to some wall surfaces. An earlier color scheme of gold and red was accentuated through new furniture and draperies. Marble-topped European furniture pieces filled the main room. This, of all the rooms in the house, was visually the richest. The immense lava-rock fireplace, the filled bookshelves lining the walls, and the rustic bark wall surfaces contrasted with the golds and reds of the floor, furniture, draperies, and incidentals.

The ghost, "Clifford" Hall.

The Highland Park "log" house was a showplace during the 1930s, '40s, and '50s. Clifford McCallum spent a great deal of her time, money, and energy maintaining the house and its surroundings. She opened her home to many people, among them William Lovelace, who brought his international guests to view the house. The Mayo brothers, whose clinic is known worldwide, were frequent visitors. William Keleher, Clyde Tingley, and even Clinton

Anderson, in his early political years, were friends and visitors to the house.

In 1960, Clifford McCallum sold the house. Her increasing age, the extensive upkeep on the structure, and numerous other reasons contributed to her decision. The house was purchased by Zeta Mu Zeta House Corporation of Lambda Chi Alpha Fraternity.

In 1973, the Whittlesey House was purchased by the Albuquerque Press Club for use as a private club. A fire in February 1974, which originated with the wiring, destroyed the old bar and kitchen wing in the southwest corner of the structure. Following the fire, the Albuquerque Press Club House Committee established a long-range plan for improvement of the building.

All work, now being done or planned for the future, takes into account the historical nature of the building and strives to maintain and, in fact, enhance the historic structure. It is the desire of the Albuquerque Press Club to maintain the building in such a way that not only the Press Club, but all of Albuquerque, will be proud.

CHARLES F. WHITTLESEY, ARCHITECT

Charles Frederick Whittlesey was born on March 10, 1867, in Alton, Illinois. He studied architecture in Chicago under Louis Sullivan, whose influences can be seen in Whittlesey's later concrete structures in California. The extent of the friendship between Whittlesey and Frank Lloyd Wright, who also worked in Sullivan's office

215

during this time period, is unknown. The expertise that Whittlesey was to later gain in reinforced concrete in California, prior to its extensive use by Wright, might suggest that the two friends shared information when their paths crossed again in California.

CHRISTINA FLORENCE'S STORY

I began working here in August of 1994. It took me some time to learn where each room was located in this old two-story place. There are lots of stairwells and hallways that can play games with a person's memory and steer a person this way and that. Also, several low doorways split off from a central hall, which add to the confusion. I know the house has been

remodeled since the original owner, Mr. Whittlesey, designed and built it more than 100 years ago.

I recall that, when I had just started working here, I was a bit nervous, because people told me the place was haunted. I could tell they were not joking with me. They were serious! During my first five months on the job, I eventually became more and more at ease and made sure someone was in the house with me. Since I hadn't heard or experienced

"Just leave her a shot of gin on the bar, like I do."

216

anything unusual during this time, I became more relaxed and didn't think about ghosts or things like that. Until one night. . . .

At about three one morning, Kent, the president of the Press Club and co-owner, and I were talking by ourselves in the bar area. I know we were alone, because all the patrons were long gone, and the house was locked up for the night. We were leisurely caught up in our conversation, when suddenly I noticed someone looking at us from one end of the room. Without making a big fuss, I stood to face this person and clearly saw a woman in a black dress. She quickly moved away from where I had seen her. It all happened very fast. I sat back down on my chair. Kent asked, "What's going on?" I answered, "Oh, no. I think I just saw a ghost!" He responded nonchalantly, "Oh, that's just Mrs. Em, Emma Hall. Just leave her a shot of gin on the bar, like I do." Once I'd recovered from my initial shock, he told me about his experiences seeing the ghost in the house. He said that the only thought he was able to come up with at the time to pacify the ghost was to leave her a shot of gin at the bar. Still in a bit of a daze, I decided to do as he suggested. I filled a shot glass with gin and placed it to one side of the bar. Not wanting to think about ghosts, hauntings, or anything more about the supernatural, I decided to lock up everything for the night and head home. Kent once again made sure every door and window was secure and home we both went. At nine the next morning, I returned to the house and I sat with a cup of coffee at the bar and proceeded to work on some paperwork for the accountant. Not long after I had sat down, I remembered the shot glass of gin I had left for Mrs. Em. I got up from my chair and walked over to the glass. It was empty! I picked it up and, holding it to the light, I examined it for any lip prints on the rim. There were none. Later in the day, I met with Kent and told him about the shot glass and the missing gin. He responded, "Well, you know, I'm used to leaving a shot of gin for Mrs. Em. I've done it several times before you even came to work here. Some nights she drinks the liquor and some nights she doesn't. I don't know why. That's just Mrs. Em." Now, from time to time I place a shot of gin for Mrs. Em, and just like Kent's experience, sometimes she drinks it, and sometimes she doesn't.

Here at the Press Club, we have a resident cat, which we named "Emma" after the ghost, Mrs. Clifford Emma Hall. Emma Hall's picture hangs next to the bar. I'll notice Emma at times walking through the bar area. Suddenly, she'll stop dead in her tracks, and sit and gaze at thin air. It's as if an invisible person has caught her attention, because she stares in one direction, and then her eyes follow this invisible thing as it moves across the room and back again. She puts her ears back on many occasions, as if ready to make a run for the door. This, more than anything else, gives me the willies. It's so strange to see an animal react to a ghost. It's spooky.

"She'll stop dead in her tracks, and sit and gaze at thin air."

One day, on my day off, I came to the house just to feed Emma. I poured her food into her bowl and decided to sit on a couch to watch her eat. Soon, she jumped on my lap and rubbed her head against my hand. I began to stroke her back. It was a sunny, quiet day and, if you can picture the scene, I was relaxed and began to daydream. I was alone in the house and was thinking of nothing in particular. Suddenly, Emma stood up and stared intently at one area of the room. She just stared and stared, her ears went back, and immediately I knew something was in the room with us. I could feel the presence of someone standing with eyes focused on us. That was enough for me. I grabbed my purse and promptly made my way out the door, leaving the cat to take care of herself.

The last experience I had at the house went like this: I was with a friend, everyone else was gone, and I was getting ready to leave. We were talking at the bar area and abruptly we both became silent. There is an old piano in the main room of the house, several rooms away from the bar. Well, we heard someone playing the piano. Just three notes sounded. We looked at each other and not a word was spoken between us. The notes continued, so my friend and I jumped off the barstools, ran to the main room, and found the piano quiet as could be, with no one in sight! That was enough for us. We decided to head home and leave the place to the invisible piano player.

"We heard someone playing the piano."

MARY OLSON'S STORY

When I had my first encounter with the ghost, I was a bartender. I must say that this encounter scared me so badly it left me speechless. One evening at around 8 p.m., I was behind the bar rinsing the glasses I had just washed. There were three patrons seated oppo-

site from where I was working at the sink. One of these patrons was my husband, who was keeping me company. The three guys were having a light conversation between themselves and I was busy doing clean-up work. There I was, rinsing a glass, when without warning, I felt a strange, uncomfortable feeling come over me. This ill-at-ease feeling caused me to stop what I was doing, and I just stared straight ahead. With my hands dripping with water, I suddenly heard footsteps to the left of me. As I turned to focus on the sound, I caught the shadowy image of a woman dressed in a black cape or dress of some bygone style. I was frozen with fright. My husband noticed my terror-filled eyes and said loudly, "Mary, what's wrong? Are you all right?" I was unable to answer him. He looked to the area of the room at which I was staring and cried out, "There she is, the ghost! Look!" The woman in black turned away and made a quick exit towards the far wall. As she faded away, the sound of high heels on the wood floor was unmistakable! I'm telling you, the hair on the back of my neck stood straight up! We were all visibly shaken. My husband came over to me and gave me a hug to reassure me that everything was all right. There was no mistaking what we all had witnessed. We had just had an encounter with the ghost of the house, Mrs. Clifford Hall, "Emma."

The second experience I had with the ghost was around 10 p.m. I was wiping down one end of the bar, and once again there were three patrons seated on stools. This time, without any prior warning, I heard the unmistakable sound of footsteps, the sound of high heels on our wooden floor. Once again, I stopped what I was doing and, holding the limp dishcloth in one hand, stood motionless. Observing my strange behavior, one of the patrons moved towards me and, without warning me, he grabbed my stiff arm. I just about died! I let out a scream and threw my hands up into the air. The wet dishrag landed, who knows where, and I nearly fell to pieces. Of course, everyone wanted to know what was going on, so I told them all about my previous experience with the ghost. After a few laughs, I slowly regained my composure.

The third and last time I experienced the ghost took place during the afternoon. This experience, I have to say, was my worst. It was about 5 p.m. I was again at the bar, this time counting the money, preparing the cash register for the evening's business. Finishing up, I decided to open the newspaper to read the events of the day. I was alone in the house, sitting on a barstool and puffing on a cigarette. Quite suddenly, I heard the now-familiar high-heel footsteps. The sound was in one area of the room, but slowly the steps began to move towards my direction. The newspaper was shaking in my hands. When the sound stopped, about six feet away from me, I can't begin to express the terror I felt. Pardon my language, but this was scaring the living crap out of me! I listened as the footsteps moved away, then suddenly, once again, they began to move in my direction. I don't know where I got the strength to open my mouth, but in order to keep my sanity I spoke, "Mrs. Em, would you please relax? You're making me nervous!" Just at that instant, the footsteps stopped in their tracks. I heard nothing more.

Since that time, I have never had any more experiences with the ghost. Because I had a job to do, I decided to put this ghost stuff all behind me and get on with my work. I didn't want to allow the ghost to get the better of me. I decided to overcome my fear as much as possible, and to deal with things as they came, be they ghosts or whatever.

THE BERNALILLO TREASURE

VICENTE RAMIREZ'S STORY

My experience with ghosts took place about 34 years ago. My family moved into a house on a ranch that we had bought in the city named Bernalillo, north of Albuquerque. The property was in real need of care. Apparently, the family that had previously owned it had stopped caring for the numerous fruit trees and rosebushes planted throughout the property, because it looked like it had been years since they had been pruned and fertilized. On the six-acre property was a barn, a small shed, and our three-bedroom house. During the real-estate transaction, the realtor informed us that the property had belonged to a family of Anglos with three children, including an infant girl. The realtor also informed us that this family had relocated to somewhere in Utah.

I guess my parents had the keen foresight to see beyond the neglect of the buildings, because it only took us a little more than a year to turn our six acres of neglected land into a property that the neighbors marveled at. My father began to prune and water the apricot, apple, and pear trees that fall, so that by spring the next year they were all in a carpet of blossoms. Most of the roses, however, were beyond help and had to be removed. My father attached a chain to the back of his pickup and pulled them out, roots and all. My mother did yard work and turned a patch of ground, which the weeds had claimed, into a flower bed of zinnias and sunflowers. She was very proud of her hard labor and glowed with pride when the women from the neighboring properties visited and commented on how beautiful her flowers looked.

My father took all the dead and diseased trees and rosebushes into the pasture and placed them in a large pile where they remained for a week. We all went to the pasture at the end of that week to watch as my father lit a fire at the base of the monstrous pile of branches and roots. The mountain of rubbish was soon flaring high into the evening sky. My mother's *comadre* (friend), who lived a few properties away, came by to witness the event, as did other neighbors. Being a young boy, I was fascinated by the flames.

The simply constructed barn and shed on our property were in need of replastering, so my father got about 10 men together one weekend, and the replastering work was begun and finished in that weekend. There was much work to do in order to get our property looking civilized. The first year proved to be the most difficult, but when it was done, there was no doubt about it—we had a farm we were very proud of.

One day, I was out in the front yard playing with my younger brother, Antonio. Antonio spotted a small dog that had wandered close to our fence, and called to it. The dog immediately crawled under the wire fence and came running to him. Since that day we adopted the dog as a family pet. We named her "Chamisa," after the native New Mexican plant that grows wild in the state. We assumed she had escaped from her owners because of the muddy rope around her neck, which looked as if she had chewed through it to escape.

One night, at about 10 p.m. Chamisa began to bark over and over. She was tied to an apricot tree in our backyard. I went outside when my father asked me to investigate. Chamisa was pulling on her chain and wanted to be set free. As far as I could tell, she wanted to run in the direction of the shed. Perhaps, I thought, she had seen a skunk or opossum that had caught her attention. I ran back into the house and located a flashlight. When my mother asked me what all the commotion was about, I told her that there was an animal out back by the shed. She warned me about staying far away from any skunks. With that warning I ran out the door, with flashlight in hand, and returned to Chamisa. I let her loose from her chain, and she immediately darted away into the darkness towards the shed. I called to her as I took up the chase. I picked up a stick, thinking I could use the stick to fend off any skunk we might encounter. Before I had made another move, Chamisa returned to my side and began to bark uncontrollably at the shed. At that point my mother opened the back door and said, "What's going on with that dog? Why is she acting so crazy?" I answered, "There's something back there that's scaring her." My mother said, "Let's go see what all the concern is about. Bring the flashlight." As my mother and I went around the side yard and approached the shed, we spotted a woman standing as still as could be, dressed in a long black dress, her face completely covered with a black cloth. I shined the light beam on her body as my mother asked her in Spanish, "*¿Quien esta?*" ("Who's there?") The woman did not answer. My mother asked, "*¿Necesitas algo?*" ("Do you need something?") Then the woman made a movement. She slowly began to raise her arm, which had been against her side. She pointed directly to the area of ground beside the stump of a dead tree. As she pointed, we noticed the woman was wearing a white glove. My mother asked once more, "*¿Senora, que necesitas? Diga me.*" ("Lady, what do you want? Tell me.") The woman did not answer, but continued to point with her gloved hand at the spot by the tree. Then my mother took the flashlight away from me and shined the light at the spot by the tree as we took a few steps closer to this woman. We saw only a few weeds and nothing more. Then my mother moved the light towards the woman's hand. What we had assumed was a gloved hand was instead a skeleton arm with outstretched bone fingers. Quickly, my mother moved the light up to the woman's face and, although her face was covered in a long black lace veil, we both could see unmistakably the white outline of a skull and the dark circles of the empty eye sockets! My mother let out a scream, and threw the flashlight at the ghost. Grabbing my left forearm, she and I ran like the wind into the house. To say that we were scared would be an understatement! My arm developed bruises from my mother's finger marks. My father was unable to control my mother's crying, so he phoned her *comadre* who soon showed up with her husband. We both related in detail what had happened and my mother's *comadre* and husband spent the night with us in our small house. I couldn't stop shaking and asked everyone to not mention the ghost anymore. We soon decided to pray instead of talk about what we had seen.

My father opened a drawer and brought out two candles. One candle we lit for Santo Niño de Atocha (baby Jesus) and placed his statue in our living room. The other candle we lit for San Miguel (St. Michael the Archangel) and placed his picture outside our back door. During the night, whenever we would hear Chamisa barking, we would all make the sign of the cross over our chests. Eventually, we got to bed and fell asleep. My father was at a loss about what else to do and simply announced to us all, *"Dios esta con nosotros. No debemos de tener miedo."* ("God is with us. There is no need to have fear.")

The following morning we all greeted the comforting light of the sun. After gathering our emotional strength, my mother took my father and her *comadre* to the spot behind the shed where we had seen the

"One candle we lit for Santo Niño de Atocha."

ghost. Not far beyond was the flashlight lying on the ground.

Searching for an answer to the ghost's appearance, my father said that perhaps it was attempting to relay a message to us. My mother's *comadre* stated, "Perhaps there's a *tesoro* (treasure) buried there where the ghost was pointing!" We all agreed that perhaps there was a buried can of money or jewelry. Wasting no time, my father went to the barn and quickly returned with a shovel. He said, "I'll find whatever is here, even if it takes all day." Both he and la *comadre's* husband went to work, taking turns digging. Very soon they had a hole three feet deep. Deciding to take a short break among the twisted roots of the tree, they began to discuss the wondrous treasure that lay beneath them. Taking up the shovel once again, it was not long before my father cried out, *"Aqui, aqui hay algo!"* ("Here, there's something here!") Sure enough, he had uncovered a flat stone about three feet long and two feet wide. My mother was uneasy about what was happening before her eyes. Was this the right thing? What if the treasure brought bad luck to the family? She was voicing her thoughts to everyone. But soon everyone decided that it would be best to continue. Directing their energies towards enlarging the hole and uncovering the stone slab from the dirt, they soon accomplished their task. Carefully, they lifted the stone, which appeared to be about two inches thick. When they removed the stone slab and placed it on the grass, we could all see that underneath the stone were the remains of a wooden box. My mother's *comadre* said, "There it is. You're rich! It's the treasure!" Using the point of the shovel, my father began to remove the decaying planks of wood and place them to the side. Within the small oblong box was a thick layer of mud. Reaching his hand into the soft, moist mud my father felt for coins or jewelry. Then he yelled, "I've got something!" My mother responded, "*Eliseo, cuidarse!*" ("Eliseo, be careful!") He drew back his arm and, we all could clearly see, he held in his hand a round ball of mud. Quickly, someone brought a bucket to him, and he carefully placed the small round object into it. Crawling out of the hole, he called for someone to bring him another bucket filled with water. When this was done, he slowly poured the clean water into the bucket that contained the "round treasure." As the water rolled over the muddy object, we recognized that it was a child's skull. My father dropped the skull into the bucket of water and quickly washed his hands. He asked, "God, what does this all mean?" We were speechless. My mother was crying and said, "What was the woman in black trying to tell us?" Perhaps, the ghost was the mother of the child, wishing for her baby to be given a decent burial. Or, as my mother's *comadre* said, "The baby was murdered and the ghost wanted to make this known to everyone." My mother collapsed into the arms of my father. The only other things I remember were the uniforms of the police when they arrived at our house.

The coroner, who arrived with the police, dug out the remaining bones. No one dared mention the woman in black who had prompted the digging. My father just said he was attempting to remove the old tree stump when he came upon the tragic scene. The police drove off and began their investigation. They returned the next day and asked the neighbors questions about the previous family, who had occupied our property. The results of their investigation were never shared with us, and as far as we know, they have never been made public. When the police drove off with the baby's bones in a cardboard box that day, they also drove away with any answers we might have had.

A couple of weeks after the police had left our home, my father made a small wooden cross, which I painted white. We placed it at the base of the tree and said a few prayers.

If the woman in black wanted to inform us about the child in the grave, I guess she accomplished her task. We never saw her after that night. I like to think that the dead do not rest until their loved ones are at peace. Well, that's what I believe.

★ ★ ★

THE ARCHANGEL MICHAEL

The Archangel Michael is distinguished in three of the major religions: Judaism, Islam, and Christianity. His place in heaven is in the center,

before the throne of God, armored and golden-winged. Michael is such a mighty power that he has the ability to rescue souls from Hell. In his right hand he holds the sword of divine wrath; in his left he carries the prominent scales of divine judgment where souls are to be weighed at the final Day of Judgment. In the Last Days of the World, Michael is destined to do battle with the Devil, and to banish Satan deep down into the bottomless pit of Hell.

MARIA TERESA RESTAURANT

THE SALVADOR ARMIJO HOUSE

Maria Teresa Restaurant occupies one of the most historic homes in Old Albuquerque. Few of its contemporaries are left. They have succumbed to old age, the bulldozer, changing tastes, and the needs of a growing city. Fortunately for this house, it has been owned and occupied by members of the same family through seven generations, who have sustained and nurtured it.

It has been changed and remodeled several times, but most of the basic house is intact. Though the individual rooms in most cases serve different purposes from their original intent. Since 1977, when Tinnie Mercantile Company acquired the Salvador Armijo House, it has been a public restaurant. Some of the family's furniture remains in the house, along with many other antiques added by John Meigs and other Roswell artists and decorators, who restored the house for Tinnie. When Maria Teresa Restaurant was taken over by Old Town Development Company in 1984, they, too, have respected the integrity of the house and period. They have gone one step further, making it even more of a public property by making available the history of the house, its furnishings, and the people who built it and cared for it all these years.

Picture it as it was originally—a 12-room hacienda enclosing a central patio. It faced south toward the Old Town Plaza and San Felipe de Neri Church, which was the heart and soul of Albuquerque. A few small adobe houses clustered around the plaza, and several farms and haciendas were up and down the river. But New Town, which grew up along the railroad two miles east, didn't exist yet. Between this house and the church there may have been a few small homes and gardens, but the area was mostly open fields.

The mid-1800s were momentous, even traumatic, days in Albuquerque. After 10 years of revolution, Mexico had won its independence from Spain, and New Mexico had become part of the new Republic of Mexico. The Civil War had not been fought; the railroad had not arrived. The new concepts of a unified industrial nation had not permeated the provincialism of the neglected, isolated territory of New Mexico. Salvador Armijo, builder of Maria Teresa, was part of the drama, ready to accept and become part of the change.

Important people came to this house—leaders of caravans on the Santa Fe and Chihuahua Trails, church dignitaries, missionaries on their way to and from Mexico, government officials, and friends who were like Armijo, who were merchants, farmers, and stockmen.

But what about Salvador Armijo, the man who had built this house and whose stamp is still upon it, and Doña Maria de las Nieves Sarracino, the woman who had ruled it for so many years?

The family's founder, the first Salvador Armijo, came to New Mexico in 1695. General Don Diego de Vargas had recently reconquered the province, and the Spanish government was making every effort to resettle it after the Native American Revolt of 1680. There must have been lucrative incentives to lure the young widow with four sons to an unknown and dangerous hinterland. They succeeded well, for less than 100 years later, in 1790, the great-grandson of this woman had established himself as part of the landed gentry in the Alameda area. This was Vicente Armijo; he and his seven sons all became prominent in politics

and business in the Río Abajo, the "down river" part of New Mexico, the agricultural area where families had roots deep in the soil, where generation after generation they accumulated wealth and social standing.

Four of Vicente's sons were mayors (*alcaldes*) of Albuquerque during the 1830s. One, Manuel, was three times governor of New Mexico during the Mexican regime, and Ambrosio, father of Salvador, was a leading merchant, sheep man, and trader on the Santa Fe Trail. This was the family Salvador was born

Salvador Armijo.

into in 1784. From pictures, we know he was strong and stocky with thick reddish hair and a beard. He joined his father and older brothers in the family businesses, taking many wagon trains of goods to and from Missouri, and down into Mexico. We get a picture of a swashbuckling man, riding hard, overseeing shearing and shipping, making deals for thousands of dollars worth of goods with Yankee merchants in St. Louis. Somewhere along the line he was given an education, for he was fluent in both Spanish and English, and understood a good deal about law and economics, judging from his career. Most sons of wealthy families, like the Armijos, were educated in St. Louis, and it is likely Salvador was too, which probably made him receptive to the transition of governments from Mexican to North American.

He was a product of that time in New Mexico's history when allegiance to the mother country had to be changed. Two years before he was born, Spain uttered its dying gasp in New Mexico, but the cultural ties remained strong. Salvador was a child and a young man during the turbulent times when Mexico was trying to establish a republic. He was 23 when the Americans came, old enough to understand the insecurity New Mexico had endured under Mexico, and pragmatic enough to know that his and his country's future lay with the United States, no matter what ties bound his heart to his Spanish heritage.

In 1847, Salvador married Paula Montoya of another Río Abajo family. He may have already begun acquiring the land where Maria Teresa now stands, and some historians say the house was built as early as 1793, and indeed, that is very possible. This was prime agricultural land, not far from the plaza and church, and it seems likely that someone would have built a home here soon after the founding of the city. But the family believes that Salvador Armijo built this house "sometime in the 1840s."

Salvador's building plan was a traditional rectangle, a 100 feet from north to south, and 70 feet east and west, enclosing a *placita*, or inner courtyard. *Zaguanes*, covered passageways big enough for a wagon, with people-sized gates set into the big gate, were on the south, east, and north sides. Each of the 12 rooms opened to the *placita* rather than to the outside. Even in 1840 this was still the style in New Mexico, a carryover from Spanish Colonial times when each hacienda was a fortress, self-sufficient and defendable. The well was in the *placita*, stables and storerooms to the rear, and when nomadic Native Americans attacked, the gates were closed, and the family could withstand siege for a long time. There is no record that this ever happened to the Armijo family, but it was a custom to build homes in this way.

Anglo visitors often disliked the darkness of the rooms, which had neither outside doors nor windows, but once they experienced the summer coolness or winter coziness, they found them comfortable. Until the railroad reached New Mexico in 1879, glass for windows, milled wood trim, and metal trim and tools were scarce, so the traditional adobe homes were practical.

The original house had adobe walls 32 inches thick except for the west side, which was built of stone. That part of the house, having no foundation, settled a great deal and was later taken down, but the rest of the original house remains, recognizable today even after many additions and remodelings. The house was plastered with mud, inside and out, and had a thick layer of dirt on the roof, drained by long wooden canales that stuck out on all sides. In the rear (north) were the granary, winery, storage rooms, wood room, carriage house, stables, and living quarters for servants. In the main house was a family chapel on the southwest corner, which no longer exists.

Don Salvador bought more land around his house, to cultivate about 100 acres for vineyards, orchards, and vegetable gardens. The *acequia madre*, mother ditch, was his eastern boundary. To the west he had pastureland for sheep, horses, mules, and oxen required for his ever-growing mercantile business.

During the first five years of American occupation, the army spent $12 million in New Mexico, and it is easy to imagine that Salvador Armijo got his share for the flour, beans, meat, and other provisions he had sold them. In addition, he sold wine, produce, staples, and supplies locally, and manufactured goods he brought in on the Santa Fe Trail. He ran wagon freight trains as far south as Culiacan, Mexico. He also dealt in real estate, leasing property north and south of town to the Army for a garrison and a hospital.

During these years of expansion in his businesses, his personal life was in turmoil. He and Paula separated in 1848 after just one year of marriage. He developed a volatile relationship with Doña Maria de las Nieves Sarracino, a member of another prominent family from Los Padillas, south of Albuquerque, who played a major role in the Armijo family affairs until her death many years later. Even her name suggests a fierce strength—Saracen of the Snows. While Don Salvador was gone on his frequent and long business trips, Doña Nieves had full responsibility managing the homes and farms. They had only one child, a daughter named Piedad, who was close to both parents, even after they separated.

The 1860s were as full of turmoil as the decade earlier had been. Some leading citizens of New Mexico, and many of the officers at forts throughout the territory, were sympathetic with the Confederacy, and it was mistakenly assumed that New Mexico would side with the South when Civil War broke out. If this had happened, it would have given the Confederacy a clean sweep to the seaports of the Pacific, control of forts and military supplies in the Southwest, and access to gold fields of the Rocky Mountains, which they so desperately needed. Such was not the case. With few exceptions New Mexico remained loyal to the Union.

One of the most loyal was Salvador Armijo, who enlisted as a private when he was 38 years old, though there is no record of his having been called to active duty. He did, however, feel the Confederate invasion economically. As Confederates defeated Union troops at La Mesilla, and fought to a draw at Val Verde, Union troops withdrew to Fort Union, and orders were given to destroy supplies in Albuquerque, which Confederate soldiers would need. Salvador, his brother, and one other merchant suffered the heaviest losses. When the war was over, Salvador submitted a bill to the government for goods taken, almost $8,000 worth of corn, wheat, flour, sugar, coffee, beans, whiskey, brandy, horses, mules, and oxen. In less than two months the Confederates were defeated and retreated back to Texas. Life returned to normal.

In 1862, Salvador's daughter, Piedad, married Santiago Baca in the first wedding to be held in San Felipe Church since the Confederate invasion. Santiago and his father-in-law became close friends, and called their business *Armijo y Hijo*, Armijo and Son. They opened branch stores in Cebolleto, Cubero, Jarales, and Peralta.

Don Salvador left much of the business to his son-in-law, devoting more time to his farms and real estate transactions in Albuquerque. He bought more land adjoining the home place, property west of the river at Atrisco, near Alameda, at Tijeras and Cañoncito in the Sandia Mountains, south of town at Barelas, and near Old Town in

Los Duranes. He also bought property on the plaza for warehouses and a store. In 1866, an article referred to him as the only farmer in New Mexico to spread manure on his fields, hauling as much as two thousand wagonloads a year from his sheep corrals. He also used the new-fashioned steel plow and seed corn from "The States." His vineyards produced heavily, and the wine presses were busy. By 1870, he was the most successful farmer in the Albuquerque area, and the largest agricultural employer with an annual payroll of more than $4,000. Soon after Piedad and Santiago were married, and had settled in Pecos, Don Salvador and Doña Nieves separated and began a 10-year process of dividing their property. He sold the house and part of the farmlands to her for $10,000, a large price for the time. Part of the settlement agreement was that the son-in-law should have power-of-attorney for Doña Nieves. In late 1874, Piedad, Santiago, and their three children moved from Pecos to live with Doña Nieves. Don Salvador moved to Peralta and married a young woman who bore him three more daughters. In 1878, he moved back to Albuquerque, built a big home in Los Duranes, and continued to be active in civic and political circles in Albuquerque until he died in 1879.

In 1875, Piedad and Santiago began an extensive remodeling of the home. Dark, fortress-like homes of a generation earlier were no longer stylish. For those who had money, anything could be ordered, even heavy furniture. More important than the materials were the new ideas brought from the Midwest and East by the increased traffic and communication made possible by the railroad. They did the house over in what has become known as Territorial style, an adaptation of Greek Revival. The *zaguan* on the south side was now a hall opening to the rooms on either side. A door was hung on the new outer wall of the *zaguan* with glass panels on each side and above. The north *zaguan* was enclosed the same; many windows were set into walls facing the *placita* as the exterior. *Portales* (covered porches) were built along the east, south, and west exterior walls, and all around the interior courtyard. Wooden flooring replaced the earth-and-oxblood floors of the Colonial period. Once again the house became an up-to-date hacienda befitting the station of its occupants.

Santiago Baca was a handsome, fine-featured man, who stepped easily into a leadership role in Albuquerque. He had been educated in church schools in Santa Fe, had served as Clerk of the Senate, and had been elected senator for two terms, representing San Miguel County. He brought extensive sheep flocks into Armijo y Hijo. He imported a fine stallion and good brood mares from the East to improve the draft and saddle stock. He began a sawmill in the Manzano Mountains, which supplied much of the lumber for expanding Albuquerque, particularly now that the Victorian styles using more fancy milled lumber were popular. Also, in the Manzanos he found a beautiful fresh spring that he bottled and sold as Coyote Springs water for drinking. This water was so well liked by Albuquerqueans that it was sold for many years, even after Santiago had died. Several generations of the family enjoyed going to Coyote Springs for family outings in the mountains.

Piedad and Santiago became wealthy. They bought and sold hundreds of pieces of real estate in Albuquerque; he was elected to the Territorial Legislature from Bernalillo County, and sheriff and tax collector of Bernalillo County. During all the political activity, he continued to operate the farm, winery, sheep ranch, and the store at the intersection of Rio Grande Boulevard and Mountain Road. What is now Romero Street was named Don Santiago Street, after him.

In the 1890s his fortune began to decline. He was involved in political battles, usually on the winning side, but he made enemies, nevertheless. An employee in the tax collector's office was suspected of spending public funds, and an investigation showed serious shortages. Civil judgments went against him, and like dominoes, mortgages began to be called in, causing him to lose some of the home property during the next several years.

During these same painful years, there were also family problems. Never easy to get along with, Doña Nieves, with whom they lived in the big house, became more difficult as she got older. In 1895, Santiago and Piedad's son, Bernardino, and his wife also moved into the house, causing more problems. Playing grandmother against parents, the son succeeded in causing an irreparable rift, and when Doña Nieves decided to deed the western portion of the house to her grandson, Santiago and

Piedad moved out in anger, and terminated the power-of-attorney he had held for 20 years.

Bernardino sold off some of his grandmother's property without her knowledge, and she filed charges of fraud against him. While the suit dragged on, Doña Nieves went to live with her granddaughter, Francisca, who was married to Meliton Chavez, a prominent banker. She died there in April 1898, with her personal affairs in chaos. The house had deteriorated; her beloved daughter and son-in-law had moved out; the grandson on whom she had doted had cheated her and left town—the estate was in ruin.

But the thread of family ties was not broken. On August 13, 1899, Meliton Chavez bought the house and what was left of the property when it was auctioned off on the steps of the Old Albuquerque post office for back taxes and debts. He paid $1,125 for it. Santiago and Piedad returned to the house to live out the rest of their lives. She died in 1907, he a year later.

Francisca and Meliton Chavez, with their daughters Piedad and Soledad, moved back into the family residence and began to restore its grace and beauty.

For the third time the house took on a new life, and became a gathering place for family and friends, a social center for the community. The Chavez's daughter, Piedad, married Alejandro Sandoval from Sandoval County, and they lived in one wing of the house. Their granddaughter, Frances Wilson, present holder of the lease/purchase agreement on the property, has spent most of her life in this house. When her grandfather, Meliton Chavez, died in 1933, he willed the south half of the house to her mother, Piedad Sandoval, and the north house to Frances. In the midst of the Depression, they were faced with the maintenance of a very large and very old house, so they converted it into seven apartments. When her mother died, Mrs. Wilson became sole owner. In 1977, she accepted a lease/purchase agreement with Tinnie Mercantile Company, who opened Maria Teresa Restaurant that year. Interior design was under the direction of Roswell artist John Meigs, who sensitively augmented family heirlooms with antique pieces of comparable periods, keeping the flavor of the house intact. In 1984

Old Town Development Company acquired Maria Teresa, and it has preserved the ambiance of the house as carefully as if it were part of the Armijo clan.

Flamboyant, redheaded, swashbuckling Salvador Armijo would be delighted if he could walk into Maria Teresa today. (And who's to say he doesn't?) Seven generations of his descendants have loved the house. Through happiness and sorrow, disappointment and victory, the house has held the family together and sustained it, and it, in turn, has sustained the house.

Each generation has left its mark. There is a whisper of old Salvador, and his passionate arguments with strong-willed Doña Nieves; of the handsome Don Santiago who made and lost a fortune; of gentle Piedad; of misguided Bernardino; and of the children who romped in the *Quarto de Leones* (the Lions' Room).

Though it has undergone four major remodelings in its 130 years of life, the basic plan is still recognizable, and it is fun to imagine how it used to be.

LEO BRYANT'S STORY

I've worked at the restaurant now for about 10 years. My first job was dishwasher and now I'm the night manager. The restaurant is a great place to work. I'm surrounded by antiques and a beautiful house, filled

with the history of the family that built it.

I've not experienced anything unusual in all the years I've worked at the restaurant, but the staff I've known sure has. Several employees have come to me with their own stories of strange goings-on. I personally know these individuals to be honest, and they would not make up such stories of ghosts and such things to please themselves. One incident I recall happened several years ago when I was a busboy. I had a fellow employee named J. D. Romero, also at the time a busboy. He abruptly quit after experiencing, as he put it, ghosts.

It was late at night, and both he and I were left alone in the restaurant. We had been put in charge of making sure all the doors and windows were locked. After checking each room for the possibility of a "lost" guest, we determined the house was, indeed, empty. All the lights were turned off except for where we were standing in the lobby area. Quite unexpectedly, we heard the soft sound of voices coming from the north boardroom. J. D. decided to investigate. He left, and I stayed in the lobby, awaiting his return. Soon he returned, and informed me that there were some people sitting in the boardroom at the table. He had taken a quick look inside, but had decided to have me ask them to leave, since I was the one in charge. I was perplexed as to why these folks had not cleared out of the restaurant. I decided to check for myself and tactfully ask them to leave for the evening.

Making my way to the boardroom, I rehearsed over and over how I would ask these people to leave. I opened the door of the room and found it dark and empty. I did a thorough check. I looked inside closets and under tables. The room was totally empty. Why would J. D. play a joke like this? I turned off the lights in the room and returned to the lobby to confront him. "What are you up to, J. D.?" I asked. He answered, "What do you mean? Did you tell them to leave?" I told him either he was playing a joke on me or he had imagined the people in the room. He left the lobby and after checking the boardroom for himself, stated emphatically that there had been people in the room, but he could not explain why they had disappeared. He was very shaken by what had just happened, and refused to stay a minute longer at the house. He even gave me a couple of dollars if I would finish doing both his and my own for the night. The following day he gave his notice to our supervisor, terminating his employment.

There was another time, just about two years ago, when one of our waiters named Daniel Lamb reported a weird experience one evening. It seems that some patrons he was waiting on pointed to a mirror in their dining room and said, "What is this?" Dan asked, "What do you mean?" They said a woman had appeared in the mirror, seated at the table with them. She was only reflected in the mirror, but they could not see her in the room.

I had another fellow employee who shared his strange experience at the house with me. This particular employee was like myself, a shift manager. His ghost experience took place in the dining room, called The Armijo Room, named after the original owner of the house. From the opposite end of the house, he heard the antique piano that belonged to the original owners of the house, playing in the Armijo dining room. The piano currently stands against the west wall of the room. Knowing that he was the only person in the house, immediately he thought a burglar was in the restaurant. The eerie music continued as he quickly, but quietly, made his way to the rear of the restaurant and locked the door from the outside to enclose anyone in the house. Then he found a public phone and called the police. As he put it, "The police were there in a flash!" He opened the door for them and with drawn weapons they shone their flashlights to completely probe and explore

"I heard someone call my name."

every room in the house. They were unable to find any evidence of burglars. Everything in the house was as it should have been. This manager was totally convinced he had heard the piano. There was no way of convincing him otherwise. His explanation, after all other possible explanations had been exhausted, was that a ghost had been the musician that night.

One unusual incident that took place here in the restaurant last year occurred in the cocktail bar. The water pipes underneath the floor needed replacing. A crew of plumbers came in one day and proceeded to remove the floorboards in the bar for access to the pipes below. When the boards were dismantled and the bare ground underneath exposed, the work crew began the grubby task of digging down through the dirt. Very soon they came upon some old bones.

The bones were of various sizes and, from their timeworn appearance, must have been in the ground for many, many years. As was our good fortune, we had an employee who was attending the University of New Mexico, majoring in anthropology. She gathered the bones in a box and took them to the university. She presented them to a professor who examined the bones and determined that they were from a large animal, perhaps a horse. Mixed in with these bones were also human bones. As you might imagine, there was much talk among the employees when word got back to us about the bones. Whether the bones were reburied where they were found or if they remained at the university, I do not know. If they are connected in some way to the hauntings, I'm not sure. The fact that they were found where they were is enough to cause a bit of uneasiness, wouldn't you say?

Without a doubt, I've had many staff come to me with stories of their experiences with what they call ghosts. As I've said before, I've been employed at the restaurant for over 10 years, so that's quite a lot of experiences with ghosts.

DANIEL L. LAMB'S STORY

I began my employment as a waiter with the restaurant about three years ago. After a few days on the job, some staff members told me about the spirits of the original owners of the house haunting the restaurant. Of course, I was skeptical of what I had been told. But after so many personal encounters with the supernatural, I now believe the house has spirits that look after the place.

I've known waiters and waitresses like me who have come to work with negative attitudes about a variety of issues; they don't like their supervisors, their work hours, other waiters, or the house itself. I clearly recall one employee in particular, who didn't like working in the dining room, named The Armijo Room. In the room hangs a small portrait of a woman, one of the original family members of the Armijo family. The woman has light-colored eyes. Well, this waiter for some personal reason disliked the dining room and especially the portrait of this woman. He at times made rude comments about the woman, including some off-color jokes. An obvious pattern began to develop. Soon after he said something negative about the portrait, he would have a mishap of some kind. This waiter was usually quite capable, but he dropped trays of food, tipped over glasses of water or wine, etc. These "accidents" took place directly in front of the portrait, in a dining room filled with guests. Eventually, to no one's surprise, this waiter left his employment at the restaurant. My personal encounters with the ghosts were not so unpleasant, but they were spooky and weird, nonetheless.

My first ghost experience occurred three weeks after I had started working at the restaurant. I was assigned to the dining room named The Chacon Room, a room with many mirrors on its walls. Other waiters had told me that this room was known to have the ghost of a man in a dark suit. Apparently, this is the only room in the house in which he has ever been seen. I was told that typically the back of this man is reflected in the mirrors when he is seated at one of the tables. The man is elderly, and somewhat stooped over because of his advanced age. Strangely, only the upper back and head of this man is seen.

As I began my third week of employment, I was tending a table of customers in the room adjacent to The Chacon Room. It was 6 p.m. After taking the customers' orders, I excused myself and made my way to the kitchen. When I entered the corridor towards the kitchen, I was strangely compelled to look into the adjacent Chacon Room. There, in the empty room, I looked at a large mirror on one of the walls. To my amazement, I saw the reflection of the figure of the man in the dark suit, seated at the table! The room was more than adequately lit. Very distinctly, there was the ghost. I was surprised to see how clearly he appeared in the mirror. I could see his white shirt collar and his full head of dark gray hair. As I changed my focus from the mirror to the table, his image was not visible at the table but I could see his image in the mirror. As I said before, others have seen this man in the same situation as I. Among the staff there is a saying, "The house accepts you when the ghost appears to you." To my knowledge, the ghost of the man in the dark suit has a history of appearing only to people in The Chacon Room and nowhere else.

I must admit that I was more than a little surprised to have seen the ghost. At first it took me some seconds to collect my thoughts and to react rationally. It's not every day I see a ghost. I tried to handle myself with as much poise and normality as possible. I acted as if nothing had happened. But soon it was all too much for me to contain. I began to question my sanity, so I mentioned my experience to a fellow employee that evening. She informed me that there have been other workers who had encountered the same male figure. Very soon I found out that most of the employees here had encountered the ghost at one time or another. They were open to discussing their personal encounters and reactions. I found it strange that none of the witnesses had ever seen the complete figure of this ghost. He keeps his arms to his side, he never makes a move, and he sits quietly, as if awaiting someone to join him.

I've had another experience in The Chacon Room, which might be related to the man in the dark suit. On several occasions, I've meticulously arranged the table settings including the flatware here, napkins there, knife over there, etc. Afterwards, I've moved on to another task in another dining room, and returned only to discover all the flatware I had arranged was now piled haphazardly in the center of the table. This has happened to me when I've been alone in the house or when I have been at the opposite end of the house and the cook staff is in the kitchen. What all this means, I'm not sure. It's as if the ghost has felt things are out of place and he has taken it upon himself to correct matters.

My third, and most dramatic, ghost encounter happened the day before the Thanksgiving holiday in 1993. It was about three in the afternoon, and I was the only waiter on the floor at the time. There were no busboys, and aside from myself, only the bartender was in the house. As I was attending to a young couple's meal order in the dining room adjacent to The Chacon Room, I found out they were from New York and this was their first visit to New Mexico. They had just arrived, and were anxious to have an authentic New Mexican meal. After taking their order, I made my way to the kitchen. On my return to the couple, I distinctly heard a woman's voice ask me, "Can you help me, sir? I need your help." I turned to face the direction of the voice and looked around. No one was in the room. I walked to another dining room and peered inside; the room was also empty. Involuntarily, the hair on the back of my neck stood up! I instantly knew something was going on, something weird. I decided to continue my walk back to the young couple's table, picking up the pace as I walked. As the seated couple came into view down the corridor, I noticed the woman began waving her hand at me excitedly, saying, "Did you see her? Did you see her?" Then it hit me like a stone. I got the strong whiff of flowery perfume. The smell reminded me of a sweet-rose or lilac scent. As I arrived at their table the woman once again asked me, "Did you see the lady?" I responded, "No, I didn't see a thing." Then the couple described to me a middle-aged Hispanic woman with light-colored eyes and dark hair, wearing a red dress, who had appeared at the doorway leading into the dining room. She had paused, and just stared at them. Then, the woman turned away from them and faced the direction of my approach. The couple continued to say that as I walked closer towards the dining room, the woman in the red dress had disappeared into thin air. Apparently we had passed each other in the doorway. I did not see any woman, although they described her in detail. The couple remained excited about their new experience with a ghost. Being they were new arrivals to the state, I'm sure they had something unique to tell their friends and family about back in New York.

Like the man in the dark suit, other waitstaff have seen the woman in the red dress. We all believe she might very well be one of the daughters of Mr. Armijo, the original owner of the house. People who have had encounters with the ghost have pointed to the original pictures that hang in the Armijo dining room and have singled out one of the daughters as the ghost.

The management's position about these sightings remains one of skepticism. They believe that the employees make up these stories to entertain the patrons and guests. As far as I'm concerned, they can think whatever they wish. I know what I've seen and I know ghosts do dwell in this house.

My fourth experience involves the ghost of the woman in the white dress. She appears in The Armijo Room. This dining room contains the majority of the original furnishings that belonged to the house before it became a restaurant. The most noteworthy of these furnishings is a Chickering grand piano. Don Santiago brought this piano into the house in the 1880s for his daughter, Francisca. Don Santiago was the son-in-law of Salvador Armijo, for whom The Armijo Room is named after. I've been told that all of the daughters, since the time of Francisca to the present, studied on this piano. Francisca was the one known to be quite accomplished in her playing, and she practiced every day.

One evening, I was once again attending to patrons in this dining room. Nothing appeared out of the ordinary. Everyone had finished their meals and after the dinner plates had been cleared, I returned to ask if anyone wished to order dessert or coffee. I was carrying the silver tray, which had a selection of beautifully decorated desserts for their choosing. As I arrived at a guest's table, I was informed that a woman in a white dress had already taken their dessert order. I was perplexed. I had no idea who this woman in a white dress could be. I had no extra helper that evening to assist with dinner. Furthermore, all of the restaurant's female staff dressed in maroon dresses. I immediately knew that the person described to me, who had taken the order, was not part of our waitstaff. I did recall a conversation with a fellow waiter who had informed me of a similar situation involving her table. Apparently, the ghost of a woman attired in a white dress had taken the meal order of her patrons. When I asked the people at my table what this woman looked like, they described her in great detail as middle-aged, Hispanic, about 50 years old, dark haired with streaks of gray, which she wore in a Gibson bun. Her full-length white dress was decorated with small white beads about the collar and bosom. I believe the woman in the white dress is the second wife of the original owner/builder of the house,

Mr. Armijo. Apparently, the woman in the white dress also frequents another dining room named The Wine Press. I have been informed that she is typically seen by busboys in an area outside the restrooms. The busboys describe the fleeting image of a woman dressed in white, which is followed by a chilling gust of air.

I recall one Easter Sunday evening when I returned to a table of guests after dinner, and asked them if they wanted dessert. They responded by saying that a woman in a white dress, pushing a dessert cart, had already taken their order. I knew that the restaurant did not use or own a dessert cart and that, once again, the ghost had visited us. The patrons described in detail the woman's long, white-beaded dress and her distinctive hairstyle.

The piano in The Armijo Room, which I described earlier, has some more interesting history. This old piano has been heard playing on several occasions. Employees have been in the restaurant after it has closed for the night and the dining rooms are empty of patrons. Quite

strangely, and without explanation, the sound of several keys can be heard from across the house. Whenever employees went to The Armijo Room to investigate, they found the room dark and empty. I recall my very own experience when I heard the piano keys being struck, not once, but on several occasions late at night.

On one occasion, not long after I began my employment, I was alone in the lobby area. I heard soft piano music originating from The Armijo Room. I decided to investigate. All the lights were turned

"When I reached into the room to turn on the lights, the music stopped."

off in all the dining rooms, including The Armijo Room. While I made my way through the house, I reached blindly into each dining room, located the light switch, and turned on the lights. As I approached The Armijo Room, the piano music continued to play. When I reached into the room to turn on the lights, the music stopped. I turned on the lights and the room was empty. I was terrified. There is only one way into the room and one way out, and I was standing in that doorway. Whatever or whoever was in The Armijo Room playing the piano had to pass by me. Quickly, with shaky knees, I made my way back to the lobby. I didn't even bother to turn off the lights. It took all my emotional strength to keep from running out to the lobby.

A longtime employee of the restaurant, Rose Dinelli, told me the ghosts of the house were more interactive and expressive in years past. Rose related stories of ghosts knocking guests off their chairs and even turning over tables. I have not personally encountered this extreme behavior but, knowing Rose as I do, I don't doubt her word.

I am not afraid of being alone in the house any longer, because I know the spirits have accepted me as nonthreatening. I know this might sound strange, but I believe the house actually likes me. I find comfort in this belief, and feel quite at home here.

FRANCIA-GALE SEYMOUR'S STORY

I've been working at the restaurant for four months now. I'm currently a waitress, and can usually be found in the Zamora dining room. Three weeks after my first day of employment I had my contact with the ghost of the house. The house is filled with original antiques that belonged to the original owners of the house. These personal pieces of furniture and whatnot somehow have given me the feeling that something was "special" about the house. As I said, I had been working for only three weeks, when one evening the strangest thing I've ever encountered took place.

That night, I was taking dinner orders in The Zamora Room. I remember I had a large table of six patrons, who were seated directly below a large antique mirror. After taking their orders, I collected the menus and made my way to the kitchen. Suddenly, one of the patrons, who was seated at the table, got up and ran after me. She was excitedly saying to me, "Come here, come here! How do you do that? This is great!" Bewildered, I answered, "How do we do what?" She asked me to follow her back to the dining room, and pointed to the large mirror, saying, "That, look!" Everyone seated at the table was happily smiling. I looked at the mirror and saw the reflection of the patrons at the table. Then, in an instant, I knew what everyone was so excited about. Reflected in the mirror, seated between two of the patrons, was the clear figure of a woman I'd not seen before. But what made this all so weird was that, when I turned my view away from the mirror to the table, this woman was not to be seen! She was not physically present in the room, although her ghostly image was in the mirror! Everyone assumed that it was all a special-effect illusion provided by the restaurant. I was at a loss for words, so I decided to play along as if it was some kind of prank put on by the restaurant, though this was not easy for me to do.

"Reflected in the mirror, seated between two of the patrons, was the clear figure of a woman I'd not seen before."

As I said before, the ghost was seated between two people, and I could clearly see her from the waist up. The details of her dress and face were also visible, and I was able to study her mannerisms. She had poise and was obviously a woman of refinement. She had long black hair, and was wearing a white dress with long sleeves and no jewelry. The white dress itself was very sheer. Her face was slender and her eyes were a very clear hazel. I venture to say that her age was somewhere in her early 30s. She had a healthy color to her face and was not overly pale as I might imagine a ghost would look. The entire body of this woman was transparent, and aside from this oddity, she appeared to be quite normal and real. Although she appeared to be seated between two of the patrons, she did not use a chair. She just sat in space and was not bothered by not having a chair. Seated at the back of the table, she directly faced the mirror and was very curious as she examined each plate of food presented to the patrons. I saw her lean over the dinner plates closest to her and inspect each dish with a critical eye. Apparently, she liked what she saw, because she nodded her head with approval. I remember her being very animated, moving her hands and arms regularly. Overall, she was very pleasant and genuinely concerned about how the patrons were being served and cared for. At one point, our eyes met and she fixed her gaze on me. I looked away, filled with apprehension. The patrons were thrilled and amazed at what they believed was some form of "extra added entertainment." They even went so far as to accommodate the ghost by passing butter around her and not *through* her. They were really having a great time with their "entertainment." I, on the other hand, was at a loss for words. Astonished by everything, I forced a smile, and kept my anxiety to myself.

For about an hour and a half, the ghost remained seated during the meal. Routinely, I walked out of the dining room area into the kitchen where I stayed for minutes at a time. Each time I returned, she was still at the table. Sneaking glances at the mirror, I could see her carefully, as I brought food to the table and when I removed the plates. When it came time for me to offer dessert, one of the patrons said, "Look." I watched as she slowly disappeared.

Since that time, whenever I am in the Zamora dining room, I always take a quick glance at the mirror in the hope of seeing her again. The

"I watched as she slowly disappeared."

whole experience has left me with a strange, but good feeling. I guess, if I were to see her again, my reaction would be to acknowledge her by saying hello. I have no idea who this ghost might be, although waiters, after hearing about my experience, have told me about their own encounters with the "woman in white."

The only other strange thing that happened to me took place in the Armijo dining room. A couple of times I have been alone in the house, and have set up this particular room with all the place settings, including flatware. After rechecking all the dining rooms for the night, I have discovered that the flatware on the tables in The Armijo Room has been moved around and placed usually in one large pile upon the table. Definitely, this is not something the staff has done. I am convinced an invisible hand—or hands—is responsible.

THE BLACK DOG

FATHER HENRY'S STORY

Well, to begin with, I've been a Catholic priest for more than 40 years. I am now retired, and I have to say, I've lived a very active religious life. My faith has taken me to many parts of the world, including a 21-year spell in India where I worked as a missionary in the city of

Bangalore. I belong to the Franciscan Order of priests and brothers, and have been retired for more than six years now. My provincial felt that it would be best for me to relax for the remainder of my life. I must admit, I also think this is best since I am losing my eyesight more and more.

You asked about my experience with ghosts. I have to laugh, because such things are difficult for many people to believe in, even priests. But, I'll tell you about something that happened to me many years ago. It doesn't have to do with ghosts per se, but evil takes many forms. I believe what I experienced many years ago at the Veterans Hospital in Albuquerque will prove this.

It happened in August 1943. I had taken my final vows in July and was ordained to the priesthood. I was young and excited about my vocation as a pastoral minister. Among my first official duties as a priest was celebrating Mass for the patients and staff of the Veterans Hospital in Albuquerque. I offered Mass at 7 a.m., and then I made visits to the patients' rooms for personal counseling, confessions, etc. There was no

The original building that housed the Albuquerque Veterans Hospital.

set schedule of activities around the hospital and I often received late-night and early morning emergency calls to perform last rites. Very soon I had made good friends with several of the staff and patient families.

One afternoon, while at the hospital, I was summoned to a 15-year-old girl's bedside by her family. A nurse informed me that apparently the family was convinced their daughter was under the influence of an unseen evil force. The parents described in vivid detail several

incidents that had occurred within a short time leading up to their daughter's hospitalization. According to the parents, they no longer recognized their daughter. Her personality had changed to such a degree that even her facial features had altered.

About seven weeks before, their daughter, Lisa, began to complain about hearing a small, whimpering puppy in her room. The sound was loud enough to wake her from sleep. Lisa would get out of bed, turn on the light, and search behind her dresser, under her bed, and not be able to discover any evidence of a puppy or animal. Eventually, the whimpering noise became so loud that poor Lisa would sit wide awake in bed with tears in her eyes concerned about the invisible, crying puppy. The parents never heard the cries of the puppy and, as the weeks progressed, the nightly episodes of Lisa's fruitless searching escalated to the point that the poor girl was screaming for the dog. Her parents concluded that their daughter was imagining everything. Lisa became obsessed with the task of locating the puppy. She refused to leave the house, and only walked out of her bedroom to use the bathroom. Her mother brought her food to her bed. Lisa became so preoccupied that she soon lost all interest in bathing and eating. Her parents sought the advice of friends to no avail. One night, Lisa's parents discovered her sleeping under her bed. Lisa told her parents that a man's voice had told her to crawl under the bed and that the puppy would come to her. Lisa did as she was instructed by the voice. The very same day her parents sought the help of a psychologist. They found a doctor who had a private practice in Albuquerque, but who also worked part-time for the Veteran's Hospital. The psychologist evaluated Lisa and diagnosed her as schizophrenic. Lisa was placed on medication, but the medicine caused her to become drowsy most of the day. After two weeks had passed, poor Lisa worsened to the point of yelling obscenities at her parents and staring for hours at a time at her image reflected in a mirror. She also began to recite the Lord's Prayer, also known as the "Our Father," backwards! She began by yelling loudly, "Amen, evil from us deliver, etc." When she reached the first word, "Our," her father took his daughter by the shoulders and shook her, pleading for her to stop. Lisa's reaction was to open her mouth wide and scream out a wild, explosive laughter. She was beyond the point of being reasoned with, and her parents could think of no other response but to take their daughter to the Veterans Hospital to visit the psychologist on an emergency basis. It was during this visit that I got to meet Lisa and her parents personally.

As I approached the hall where the hospital staff had restrained Lisa to the metal bed with linen ties, I could not help but notice the despair on her parents' faces. Lisa's arms and legs were tied firmly to the bed, as if she was a savage beast. Since the psychologist was unavailable, and Lisa's parents were Catholics, they asked for a priest. The parents asked me to bless their daughter with holy water.

Lisa had been given a shot of morphine and was quite tranquil in her bed. I assured her parents that everything would be fine. I went to my office and located a small bottle of holy water and then returned to Lisa's bedside. Arriving in the hall where I had seen her just a few minutes before, I saw Lisa moving hysterically and yelling, "Get away from me! Don't come any closer!" Automatically I paused, but her parents bid me approach their daughter. I must admit that I had mixed emotions about the situation before me. I decided to do a simple blessing over the child. I unscrewed the bottle containing the holy water and placed a few drops on my hand. Quickly, I recited a short prayer and placed my moist palm on Lisa's forehead. Immediately, the young girl yelled out the words, "Stop! You're killing me! You're killing me, you son of a bitch!" I backed away in shock! Then I immediately said, "Child, be at peace with your Savior who will deliver you." She opened her eyes wide and stared at me with what appeared to be the eyes of the devil himself. At that point, there was no mistaking that I was in the presence of evil. I'll never forget the intense hatred directed at me in those large brown eyes. Being a young and inexperienced priest, I was shaken. Attempting to gain control of the situation before me and of my own emotions, I said aloud, "The love of our Father in Heaven and of his son, Jesus Christ, bless you." At that point Lisa went crazy! She broke away from the linen restraints, and we backed away as she sat up in bed. By this time, there must have been about five nurses looking on. No one made an attempt to intercede. Everything was happening so quickly, we did not have time to react. Suddenly, Lisa reached past her extended legs with both hands, grabbed her left foot, and began to pull the foot towards her as she repeated these words, again and again,

"Jesus loves me, Jesus loves me." I began to hear the bones in her foot dislocate and break. There was no indication on her face that she was in any pain, just a wild, unearthly smile. The sight of this poor girl doing such physical damage to her foot was horrible to watch. Both her father and I lunged towards her. We took hold of her arms and pulled with all our might. Her strength was unbelievable! Lisa's mother yelled for me to throw holy water on her daughter. I took the glass bottle out of my pocket as the nurses took my place holding her. I doused Lisa with the water. Instantly she fell back on the bed and let out a terrible scream. It was awful. No one in Lisa's hospital room was prepared for what took place next.

As Lisa collapsed on her bed, we saw a large black dog crawl out from under the bed. Its ears were bent back, its long tail was curved tightly down between its legs, and the hair on its back was standing straight up. As soon as it had cleared the bed frame, the dog bolted towards the door and down the hallway. Several courageous nurses went in pursuit of the animal, but amazingly it was never found. There was no way for it to escape. The hall doors all had handles and latches, which needed to be turned in order to open them. The black dog had simply disappeared.

Lisa was shaking and crying in her mother's arms. After spending a night in another hospital under observation, Lisa regained her composure and was well enough to be released. Her foot was in a cast, but aside from that she looked fine.

I kept in touch with Lisa and her parents for a few years following the incident, and can give my personal assurance that she turned out to be as normal as can be. Lisa was unable to recall much of her brush with evil. Both her parents are now deceased, and Lisa is employed by the Albuquerque Public Schools. Well, there you have it. I've not much more to add except please, let the readers of my story know that evil is very real and always ready to grab the opportunity to challenge God. May you all be blessed and protected.

THE HOUSE IN MARTINEZ TOWN

I met Manuela outside her home in Martinez Town. We spoke briefly. Then she invited me inside, where I began the interview. We were joined by her two grandchildren, who sat with wide, amazed eyes at the story she told. The interview was conducted in Spanish, and at times during her story I glanced away and looked intently at the ceiling in her kitchen, which was in clear view from where I sat. Why, you might ask, would an ordinary kitchen ceiling draw my attention and concern? My answer: read on, read on.

★   ★   ★

★   ★   ★

MANUELA HERNANDEZ Y
VALADEZ LOPEZ'S STORY

The story I will tell you happened to me in 1952. Everything that happened way back then is still very clear in my memory. Most people do not believe in such things, you know, ghosts. But as sure as I am standing right here in front of you, I tell you, it happened to me!

In 1952, I had arrived from Tucson, Arizona, to settle in Albuquerque with my family. We found a nice house in this part of Albuquerque that is now known as Martinez Town. It was perfect!

One afternoon, I was doing my general housework—sweeping, dusting, etc. Then I decided to begin the evening meal's tortillas, so I filled a bowl with flour, water, salt, etc., and finished the dough. I rolled out a tortilla on the kitchen table and placed it on the stove. Quite suddenly I heard a woman's voice. I could not dismiss it, because it called out my name. I stopped, and turned in the direction of one of my kitchen walls. Again, I heard my name. But this time it came from up above, towards the ceiling. Before much longer my instinct told me that this thing I was hearing was evil. I got a little scared and yelled out, "Whoever in God's name you are, show yourself to me. I am not afraid of you!" Then I heard a woman's voice say to me clearly, "I am not from here, I am from another world, and I am going to bring you lots of money." Slowly, a dark cloud began to form on the ceiling. It started as a light color gray and, as I watched it, it turned darker. Strangely enough, I was more fascinated by it than of being afraid. I spoke to this "thing," saying, "In the name of God, if you are not of this world may God help you, but please be at peace and, if you are going to bring me money, then show it to me."

Immediately, I smelled burning on the stove. My tortilla had caught fire. I took hold of it, and threw it to the floor, and then kicked it out the door. When I turned and walked back to the table, the dark image was still there on the ceiling. It spoke once more, "I will tell you where the money is." This time I walked closer and said, "What are you?" Once again it spoke to me in a muffled voice, "There are two cans that were placed in the ceiling above me." Suddenly, the cloud formed itself into a woman, with outstretched arms and a flowing white dress. I yelled out, "Who are you? God help me! What is all this?" The image began to extend her arms even more and to move her fingers spider-like. I said, "Why are you speaking to me? Why did you appear to me? Are you trying to scare me?" She said with an authoritative voice, "I'm not trying to scare you. I'm telling you to destroy the ceiling above me and there you will find the money inside the two cans. Quickly destroy the ceiling and between the boards you will discover the money. You are not to tell anyone of this, do you understand? Do it now!" she exclaimed. Then, in an instant, the woman disappeared.

"It called out my name . . . but it came from up above, towards the ceiling."

I'm not sure why I did as she demanded, but I guess it was because it was her strong voice. I located a hammer and moved a chair below the ceiling. I began to hit the ceiling with all my strength, blow after blow, until I had made a hole. With my fingers, I tore at it, and began to pull away larger and larger chunks of ceiling material. Sure enough, I eventually found a metal can and then another. I got down from the chair and placed the cans on the table. My kitchen was a mess and so was I. Plaster dust and bits of wallboard were everywhere.

I'm sure I must have looked like a ghost! I grabbed a knife, and pried the lid off each can. Inside, I found coins of silver. I lifted a handful of coins to my eyes and in a normal voice, said, "What do I do now? Come and tell me, what am I to do with all this money?" The ghostly woman did not reappear to me, but her unmistakable voice answered, "I have nothing more to say to you. The money is yours. Do with it what you wish." I used the money to repair my ceiling and to make improvements to the house.

A few days after this experience, I asked a known spiritual expert, a *curandera* who lived in the neighborhood, to visit our home. As soon as she walked through our door, she cried out in Spanish, "*Aqui en esta habitacion hay una fuerza negra.*" ("In this house exists a negative force.") She went on to say that the devil's hands had left their fingerprints on the walls and that there was, hidden in the house, wealth that belonged to a dead person, and that we should avoid the temptation to look for it. More was told to me, but I'm bad at remembering, so most of what this woman told me I have forgotten.

Another neighbor, Mr. Perrea, told me that on the exact spot where my house now sits was a previous house belonging to a woman who was a known witch. A Mr. Cristobal was married to this witch's daughter. Mr. Cristobal was given to heavy drinking, and rarely kept his wife happy and satisfied (if you know what I mean). Well, as the story goes, the mother-in-law witch hated her daughter's husband, and she decided to teach Mr. Cristobal a lesson. This witch was a mean one. She had a tattoo of the devil himself on her back and, as the neighbors say, she caught spiders that nested under her porch and actually ate them! Well, her son-in-law had six large pigs. The witch cast a spell on them and one night they all disappeared without a trace. Not long after, her daughter left Mr. Cristobal. So the witch got her way. I was also told about a woman who lived in the neighborhood whom the witch hated. As the story goes, the witch caused the woman to go blind. As time went on the evil witch died. Soon after this, the woman who had lost her sight regained it.

There are people who believe in these things and I am one of them. Yes, I am a believer, because I've seen with my own eyes what ghosts can do. I am not sure if I should have spent the money I learned about from the ghost that I saw on my ceiling, and God help me if I was wrong to do it.

When I think of these things I just pray, "Our Father in heaven, the holy presence of St. Peter and St. Paul protect me." I know there are people who do not believe, but these things exist. I tell my children to watch out for such things. It's only when you have a pure heart that evil does not approach. If you come across a person in need, if all you have is a glass of water, offer it with a pure heart. That's all. I have nothing more to say.

★　★　★

SOUTHERN NEW MEXICO

LAS CRUCES AND LA MESILLA

Las Cruces is situated in a broad valley (the Mesilla Valley), sculpted by the Rio Grande over millions of years. To the east, the city is framed by the Organ Mountains (named for their resemblance to pipe organs), the physical feature synonymous with the city's identity. To the north and northwest are the Doña Ana and Robledo Mountains; to the south, the Franklin and Juarez Mountains; and on the west side of the valley is Picacho Peak, once an active volcano. In the valley, surrounded by these mountain ranges, softened by groves of centuries-old cottonwood and pecan trees and green agricultural fields, there is a cozy, protected feeling to the landscape.

People have known about this special area for centuries. A fingerprint, carbon dated to about 28,000 years ago, was discovered in a cave about 50 miles east of Las Cruces, near Oro Grande in the Tularosa Basin. It is the earliest known evidence of human presence in all of North America.

It is accepted that the first European man in the region was Spanish explorer Alvar Nunez Cabeza de Vaca. He is believed to have passed near the site of what is Las Cruces as early as AD 1535. In 1581, two explorers, Franciscan friar Augustin Rodriguez and Captain Francisco Chamuscado, are generally recognized as being the first explorers of the Mesilla Valley. They came with eight soldiers, two friars, and 19 servants. Early Spanish accounts named the valley Estero Largo (long estuary).

European colonization of the region began in 1598 under the leadership of Don Juan de Onate. He is credited with naming the valley

Mesilla, or "little table" in English. The Robledo Mountains to the north were named after Pedro Robledo, a soldier whom Onate buried there.

At one point, the historic town of Mesilla served as the capital of a gigantic territory that included all of present-day New Mexico, Arizona, and portions of Colorado and Nevada. The Mesilla Valley was a powerful center of commerce and political activity. Las Cruces itself did not officially come onto the scene until the mid-1800s. The Santa Fe Railway bypassed Mesilla because landowners with greed in their eyes made it too expensive for the railroad to purchase a right-of-way through the town.

The name Las Cruces dates from 1830 when a group of travelers from Taos was surprised and killed by a band of Apaches, who were protecting their homelands from outsiders.

A grouping of crosses on a hill overlooking the site of the battle provided the name of the town—Las Cruces means "the crosses." La Placita de las Cruces, "The Place of the Crosses," has grown over the years to become the second largest city in New Mexico.

During its early days, the Mesilla Valley had its share of tough characters. The roster includes legendary Billy the Kid, a misdirected New Yorker who played a significant role in the nearby Lincoln County range war during the late 1800s. The outlaw's nemesis, who tracked and finally gunned down the Kid, was famous lawman Pat Garrett, another Las Cruces resident.

LA MESILLA

Mesilla is the best-known and most visited historic community in southern New Mexico. Before it was bypassed by the railroad in 1881, it was the largest town between San Antonio, Texas, and San Diego, California. It served as a major regional center for commerce and transportation in the Southwest. The traditional adobe buildings remain as a tangible reminder of the town's long and significant past.

After 1800, the vicinity of Mesilla was only a camping spot for both the Spaniards and Mexicans. It wasn't until after the treaty of Guadalupe Hidalgo in 1848, that the first permanent settlers came to Mesilla to make it their home. By 1850, Mesilla was a firmly established colony.

The constant threat of attack by the Apache put these early settlers on constant alert. Apaches periodically swept through the Mesilla area, taking livestock and foodstuffs, killing colonists, and seizing captives. Just as frequently, the villagers retaliated by sending out the Mesilla Guard, a militia comprised of a man from each household. Time after time the militia wrought revenge on any Apache in the area.

In 1851, Apache attacks in the Valley caused the United States government to establish Fort Fillmore to protect the newly conquered territory and its people. As a result of the Mexican War and the Treaty of Guadalupe Hidalgo, Mesilla was within the strip of land claimed by both the United States and Mexico to be a "no man's land." In 1854, the village of Mesilla became the supply center for the garrisoned troops, providing entertainment, food, hay, and building materials because it was closer to Fort Fillmore than either Las Cruces or Doña Ana. The Mexican inhabitants of Mesilla also provided the knowledge needed to build a fort of adobe. The colony of Mesilla flourished, and was a major stop on the crossroads of the Chihuahua Trail. Business prospered and Anglo merchants such as Reynolds, Griggs, and Bean—many of whom had come with the first armies—were among those who reaped the profits of commerce.

In 1854, the Gadsden Purchase determined Mesilla was officially part of the United States. As Mesilla was the most important community in this parcel, the treaty was consummated by the raising of the American flag on the town plaza with much ceremony on November 16, 1854. The United States government now had a reliable route to the West Coast and encouraged stage and freight services that connected California with the Eastern states. The San Antonio–San Diego Mail began offering mail and passenger service in 1857. The Butterfield Overland Mail and Stage Line, established in 1858, set up its regional headquarters in Mesilla where El Patio Restaurant is today. Some of the finest hotels and restaurants in the region, such as El Meson and the Texas-Pacific Hotel, did booming business during this period. Within 10 years of settlement, Mesilla had gone from a tiny colony struggling for survival to the largest and most important town in the area.

The Civil War interrupted this bustle of activity. On July 25, 1861, Confederate Colonel John R. Baylor and 220 Texas Mounted Troops entered Mesilla. Following a skirmish on the outskirts of Mesilla, the 500 or so Union troops garrisoned at Fort Fillmore surrendered to Baylor a few days later near San Augustine Springs, in the Organ Mountains. The Confederates set up their regional headquarters on the site of the present Fountain Theatre, and proclaimed Mesilla the territorial capital of Arizona, which then encompassed what is now southern Arizona and southern New Mexico. An uneasy quiet prevailed over the town for the year the Confederates were in control. Texans, who had repeatedly attempted to take over the territory, continued to be the traditional enemies of New Mexico.

By early July 1862, the Confederates had fled from Mesilla, and returned to Texas. A few days later, the California Column, a Union army composed of 1,400 troops and civilian employees, began arriving in the valley. This area impressed many of them, and some returned to make it their home at the end of the war.

Following the Civil War, Mesilla resumed its role as the commercial and transportation center for the region. It outfitted the profitable mining activities and ranching operations that had become important industries in the territory. An even greater number of passengers and freighters made the town a vital link in the important and sometimes dangerous transportation network of the West.

Mesilla was a lively social center in the 1880s. People came from as far as the cities of Chihuahua and Tucson to attend *bailes* (dances), bullfights, cockfights, and theatrical presentations. The town also had more than its share of violence. It was not uncommon to see differences settled in the streets with guns. Outlaws such as Dutch Hubert, Nicolas Provencio, and Billy the Kid frequented many of the bars and dances in town. It was at the jail and courthouse on the southeast corner of the plaza that Billy the Kid was tried and sentenced to hang in 1881. The town of Mesilla was as wild as the West ever was.

In 1881, the railroad bypassed Mesilla in favor of Las Cruces, four miles to the northeast. With this event, the county seat was moved to Las Cruces and Mesilla's importance was soon overshadowed by its neighbor. As a result, Mesilla has experienced little growth until recently, and so has retained much of its original 19th-century character.

The 1950s and 1960s saw new construction using more modern styles. Citizens of Mesilla, wanting to retain the character of the original town, enacted a historic zoning ordinance to promote the preservation of this lovely old town. Because of this action, the town retains the physical proportions and scale that it had a hundred years ago. Stabilization, restoration, and rehabilitation projects undertaken by individual property owners have, for the most part, retained the architectural character of the structures.

THE MESCALERO APACHES

Far and wide the Apaches roamed over the region known today as the Southwest. They ranged from Texas to central Arizona, from far south in Mexico to the peaks of Colorado. For centuries, before the first Spaniards and other explorers, the Apache people knew the secrets of the mountains and the deserts as no other people have, before or since. Proud always, and fierce when need be, the Apaches bowed to no one except their Creator. They lived off the land, and cared for no possession except their land.

The Mescaleros took their name from the "mescal cactus." The mescal, a desert plant, in earlier days supplied the Apaches with food, beverage, and fiber. Literally, it was their staff of life.

For the Apaches, the 20th century was a period of violence. Before it ended, the Mescaleros and other Apache bands had lost much of their Southwest empire. The Mescaleros were more fortunate than some other Native American groups, who were also dispossessed. They could still live in sight of their sacred mountain, White Mountain, which was, and remains, the source of their wisdom.

Today, the Mescalero Apache Indian Reservation is located in the south-central part of the State of New Mexico, in Otero County.

The Mescalero Apache Indian Reservation was established by Executive Order of President Ulysses S. Grant on May 27, 1873. Subsequent Executive Orders and Acts of Congress have altered the area and defined the boundaries, fixing the gross area at 720 square miles of 460,661 acres, all of which is in Tribal Ownership status.

The United States never specifically obligated itself by Treaty, or Act of Congress, to set apart a reservation for the Mescalero Apaches. The Executive Orders that set aside these lands used the term "Mescalero Apache Indians, and such other Indians as the department may see fit to locate thereon." The Lipan Apache survivors, who suffered severely in many of the Texas wars, were taken to Northwest Chihuahua, Mexico, in about 1930. Later, they were brought to the United States, and placed on the Mescalero Reservation in early 1903. In 1913, after the capture of the famous spiritual leader, Geronimo, approximately 200 members of the Chiricahua and Warm Springs bands of Apaches, were being held

as military prisoners. They were subsequently moved from Fort Sill, Oklahoma, to the Mescalero Reservation. The Mescaleros numbered about 400 persons when their reservation was established. Chiricahua and Lipan bands became members of the Mescalero Apache Tribe in 1936, when the tribe was formally organized under provisions of the Indian Reorganization Act.

Today, the population of the reservation exceeds 4,000 enrolled members of the tribe. Several families have relocated

Apache Mountain Spirit Dancer sculpture by Craig Dan Goseyun.

off the Reservation where they have found employment. Most of the tribal families live in or near the community of Mescalero, but there are also settlements at Three Rivers, Elk Silver, Carrizo, Whitetail, and Mudd Canyon.

The visitor who comes to the Mescalero Reservation today expecting to see braves and women in buckskins and blankets is likely to be disappointed. Changes have occurred in the Mescaleros' ways of life over the last 100 years. In that 100 years, the Mescaleros, while striving to adjust to a dominant culture so different from their own, have survived stresses that might have destroyed people with less fortitude. Their adjustment to the complex ways of the white man's society is not yet complete. The Mescaleros have come far along the new road, however, and the trail should be smoother from now on.

The teepee and the buckskin garments are gone from the Reservation now, except for the four days over the Fourth of July holidays when the tribe observes the ancient "Coming-of-Age Ceremony" for Mescalero maidens. Gone too are the raids against enemy forces. Almost gone is the mescal gathering when the cactus is ripe for harvest. The deer hunt still takes place, but with rifles rather than bows.

The Mescalero tribal member of today lives in a house, shops for food and other necessities in stores, drives to the stores in automobiles, and dresses much as the neighbors do. The Native American language is largely spoken, although almost all of the Apaches speak the English language fluently. A few also speak Spanish.

Typical Native American names have gradually vanished, except for a few of the older generation. The Mescaleros are free to enter into marriage with whom they wish, thus varied surnames are now common on the Reservation. Modern first names common to the general public are given.

Tribal members work for their living, as do their neighbors. Contrary to popular belief, the Mescalero Apaches are not receiving an annuity from the U.S. Government. Not for many years have the Mescaleros, or any other Native Americans, received food, clothing, or gratuity payments from the Federal Government.

The Mescalero Apache Tribe owns "Ski Apache," the largest, best-developed ski area in the Southwest. Also owned by the tribe is "The Inn of the Mountain Gods," a luxury resort complex. The Inn opened for business on July 10, 1975, and its reputation as one of the Southwest's finest facilities has grown rapidly. The Inn plays a major role in the economy of the tribe, and indeed all of southeastern New Mexico.

LA POSTA RESTAURANT

La Posta, a restaurant today, is a 175-year-old building that served as a way station on the Butterfield Overland Mail route. The Butterfield stages ran the "ox bow" route, from Tipton, Missouri, to San Francisco, California, a distance of over 2,800 miles! La Posta is the only Overland Mail way station still in use by tourists. It serves food in dining rooms that display items of a bygone era. It also is known to serve much food for thought where ghosts are concerned.

★ ★ ★

I interviewed Juan in one of the dining rooms of the restaurant. During certain moments of the interview, when Juan described a particularly weird experience, he would rub both his arms as if he were cold. Although the room was quite warm, I asked him twice about this and he always answered, "Oh, it's nothing." The obvious goosebumps on his arms told me otherwise. After the interview was over, I asked him if he was just a little bit scared; he answered, "Well, maybe just a little." His interview follows.

JUAN MANZO'S STORY

I started working at the restaurant five years ago. I currently work as both a cook and a waiter. My first ghost experience at the restaurant took place about two years ago. It happened one night while I was waiting tables. I was at the computer, typing a food order that I had just taken from a customer. I walked over to the computer, which is located in another area of the restaurant. At the time, this dining area was empty of patrons. I was busy typing in my customer's order when I heard a chair move behind me. I thought another employee had walked into the room, pulled a chair away from a table, and made himself comfortable. Without turning around, I said, "Hey, what's going on?" I received no answer, so I repeated, "What's up?" Still no response. I turned around and spotted an empty chair in the middle of the room. I had been in and out of this room many times that evening. Since the room was not going to be used that evening, with the help of another waiter I had stacked the chairs upside down on top of the tables earlier in the day. When I entered the dining room, I knew there was not a chair on the floor. I'm positive of this! Someone had to pass me in order to enter the room, remove the chair from on top of the table, carry it to the middle of the room, and then walk out of the dining room without being seen by me. Impossible! Without any doubt, I would have noticed the person. Something invisible had to be responsible for this. I knew it had to be the ghost everyone talks about in the restaurant! I admit, the thought of having an encounter with a ghost scared me. I heard the movement behind me; all that was missing was a solid body.

I kept this incident to myself to avoid any ribbing from my fellow employees.

The second time I experienced something strange took place only a few days later. I was in the restaurant's bar one day, taking an order from patrons. Suddenly, we heard a loud noise coming from the glassware, which was arranged in neat rows on the shelf. The patrons and I witnessed the glasses fall from the shelf and break on the floor. We were amazed to see each glass, one by one, lifted off the shelf. It was as if an unseen person was having fun breaking them.

The third time I experienced something strange, I was physically touched by the ghost! I was standing next to a window ledge, where I keep my extra order receipts. While I was standing there, I felt someone come up behind me and push my right shoulder. This force caused me to take a few steps in order

"I turned around and spotted an empty chair in the middle of the room."

to keep my balance; it was that strong. I turned, but saw no one. Suddenly, I heard the angry voice of a man say something that I did not recognize. It sounded more like a series of mumbling sounds. This really scared me! My arms were covered with goosebumps. Another waiter was just a couple of feet away from me. I asked him, "Did you hear that?" He answered, "Hear what?" Apparently, I was the only one who had heard the voice. I knew the ghost with the angry voice had pushed me. This incident was enough to convince me that the restaurant was haunted. Once again, I kept the experience to myself. I didn't have to wait longer than a month for another "experience" to take place. Only this time, there were other witnesses.

"I felt someone come up behind me and push my right shoulder."

One evening, I was waiting on a mother and her 10-year-old daughter. They were seated by our restaurant's host in a room by themselves. After taking their order, I walked out of the room and towards the kitchen. Soon, another waiter came up to me and said that my patrons needed to speak to me. When I returned to their table, the mother asked, "Is this place haunted? Do you have ghosts in here?" Her question caught me off guard, but I responded, "Why do you ask?" She pointed to her daughter and said, "Something just hit my daughter on her shoulder." The little girl was rubbing her shoulder as if to soothe the pain of being struck. I answered the mother, "Yes, I do think we have ghosts in the restaurant." Not wishing to further alarm her daughter, the mother secretly winked at me and said, "Well, I know they are friendly ghosts, just like Casper!" I played along with the mother, and did not bring up the subject again. The two were able to enjoy their meals without further disturbances from the ghost. I have since spotted them in the restaurant, so I guess that a ghost is not going to keep them away from our famous chile dishes.

There are numerous times when the caged parrots, kept in a large aviary located in the lobby, will suddenly begin screeching and flapping their wings for no apparent reason. I know that birds can be noisy, but at these times the screeching birds are so alarmed that they fly right against the sides of the large cage, as if trying to escape something that is wanting to cause them harm. Not long ago, we had a large, beautiful parrot that was so frightened it died of shock! Its wings were fully extended as it hung upside down, holding on with a death grip to the side of the cage.

There have been other employees who have heard and witnessed ghostly things: doors that open on their own, then close, then open again. Sometimes, a strong smell of sulfur accompanies these experiences. I know an employee named Raul who witnessed a flying clock! Talk to him, he'll tell you his experience.

★   ★   ★

Before beginning my interview with Raul, I found him sharing jokes with his buddies at the restaurant. He gave me the initial impression that he was in a very happy mood. However, after he had sat down and begun the interview, his personality changed to that of a serious and reflective man. His answers were very straightforward as he described the violent and strange ghostly experience he once had at the restaurant. I was aware that several times during our interview he took a cautious glance at the clock on the wall. Read Raul's story below for the answer to his strong attention to "time."

RAUL A. MARTINEZ'S STORY

I've worked at the restaurant for three years. I'm both the dishwasher and maintenance man. One morning, a month ago, a fellow worker and I were seated behind the counter, located in the lobby area. We were sipping coffee and talking about nothing in particular. Because of a large skylight above the bird aviary, the lobby area is a very bright room. We were talking, and every now and then the birds squawked and made noises as they flew from perch to perch. It was a typical morning at the restaurant. Employees were busy with their tasks in the other rooms. My friend and I were not expecting anything unusual to happen.

Suddenly, we noticed that a large, plastic wall clock above us had begun to move from side to side, as if an unseen hand was attempting to remove it from the wall. We both looked at each other and fell silent. In a matter of seconds, the clock went flying off the post where it had hung for months! It hit a wall, landed on the floor several feet away, and shattered into pieces! It was clear to us that someone or something wanted our attention. With open mouths, we looked at each other in amazement. The noisy birds became quiet as we walked over to view the broken pieces on the floor. I turned to look at the post on which

"Suddenly, the large wall clock began to move."

the clock had hung all those months before. The nail that had held the clock was still in place. It was obvious that the clock had been somehow lifted off the nail and thrown with considerable force across the room! My friend and I were both convinced that not only was the restaurant haunted, but that we were both witnesses to the ghost's angry rage.

THE DOUBLE EAGLE RESTAURANT

Now on the National Registry of Historic Buildings, the Double Eagle restaurant was constructed in the late 1840s. The building has witnessed many colorful and historical events, from the Mexican–American War of 1846, to the confirmation of the Gadsden Purchase on the Plaza in 1853, to the Secessionist Convention declaration of Mesilla as capital of the Arizona Territory in 1861.

In 1972, the restaurant was acquired by Robert O. Anderson, who showed wisdom in preserving it as a private residence. In 1984, major restoration was completed by the present owner, C. W. "Buddy" Ritter, a fifth-generation Mesilla descendant. Antiques, many of which have their equal only in the finest museums, were painstakingly collected by the well-known designer John Meigs.

The name "Double Eagle" was taken from a United States gold coin minted in the 1850s. The $10 gold piece was known as the Eagle and the $20 gold piece was known as the Double Eagle.

THE LEGEND OF THE CARLOTA SALON

In the 1850s the restaurant was the home of an affluent Mexican family named Maese. The Carlota Salon was named after Marie Charlotte, daughter of the King of Belgium. Marie was born in 1840 and died in 1927. She was the wife of Maximillian, Archduke of Austria, and the Empress of Mexico from 1864 to 1867. An oil portrait of her, holding her small white Maltese dog, dominates the room. The two oval portraits of Señor and Señora Maese, the owners of their home, are of the type frequently commissioned by families of that era. The heavy gilded brass and cut crystal lamp once lighted the boudoir of famed red-light madam, "Silver City Millie."

The fabric is worn in the shape of a human body.

One day, the family hired a maid named Ines. The family had a teenage son named Armando, who fell in love with the maid, much to the distress of his mother. Love persisted, however, and Carlota, the mother, came home one afternoon to find the two lovers romantically entwined in her bedroom. Enraged at what she saw, the mother grabbed a pair of scissors and went towards Ines in order to stab her to death. In an attempt to protect his lover, Armando leaped in front of Ines, and Carlota stabbed her son in the scuffle. Armando soon died from his wound. Ines escaped the bloody scene and was not seen in the town for more than a year. Carlota became a bitter and antagonistic woman.

One evening, Ines returned to Mesilla in disguise, but was recognized in the plaza by a drunken cowboy. A confrontation occurred between the two, and Ines was fatally shot. Local citizens, unaware of her identity, brought her wounded body into Carlota's home and placed it inside Carlota's very own bedroom. It was there on Carlota's bed that Ines died.

Employees and guests alike say that the ghosts of the young lovers inhabit the Carlota Salon to this day. The ghosts apparently make their presence known in many ways. Even though modern security motion detectors are armed at night, broken glasses and overturned chairs are found by morning. There are two upholstered Victorian armchairs in the room that are rarely used. However, the cut velvet fabric is worn in the shape of human bodies, one larger than the other, but both small by today's standards.

There is a framed *Las Cruces Sun News* article of the "Young Lover Ghosts," and a photograph believed to depict the presence of the ghost lovers, displayed in the salon.

★   ★   ★

When I interviewed Yvonne, it was by chance that I was able to catch her before her retirement to Hawaii just a few days later. As of this date, she must be basking under the warm island sun. Luckily for me, Yvonne was full of information and personal stories about the restaurant, which she had no problem sharing. As you read this, it is easy to imagine the bewilderment and fear she and her staff must have experienced. Although the ghosts of the restaurant were, and continue to be, a force to be reckoned with, Yvonne, ever the professional, handled it all with professionalism and flair. Aloha Yvonne!

YVONNE THOMASON'S STORY

I am the general manager of the restaurant, and have been employed here for 10 years. My first ghostly experience at the restaurant took place in February of 1986. At that time, I was the assistant manager. One of my duties was to close the restaurant each evening at 10 p.m. My responsibilities included closing doors, and turning off the heaters and lights in each room. After securing the building, I would

spend a few more hours at my desk, doing the day's paperwork. I was told about strange sounds and so-called ghostly things in the restaurant, but I really did not pay them any mind. I honestly did not believe in spirits or ghosts. But one Tuesday night my mind was changed for good!

I finished my work for the evening and walked into the kitchen. I made my way toward the back door to where my car was parked. Upon entering the kitchen, I noticed a knife on the floor. The chefs are very careful about their tools, so to have a large butcher knife in the middle of the kitchen floor was very unusual. As I bent down to pick up the knife, I felt someone looking at me. Still bent over, I turned my head and saw a small woman about 4'6" standing by the door that led into the Carlota Salon. Holding on to the knife, I straightened up quickly and faced her. She wore her hair up high on her head, held together with long, old-fashioned hairpins. She had her back to me. I noticed her long black skirt and long-sleeved blouse. I was able to see directly through the blouse and through the woman; she was transparent! She stood not more than eight feet away from me. Without saying a word, she left the kitchen and walked into the dining room named the Carlota Salon. The odd thing about her walking was that she glided across the floor, as if on roller skates. As I looked closer, I saw she had no noticeable feet or legs. I was scared to death! As this small woman quickly moved away from me, she gradually faded as she entered the Carlota Salon. My mind was changed forever about the existence of ghosts! I tried to gather my composure as I raced out the back door. After fumbling for the keys, I managed to lock the door, get in my car, and quickly race home.

About two years ago, I was again alone in the restaurant, getting ready to make my final security rounds before leaving for the night. It was midnight and I was upstairs in the office. I was writing at the desk, when suddenly I felt the strong presence of something evil in the room with me. Immediately I grabbed the money pouch, threw it into the opened safe, and locked it! Then I grabbed my purse and rushed downstairs. As I was racing through the kitchen, towards the back door, I suddenly heard a voice say, "Don't go!" The voice was definitely masculine, so deep and low that it made the hairs on the back of my neck stand straight up! I looked around and saw no one. This scared the living Jesus out of me! Once again, I dashed out the back door, got in my car, and drove home. To this day I haven't a clue as to who the voice belonged to.

The Carlota Salon.

There were other times when very strange occurrences would take place in the middle of the night. The restaurant is equipped with security motion detectors in each room. While asleep in my home, I would wake up in the middle of the night to answer a phone call from the security company. They would tell me that the computer had detected movement in the restaurant, and the local police had been called to respond. I was expected to meet the police by the back door in order to let them in the building. Over the years, I have been called many times about the alarm going off. The odd thing was that each time I opened the door to let the police inside, they would find nothing. No burglar, no stolen items, nothing.

The only unusual signs of disturbance would be knives on the kitchen floor. These knives had been neatly placed in their proper drawers the day before. I would ask the chefs the next day about this, and they would plead innocent. Chefs, as a rule, are very particular about their knives. They had no explanation as to why their personal tools would be treated in such a careless manner.

The most unusual thing that I ever came across during one of these false alarms happened in the Carlota Salon. Accompanied by a police officer, I walked into the Carlota Salon and found, in the middle of one table, several candles lit! I thought to myself, what is this? There was no evidence that someone had been in the room. There were other evenings when I had been alone in the restaurant and had found the same candles burning brightly. It was impossible for anyone to have entered without my knowledge.

Several employees have also heard the masculine, ghostly voice that I spoke of earlier. This voice has been known to disguise itself by mimicking the voice of employees. For example, one evening, a waiter named David suddenly heard me call out, "David, David, come here!" I was obviously not in the room with him. On another occasion, employees have told me that on my days off they have heard my voice calling out to them. Another example involved an employee walking through a room, who heard her name called out by another manager. The voice was once again disguised as someone else's. Employees have also seen darting shadows in all the rooms. These strange experiences are definitely not uncommon.

At other times, the voices will begin to call our names. This has happened numerous times to almost all of our employees. Night or day, one of us will be alone, busy cleaning a table, and "someone" will come up from behind, touch a shoulder, and call out our name. We'll turn around, but no one will be there. We employees have all witnessed this.

We have also had people who claim to have parapsychological sensitivities come to the restaurant and feel for vibrations or whatever. They have told us that in certain locations of the restaurant they can "feel" a lot of pain and anguish. I think this is because the house was used as a hospital during the Civil War. At that time, controlling infection was a big problem. I think that a lot of limbs must have been amputated and this must have caused great physical and emotional grief.

I know a couple that swears they regularly see a woman appear to them in the Maximillian Room. She is dressed in a yellow dress. Slowly she appears, only to slowly disappear in the large mirror.

There was an elderly woman who came to the restaurant one day, about the time that I first started working there. She told me she was related to the Maese family and, as a little girl, she used to come to the house and play with the children. She said she remembered Carlota Maese as being a very mean woman. Carlota's personality frequently changed from pleasant to enraged.

There is no doubt in my mind that the restaurant is haunted—none whatsoever!

* * *

Interviewing Leslie was a first for me, because it was an interview that was totally conducted in her truck! Being pressed for time, Leslie was gracious enough to tell me of her experiences at the Double Eagle. I've come across stories of many strange ghostly happenings, but Leslie's is certainly one of the more unusual. I know that the next time I'm in La Mesilla, I'll think twice about "pulling up a chair" and "ordering coffee." Leslie's story follows.

LESLIE K. SNOW'S STORY

I've been working at the restaurant as a waitress for two years. My first ghost experience took place one evening around 8:30, just a year ago.

I was serving a table of three women in the Carlota Salon. After taking their order for coffee, I returned from the kitchen with a serving tray, upon which were cups of hot coffee on saucers. As I placed the cups on the table before the patrons, we noticed the cups start to move slowly by themselves. They rapidly moved around the place mats, flatware, and dishes, as if an unseen hand was pushing them along. Our mouths fell open with astonishment. The women moved away from the table. It happened really fast. Moving from the spot where I had set down the cups, to the place they eventually ended up, at the opposite end of the table, had taken them no more than seven seconds. I gave a nervous half-smile to the patrons, perplexed by the incident. Cautiously, I looked beneath the table and checked the table legs for any unevenness that may have caused the cups and saucers to move. I found nothing out of the ordinary. We laughed nervously and changed the subject.

The second ghost experience occurred about mid-morning, just a few days after the coffee-cup experience. Several other waitstaff and I were in the Maximillian Room, preparing for a banquet. My task was to push the chairs up to the tables, making sure the tablecloth was draping nicely. After completing two tables, I moved on to the next one. When I glanced over to the table I had just completed, I noticed that one chair was pulled away from the table. I thought this was unusual, because I had personally arranged it. Returning to that particular table, I pushed the chair under once again. As I turned to walk away, the chair suddenly spun around on its own and moved away from the table! I saw it with my own eyes and still could not believe it. It appeared as if someone had taken hold of the chair, and then pulled it out and away from

The Maximillian Room.

the table. Once again, I looked under the table, thinking maybe a fellow employee was hiding underneath to scare me. I saw no one. I decided to leave the chair right where it stood. This was reason enough for me to know that the ghost wanted to have its way with the chair, and believe me, I did not want to argue!

There have been times when other employees and I have been busy folding napkins in one of the dining rooms, and suddenly, we have heard doors in other areas of the restaurant loudly open and close. We knew we were alone in the building and agreed among ourselves, "It's the ghost!" One or two of the guys would run to where the noise had originated, only to discover nothing. The whole restaurant was searched, and nothing was disturbed. Another common occurrence has been the voices that we hear call out our individual names. It is so weird when that happens. We have a new employee who came up to me recently. She said, "Leslie, why do you follow me around, calling out my name?" I answered, "Brandy, what are you talking about? I haven't been following you!" She told me that she hears my voice, calling out, "Brandy, Brandy!" Another employee named Mark once came running out of the Carlota Salon. I noticed he was visibly shaken. I asked him, "Mark, what's wrong?" He said, "Someone called out my name, and when I looked around, there was no one there." Then, Mark continued, "As I stood there wondering who was calling me, I heard someone say, "Pssst! Pssst!" I told Mark he had better get used to such things. The restaurant has been known for having many ghosts, and all the employees have experienced them at one time or another.

★   ★   ★

I interviewed Cali at his home, under the watchful eyes of his very protective Doberman. "Cali," as his close friends call him, happens to be a very good friend of my family in La Mesa. This interview is the first, and hopefully not the last, I will openly conduct with a law-enforcement officer. I have had the opportunity on a few occasions to discuss the topic of ghosts with officers in other states, and do they have stories to be told! Read now the rare interview I had recently with one of New Mexico's finest, Carlos Tellez!

CARLOS "CALI" G. TELLEZ'S STORY

I've lived in Las Cruces all my life. I was born and raised in La Mesa, but make my home in Las Cruces. I am retired from the Doña Ana County

Sheriff's Department and currently work for the American Red Cross as Director of Disaster Services in Las Cruces. My experience with strange happenings at the Double Eagle restaurant took place when I was a patrol sergeant for the Sheriff's Department.

I remember one summer when I received three separate calls to investigate the restaurant. The calls indicated that the burglar alarms in the restaurant had been activated. The calls each came in between 2 a.m. and 4 a.m. The entire restaurant is equipped with motion-sensitive detectors, and when they were activated, the police would "roll-on" to the restaurant. The Marshall was first on the scene, and we, the sheriffs, were their backup.

When my partners all arrived at the restaurant, we cautiously entered the back door to begin our search. There was no indication of forced entry, a burglary, or anything having been disturbed. A restaurant manager always accompanied us during our search. We combed the entire building from top to bottom. No evidence of an intruder was ever found. The only unexplained evidence I recall finding occurred in the kitchen. As we turned on the lights and walked in, practically all the kitchen knives were lying, as if thrown about, on the kitchen floor. Large butcher knives and cooking utensils were everywhere. The manager informed us that the chefs religiously took great care to store their tools. They would never intentionally leave knives thrown about the kitchen floor. We took note that the knives were clean, and had not been used to cut anything.

The alarm company was brought in on one occasion to readjust the system to make it less sensitive, hoping to minimize the frequency of the alarms. This seemed to help, but not for very long. We still kept responding to the alarm calls at the restaurant even after this was done. Again, we searched high and low and discovered nothing.

As children, we knew the local stories of ghosts haunting the restaurant. One of these stories is of a ghost who makes itself known to people when things do not please it. I don't recall the exact details of the story, but I always felt that "something" was there in the restaurant, a "presence" perhaps. As officers, we discussed our own ideas regarding the ghosts at the restaurant. Although we each have our own personal beliefs, what some people might call a ghost we decided to call a "presence." Although I can't speak for all the officers, I know that the ones who have responded to the alarm calls at the restaurant have felt something unusual.

THE SALINAS MISSION AND PUEBLOS
OF THE SALINAS VALLEY

In the stones of the Salinas Valley pueblo ruins, one can hear the faint echoes of the communities that lived here three centuries ago. Before they left the area in the 1670s, Pueblo Native Americans forged a stable agricultural society, whose members lived in apartment-like complexes and participated through rule and ritual in the cycles of nature. Two ancient Southwestern cultural traditions—the Anasazi and Mogollon—overlapped in the Salinas Valley to produce the later societies of Abo, Gran Quivira, and Quarai. These traditions have roots that go as far back as 7,000 years ago, and were preceded by nomadic Native Americans who arrived perhaps as many as 20,000 years ago.

As the Southwestern cultures evolved, better agricultural techniques from Mexico and the migration of Tompiro- and Tiwa-speaking peoples from the Rio Grande spurred the growth of settlements in the Salinas Valley. By the 10th century, substantial Mogollon villages flourished here. The dwellers practiced minimal agriculture supplemented by hunting and gathering, made a simple red or brown pottery, and lived in pit houses and, later, above-ground *jacales* of adobe-plastered poles. By the late 1100s, the Anasazi tradition from the Colorado Plateau, introduced through the Cibola (Zuni) district and Rio Grande pueblos, had begun to assimilate the Mogollon. The contiguous stone-and-adobe homes of the Anasazis represented the earliest stage of the Puebloan society later encountered by the Spanish.

Over the next few hundred years the Salinas Valley became a major trade center and one of the most populous parts of the Pueblo world, with perhaps 10,000 or more inhabitants in the 17th century. Located astride major trade routes, the villagers were both producers and middlemen between the Rio Grande villages and the Plains nations to the east. They traded maize, piñon nuts, beans, squash, salt, and cotton goods for dried buffalo meat, hides, flints, and shells.

By 1300, the Anasazi culture was dominant, although the Salinas society always lagged behind the Anasazi heartland in the north in cultural developments. Brush-and-mud *jacales* had evolved into large stone complexes, some with hundreds of rooms, surrounding kiva-studded plazas.

Besides the domestic plants already mentioned, the inhabitants ate wild plants, raised turkeys, and hunted rabbit, deer, antelope, and bison. People wore breech cloths, bison robes, antelope and deer hides, and decorative blankets of cotton and yucca fiber. Turquoise and shell jewelry, obtained from trading, were used in rituals. The Spaniards were impressed with the Pueblos' weaving, basketmaking, and fine black-on-white pottery, a technique the Salinas people borrowed from the Rio Grande pueblos.

The Salinas pueblo dwellers were an adaptable people who drew what was useful for them from more advanced groups. But strong influences from the Zuni district, the Spanish explorers, and deteriorating relations with the Apaches to the east radically altered pueblo life.

In the end, cultural conflict and natural disaster devastated the Salinas pueblos. The Apaches, formerly trading partners, began raiding the pueblos both for food and for revenge for the Spanish slave raids in which the Pueblos had participated. The Pueblos might have survived the raids, but along with the Apaches and Spaniards they were hit during the 1660s and '70s with drought and widespread famine that killed 450 people at Gran Quivira alone. Recurring epidemics further decimated the population, which had little resistance to introduced diseases. The ability of the Puebloans to withstand these disasters may have been weakened by the direct disruption of their culture under harsh Spanish rule. In any event, the Salinas pueblos and missions were abandoned during the 1670s, and the surviving Native Americans went to live with cultural relatives in other pueblos.

In 1680, the Pueblos north of Salinas, in an uncharacteristic show of unity, revolted and expelled the Spaniards from their lands in New Mexico. In the general exodus of Native Americans and Spaniards, the Piro and Tompiro survivors of the Salinas pueblos moved south with the Spaniards to the El Paso area. They were absorbed by Native American communities there, making them the only group among the

Pueblo Indians during this historic period to lose their language and their homeland.

★　★　★

I interviewed Maria in her home, where she and her husband now live, in the city of Albuquerque. From time to time during the interview, she asked me to stop the tape recorder in order to gather her emotional strength. I could clearly see that the interview was not going to be easy for her. Maria still felt the fear of what she experienced more than 10 years before. The interview went slowly, but cautiously. The following is that interview.

MARIA DE LA CRUZ'S STORY

My first experience at the Salinas Mission ruins took place about 10 years ago, when I was 17 years old. My mother was going to spend the weekend with her sister and brother-in-law, who lived in the town of Mountainair. She asked me to accompany her on the trip. She knew I would enjoy the visit because I would also have the opportunity to visit with their children, my cousins. At the time, we lived just about 20 miles north of Mountainair, in the very small town of Estancia.

We arrived at my cousins' house at 11 a.m. My mother spent the time in conversation with her sister, and I with my cousin Delfina and Delfina's boyfriend.

After dinner, Delfina decided that we should go for a ride in her boyfriend's car. I told my mother about the plan, and she said, "Just be back before it gets real dark." Off we went.

We drove west, following the setting sun, listening to music on our cassette tapes. We were having fun just cruising along. Eventually, we came to a gate and a sign that read, "Salinas Pueblo Mission National Monument." Neither of us had ever visited the monument, but we knew a little about it from our parents. We decided to stop and look around. There was a small sign that hung on a chain, across the dirt road leading to the entrance, that read "Closed." We decided to take a chance and left the car parked by the side of the road. We then walked over to the site.

I asked Delfina and her boyfriend to take the lead. As she held on to her boyfriend's hand, I carefully followed behind. It was a warm August night, and I knew from experience that on such nights rattlesnakes like to come out of their burrows and feed. I didn't want to take any chances on getting bitten. We kept our ears open for the sound of a rattling noise. The moon was out and shining brightly, so this gave us confidence as we walked along the moonlit road.

As we got within sight of the tall ruins of the church, we noticed a soft, yellow glow coming from within the structure. We thought there must be a private party for the park rangers or a celebration of some

kind going on. As we got closer, we heard the low singing or chanting of church music. It wasn't very loud, but we could clearly hear it as we approached. Not wanting to be noticed, we carefully approached the front entrance of the church and looked inside. We could not believe our eyes!

There was a misty, yellow cloud that looked like fog. This fog floated about a foot or two above the ground. Above this cloud were several twinkling lights, similar to the flames of flickering candles. It was such a beautiful thing to witness that it didn't frighten us at all. We were amazed as we gazed at the wonderful sight. The chanting music slowly intensified; however, we were unable to make out the words. Then, from within the fog, we saw the ghostly images of people slowly emerge! Their complete forms were difficult to make out, but I could see their shoulders and small heads. I said, "Look, you guys! People are appearing in the cloud!" Delfina's boyfriend bent and reached down, picking up a small stone. Then he threw it. It landed within the middle of the cloud, and immediately the ghostly images along with the cloud and bright light disappeared!

"We heard a noise in the trees . . ."

That was all it took to send us running back to the car. Rattlesnakes or not, I didn't care where I stepped. I was determined to be the first one to reach the car and get inside! Once we were in the car, we drove without stopping until we had reached my cousins' house.

We told our parents what we had seen, and they reprimanded us for being so foolish. "You should never have done what you did. Don't you know those places are sacred? There are lots of spirits that hang around the mission, and you should give thanks to God that they did not take you with them!"

Delfina's father told us about the time that he and his friend saw some ghosts at the mission when they were children. "I remember the time that my friend Luis and I were playing in an area of the mission that had some small hills. We didn't know it at the time, but those small mounds were what was left of the original pueblo houses. We heard a noise in the trees, and then a large flock of birds flew away. Suddenly, everything seemed still; even the wind stopped. Then we saw three small shadows of people running in and out of the trees. They would look at us from behind the trees, and then they would run and hide behind other nearby trees. I got the feeling that they were playing a game with us. We never got close to them because we were somewhat afraid. I was nine, and Luis was ten years old at the time, and as far as I'm able to remember, the ghostly shadows weren't any taller than us."

Today, as an adult, I'll make sure that my baby is aware of ghosts, and that they should be respected. I never make fun of spirits. I know from experience that there are things we can't explain, so we should just leave them alone.

SOCORRO

The city of Socorro is located in central New Mexico. The city's name means "help," or "aid," in Spanish. In 1598, members of the Juan de Oñate expedition gave the name to the existing Pilabo Pueblo. There, they received assistance from the Piro people who had been the area's first inhabitants. The first mission in the town, Nuestra Senora de Pilabo del Socorro, was built between the late 1500s and early 1600s. The name was changed to its current title, Mission de San Miguel, in 1880.

The settlement of Socorro remained small until the arrival of the Santa Fe Railroad in 1880. Mining was in full swing with newcomers arriving daily. After the mining boom had come to a close, the area's economic base became predominantly agricultural.

Just a few miles south of Socorro is Bosque del Apache (Woods of the Apache). In 1939, the "Bosque" became the first National Wildlife Refuge in the United States. It was established as a "refuge and breeding grounds for waterfowl and other wildlife," particularly the Sandhill Crane, whose numbers were dwindling.

There is much history to personally experience in the town of Socorro. The people of the area are proud of their community and enjoy every opportunity to share in good conversation with visitors.

★   ★   ★

*I interviewed Mr. Jesus Hernandez in his daughter's home in the nearby town of
San Antonio, located 10 miles south of Socorro. Mr. Hernandez recalled the day
a stranger came into town with his large cage of monkeys. The year was 1920,
and Jesus was about 11 years old.*

JESUS HERNANDEZ'S STORY

My friends and I were playing in a grassy field located next to the train
station in Socorro. We caught a grasshopper, and walked to the station
searching for discarded thread or string that might have been dropped
on the ground. We amused ourselves by tying one end of a piece of
thread to the tail of the grasshopper and turning it loose, while holding
on to the other end of the thread. The grasshopper would fly around,
and we would have a lot of fun with our version of a "motorized" toy.

With my grasshopper in one hand, we were busy searching for some
string when suddenly we heard a distant whistle, which meant the train
would soon be stopping at the station. Sure enough, the train came into
view, and soon the passengers arrived at the station and their suitcases
were unloaded.

As children, we were always excited to see the new faces of people
coming through the station. It sure was something to see! The fashionable
clothes and jewelry of these strangers left us with our mouths wide
open. Children would sometimes accompany their parents as they
traveled throughout the Southwest. Unknowingly, that day proved to
be an exceptional and unforgettable one for me.

A young Anglo man got off the train and, in a rush, ran back to the
last boxcar. We noticed him instructing a porter by motioning with his
arms. Soon after, a large metal cage was loaded onto a waiting truck,
parked on the loading dock.

From a distance, we saw movement within the cage and quickly ran
to see what it contained. We were so surprised to see our first real live
monkeys! "*Changos, changos!* (Monkeys, monkeys!)," my friend yelled. I
dropped my now limp grasshopper as we scrambled to get a closer look.
Our eyes and mouths were as big as plates! I can't tell you how excited
I felt! I never saw anything like these animals. I was both interested, and
at the same time, afraid. We asked the man in Spanish, "*Como se llaman?*"

("What are their names?") But, unable to speak Spanish, the man couldn't understand us.

As we got closer, the man motioned for us to keep our distance. He reached into a paper bag and brought out a treat of some kind. As he handed it to one of the monkeys, it reached out its long hairy arm, took the food, and popped it into its mouth. As its jaws munched on the treat, it quickly reached out for more. We were so disappointed when the man draped a tarp over the cage and drove away with the monkeys, leaving us kids with many unanswered questions.

The following day, word about the monkey man spread throughout town. A few days later, we found out that the man was

Mr. Cooper with his monkeys, "Jimmy" and "Coco."

living on the west side of the city in a two-story house. My friends and I decided to walk over to the west side of town and perhaps get another look at the monkeys.

We saw the Anglo man sitting on the porch stairs of the house, talking with Señor Baca, an older Hispanic man whom we all knew. We asked Señor Baca if we could see the monkeys. Señor Baca knew a little English, and therefore communicated our request to the man. Señor Baca told us the man's name was Mr. Cooper, and that he was on his way to California to deliver the monkeys to another man in Los Angeles. These were special monkeys, trained to perform in a circus. During one performance, the circus caught fire, and these monkeys, along with a few other animals that had survived the fire, were now being sold to another circus.

The monkeys' names were "Jimmy" and "Coco." We were not allowed to see the monkeys, because they were nervous from their experience with the fire and the long train ride. But Mr. Cooper assured us that in three days we might be able to even feed them if we wished. We were so excited we couldn't wait! Our dream to see and feed the monkeys, sadly, would never come true.

Two days later, when Mr. Cooper was cleaning their cage, the monkeys escaped! They ran into the neighbors' yards and caused lots of havoc. They shrieked, howled, jumped frantically, and refused to come down off a neighbor's roof. The people were afraid of these strange animals. There was nothing Mr. Cooper could do to make the monkeys listen to him. One of the monkeys, Coco, started breaking off roof shingles and throwing them at the people below. The owner of the house screamed at Mr. Cooper, "You get those animals off my roof, or I'll take care of them myself!" The owner began to throw rocks at the monkey, and in return, the monkey began to throw more roof shingles. Mr. Cooper's hands were tied; he pleaded with the owner, but it did no good. Coco continued to tear at the roof shingles. The owner ran inside his house and then quickly returned with a rifle. We watched nervously as the owner took aim and fired. In horror, we watched as the bullet struck Coco, knocking him off the roof. His body rolled down off the roof and hit the solid ground below. The sound of the shooting gun frightened the other monkey, Jimmy, down off the roof and into his opened cage. Mr. Cooper was speechless as he ran to Coco's lifeless body. He found it difficult to forgive the death of his monkey and the loss of revenue. Señor Baca later told me that, during the night, Mr. Cooper had become drunk in a bar, 30 miles west in the town of Magdalena. While drunk, he had gotten into an argument and fought with a friend of the homeowner who had shot Coco. Two days later, Mr. Cooper and his remaining monkey, Jimmy, left on the train for California. He was so distraught that he forgot a box, which contained a few books and a broken glass photo of him and his monkeys. Señor Baca knew I was very interested in the monkeys, so he let me have the photo. I cried and cried for days. The memory of the shooting of that monkey still haunts me to this day.

One year after this whole sad affair, neighbors began to talk about hearing strange noises. They heard unfamiliar wild animal screams, and "something" running on their roofs. Their dogs were also alarmed, because they frantically barked and stared at something up on the roofs. Going outside to investigate, people would sometimes catch a shadowy glimpse of a small creature running upright on two legs!

I personally have not heard or seen this, but who is to say that monkeys don't also have souls like we humans do? After all, if what scientists say is true, that monkeys are very close to humans, why wouldn't they have spirits as well?

KINGSTON

A silver-mining boom-town in its heyday, Kingston was called the "Gem of the Black Range." In the 1880s, Kingston boasted the largest population in the New Mexico territory, home to 7,000 miners, merchants, and madams. California oil-magnate Edward Doheny had humble beginnings as a miner in Kingston, as did his partner Albert Bacon Fall, who was later implicated in the Teapot Dome Scandal.

A few historic buildings remain, notably the Assay Office, the Victorio Hotel, and the Percha Bank—now a private museum. The old village bell in front of the Volunteer Fire Department was cast in St. Louis and was originally used to announce Native American raids until the final Apache surrender in 1886. Before silver was discovered here in 1882, Kingston had been the haunt of the great Apache leaders, Mangas Coloradas, Cochise, Victorio, and Geronimo—the last nation of Native Americans to surrender their land to the United States government.

THE BLACK RANGE LODGE

You step into the Old West when you enter the Lodge's spacious lobby. Its massive stone walls and log-beamed ceilings were built from the tumbledown ruins of Pretty Sam's Casino and the Monarch Saloon, and were completed in 1940. The original construction dates back to the 1880s when it housed miners and cavalry.

Today, furnished for comfort, the Lodge invites you to relive Kingston's wild past, but with modern conveniences. Seven guest bedrooms open onto a large common room, where you can curl up with a book or watch a movie on the VCR.

★   ★   ★

I interviewed Catherine in the lobby of the Black Range Lodge. Surrounded by large stone walls, massive log beams, and a cat or two, Catherine was very knowledgeable about the history of Kingston and the Lodge. The Lodge is simply decorated and Catherine seemed very comfortable living in such an isolated, but serene, setting. On the table where we sat was a glass jar, which Catherine had filled with long jet-black feathers. Being curious, I asked her what kind of bird did these feathers come from. She answered, "Oh, those I gathered from around the property. They're vulture feathers! Those birds just hang around the village." Thus began my interview with Catherine.

CATHERINE E. WANEK'S STORY

I bought the Black Range Lodge in 1984 with my first husband, and opened it as a bed-and-breakfast in 1988. We currently have seven guest rooms and several large common rooms.

Kingston's town history is very interesting. In the 1880s it was the biggest town in the territory, and was considered to be a "boomtown." At the time, there were between 7,000

and 8,000 people living in Kingston. This number did not reflect all the women, children, and Chinese men who were not considered worth counting at the time. There were 27 saloons, an opera house, three newspapers, and a number of hotels. From 1882–1893 Kingston was the most frolicking Wild West town that you could imagine! A person would have to commit a serious crime in order to be arrested and put in jail. The primary business of the time was the mining of silver ore. In 1893, when the bottom fell out of this mining industry, Kingston and the other silver mining towns quickly lost their populations. Those people sought work elsewhere, and Kingston became a ghost town. It was a boom-and-bust situation, which in total happened over only 10 years!

When we first moved into the lodge, we had some out-of-town friends help us with our move. They stayed for several nights in the lodge with us. Each of us experienced strange events. We awoke several times during the night to sounds of cue balls being hit on the pool table. The sounds were so loud we got out of bed and walked to where the pool table was located on the second floor. Nothing in the poolroom, or on the pool table, had been disturbed. We believed what awakened us was a ghostly game of pool. On other nights, we awoke to the sound of glass breaking. Not wanting to encourage this ghost further, we just accepted the ghost as a part of the house.

I did, however, decide to investigate this ghost. I contacted the previous owner of the house, Mrs. Goforth, who at the time still lived in the neighborhood. She told me the ghost was the lodge caretaker, "Sam." Sam was not his real name. Mrs. Goforth couldn't remember Sam's real name. Sam was a one-armed bachelor, who had wandered into Kingston and was known to "hit the bottle" and chain-smoke. After living in Kingston for about 20 years, Sam died in this lodge, in his personal room, located on the third floor.

After Sam's death, Mrs. Goforth would frequently find in this room the depression of a body on the bed's comforter, as though an invisible person had been lying on the bed. She lived alone in the house, so automatically this ruled out any other person's presence. Other indications of Sam's presence in the lodge included a newly cleaned ashtray, which Mrs. Goforth had cleaned herself, full of cigarette butts. In Sam's room, she also found the windows had been opened, even

during the winter! She searched the house for an unlocked door or window and discovered all the bolts and locks in place. Periodically, she found the windows in Sam's room open, after she herself had closed them. After one cold winter's day experience, when she had discovered the third-floor window had been opened once again, she had had enough. She spoke directly to the ghost, "Now, Sam, you stop this, I can't be heating this

"Sam died . . . in his personal room, located on the third floor."

whole house just to have you open windows!" Soon after, the strange goings-on ceased. Since that time, Mrs. Goforth has never again had any ghostly encounter. She understood our recent experiences with Sam, but reassured us that he was a kind fellow who apparently still wished to keep an eye out for the property.

Not long before we opened the lodge as a business in 1986, another friend came to visit from Los Angeles. One morning, she described in detail to my husband and me an experience she had had the night before in her room. For some unknown reason, she was awakened from a sound sleep in the middle of the night. She did not hear a noise or smell anything that would have caused her to wake up. She just opened her eyes and gazed at the ceiling unafraid. A feeling made her get up and go into the large common room. As she entered, she saw a male figure at the opposite end of the room. She thought the figure was my husband, Mike. However, she knew it wasn't Mike when the figure looked in her direction then turned to go down the stairs. She followed and noticed when the figure approached a bench, on the landing, his legs simply went through the bench! Startled, but not deterred, she cautiously followed the figure as he made his way "through" the bench and down the stairs. This time she saw he had no body from the waist down; he was floating down the stairs! She was able to make out a lot of the ghost's features, except for one. She noticed that the ghost was missing a left arm!

I believe that Sam is lonely and needs to occupy himself with some job or task. What better job than to care for this lodge as he did in life? He doesn't bother us, and it's a nice feeling to know that he's here. We feel fortunate to have him.

SILVER CITY

Millions of years ago, fingers of molten rock deposited the copper, silver, and gold that would make this one of the Southwest's richest mineralized areas. Early Native Americans mined turquoise, and by 1804 the Spanish were digging for copper east of what came to be called San Vicente Cienega (present-day Silver City). In 1870, a group of American prospectors discovered silver in the hills just above the *cienega* (marshy area), and the rush was on. In 10 short months the newly christened Silver City had grown from a single cabin to over 80 buildings. Typically, the town's boom should have busted with the crash of silver prices in 1893. But unlike many Western towns, Silver City did not become simply a picturesque ghost town. Perhaps its sturdy brick architecture helped it defy such a fate. Perhaps it was the populace of Hispanics and Anglos, determined to make this their home and who were quick to exploit new industries.

At the turn of the 20th century, Silver City capitalized on its dry climate to become a haven for invalids and tuberculosis patients; one of the state's first teaching schools also prospered in town. Eventually, with new mineral discoveries, the town stabilized to become a county seat and trade center.

The myth that Billy the Kid killed his first man in Silver City is just that—one of many legends surrounding this young gunslinger's career. He is possibly the most written about Wild West figure, but little is actually known about Billy the Kid's early childhood. He was probably born around 1859 in New York City. In 1873, he was a witness to the marriage of his mother, Catherine McCarty, to William Antrim in Santa Fe. Like many New Mexicans, Antrim was a jack-of-all-trades with a burning desire to strike it rich. So within months of acquiring a wife and two sons, Billy's stepfather moved his family to the Southwest's newest and richest mining district, Silver City.

Today, Silver City is known for its retail trade and medical services and as a mountain retreat. It's also home to Western New Mexico University, which houses the Francis McCray Gallery of Southwestern art as well as the Southwest's largest collection of Mimbreno pottery and artifacts.

★ ★ ★

I interviewed Kathy in her office in the Silver City Museum, of which she is the current Volunteer Coordinator. The museum has a collection of Frontier Victoriana as well as Southwestern Native American pottery and mining artifacts. Silver City is not very big, but it has a marvelous and fantastic history. Kathy was very candid about her experiences with ghosts, and especially stated that she has a great respect for such things. After speaking with her, I left with the impression that there are many more unexplored locations of hauntings within the city and its surrounding areas. Perhaps, sometime in the near future, I'll have to return to Silver City for an extended stay.

KATHY E. BENAVIDEZ'S STORY

I lived in an apartment complex named Tinley Square, which was originally built at the turn of the century for use as a sanatorium for people who suffered from tuberculosis. It was operated by Catholic nuns. Tinley Square was only one of several such facilities in Silver City. The dry desert climate of Silver City was apparently ideal for the treatment of such ailments. Not long after medication became the main cure for tuberculosis, the large facility was turned into a complex of apartments. My apartment was located on the corner of Kelly and B streets.

Soon after my family and I had moved into our apartment, I began to hear unusual noises coming from the walls. I was awakened routinely between the hours of 2 and 3 a.m. by the sound of a constant hard thud. It sounded like a hard object hitting against a body. It always sounded as if the sound was coming from beneath the floor. This sound continued until about 6 a.m. With the first rays of the sun, the noise would suddenly cease.

Prior to giving birth to my twins, I recall that things in pairs, such as earrings, shoes, etc., would vanish as soon as I would look away. I thought this was a strange coincidence because I was pregnant with twins, and things that were disappearing were in pairs. The most significant item that disappeared was an amulet, given to me by my doctor. The amulet had an image on it of twins, a boy and a girl. A few months later, I gave birth to twins, a boy and a girl. My doctor gave me this amulet, which she told me she bought in San Francisco while on a trip. I had the amulet with me throughout my stay in the hospital. When I was discharged, I wrapped the amulet and brought it home, together with my new babies. When I got home, I placed it on the bedroom dresser. The next day, when I went to look for the amulet in my bedroom, it was gone. I thought nothing more about it; I was confident it would turn up eventually amongst my clothes. It never did, and soon I added it to my list of missing items.

One afternoon, I was sitting in the living room, holding a bottle in one hand and the baby in the other. I suddenly felt a hand pull my hair. I froze! I felt the fingers gently unhook and push out one of my earrings! I sat still as I saw the earring drop onto my chest and then continue to fall to the cushion on the sofa. My immediate reaction was to get up and flee the apartment, but with the baby in my arms I decided to maintain control. I sensed the presence of someone in the room with me, but I saw no one. I waited for several minutes for something to happen, and when nothing did, I decided to look for the earring. I searched everywhere under and around the sofa, but I never did find it.

Like the amulet, it too had disappeared. Two months later, while getting out of my parked car in the driveway, I noticed a shining object on the ground. I bent over to pick it up and discovered that it was my missing earring! How in the world had it ended up on my driveway. I have no idea. Occasionally, I feel those same ghostly fingers playing with my earrings, but now I put a stop to this by quickly taking hold of my earring and saying forcefully, "No!"

Tinlet Square, now an apartment building, was originally built for use as a sanatorium for people who suffered from tuberculosis.

My husband's favorite watch disappeared one evening, after he had placed it on the nightstand by the bed. The next morning, as he reached for his watch, it was gone! We both searched everywhere, but it could not be found. Approximately four months later, as I was cleaning under our bed and moving around some boxes, I discovered the missing watch inside a box. The unusual thing about this was that the box with the watch was itself inside another box! How did it get there? Who would have moved it without our knowledge, and why?

Two years later, while my children were eating their lunch in the kitchen and I was washing dishes at the sink, a mysterious thing took place. Suddenly, the bedroom door adjacent to the kitchen just swung open. I turned to look, but saw no one. However, my children immediately gazed at the open door and without speaking, followed with their eyes a presence as it made its way between me and the table. Once again, I had the feeling that something ghostly was in the room with us. I got goosebumps all over my arms as I watched their reactions. Whatever it was moved over behind one of the twins. They seemed not to be afraid or disturbed in any way. They just stared at the invisible presence before them in wonder. I soon felt this very cold and eerie presence surround me. Not wanting to alarm the children, I gathered my courage and cautiously walked out of the kitchen to get my husband. Whatever it was, I felt it follow me into the living room, where my husband was napping on the sofa. I felt two chilling, ghostly arms caress my body and hold me as I knelt down to wake my husband. I managed to wake him from his sound sleep and quickly told him what was happening. He was very groggy, and looked at me and said, "Don't worry about it." Thinking that my husband was too sleepy to comprehend what I was saying, I went back to my kids. When I entered the kitchen, I saw that the children were both quietly seated in their chairs, gazing at a corner of the room. I had had enough! I openly stated to whatever was in the room, "I don't know who you are or what you want, but please leave; I don't want you here, so please go away!" As soon as I said this, the kids' heads followed the unseen presence as it made its way from the kitchen, through the door, and into the bedroom. As soon as it had passed the doorway, the door began to move, and closed. Because of their young age, the children were unable to comprehend what had just taken place, but I knew better. I was emotionally shaken by it all.

A few days later, I spoke to the woman who used to live in my apartment and asked her if she had ever experienced anything unusual. I was surprised by her answer. "Oh, yes," she said, and went on to describe the following. Her three-year-old son would frequently be caught talking to an invisible presence. She often heard him speaking to someone, particularly in the bathroom. One evening, while he was taking a bath, she stepped out of the room and left him alone for a few minutes. Once again, she overheard her son talking to someone, but this time she decided to ask him who he was talking to. Her son pointed to the commode and then said, "To that man!" He said this man always visited him and that the man was sitting there, watching them both! Although *she* never saw this man, this incident left her with an uneasy feeling. After I had heard her story, I described my own experiences to her, and she was not at all surprised.

During the nights that followed, my children became more and more restless. They resisted falling asleep until about 11 p.m. each night. Physical and emotional exhaustion would eventually take over. They explained, "There are scary things in our room, hiding behind the doors and under the beds." They also spoke of a light on the wall that would keep them awake.

One night, as I walked past the children's open bedroom door, I noticed a faint glow of light coming from inside. As I walked into the room, I noticed an entire wall was lit, as if it were transparent and a lightbulb was turned on behind it. I was dumfounded, and searched the room for a possible explanation. I sniffed the air for signs of a fire or burning candle. I smelled nothing. I also looked out the window for a passing car whose light beams might be shining into the room. Again, I discovered nothing.

For several nights thereafter, I noticed that the light in the bedroom wall would glow and get brighter with each passing night. I touched the wall in an attempt to feel any heat; there was none. There was no rational explanation.

Some weeks later, we had guests who were staying with us. They were Native American dancers, in town for a local celebration. Six of these guests slept in the room with the glowing wall. None of them were told anything about the odd occurrences with the spirits in the apartment or of the glowing wall. The following morning, one guest told me that during the night, he had seen all sorts of spirits behind the wall in the room where they had slept. I told him about the glowing wall and how uncomfortable I felt. He then recommended that the room and apartment be blessed with sacred sage and suggested we say a few prayers. I agreed to this, and after gathering everyone together, he led us all in a house blessing.

Since that day, things in the apartment have calmed down, and we have not experienced any further strange happenings. I like to think that what was in the apartment has left for good. I believe many of the previous patients who came to this building, which once was a sanatorium, sought to be cured of tuberculosis. A great number of them never left the property alive. It's difficult to imagine the pain these poor people suffered. I hope they have found the lasting peace they sought in life.

★ ★ ★

I interviewed Herb in the living room of his quaint home. Herb is a good-natured man who had many stories to tell, some of them about ghosts and some not. It appeared to me that Herb is the type of gentleman who enjoys good conversation, and if it lasts way into the night, so much the better. Good friends, good stories, and a warm home, that's Herb!

HERB J. MCGRATH

When I was in my early twenties, several friends and I were walking the streets of Silver City one evening. We were checking out the girls and just having a good time. We were walking on Bullard Street, passing the Buffalo Bar, when one of us remembered a local story about a murder that had taken place above the bar sometime in the early 1900s. Apparently, a locally well-known brothel had been located in  the building before the new owners took it over. A local prostitute took a client up to her second-floor bedroom, but things got out of hand. There was a struggle, and the poor woman was thrown out of the window to her death on the street below. My friends and I commented on the story, and didn't give it any further thought. We knew the present owner of the bar and that the second floor, where the tragedy had taken place, was now used as a storage area.

As the evening grew late, my friends and I decided to call it a night, since we had to work early the following day. It must have been a little after midnight when I made my way home down Bullard Street. At that hour, the streets were empty. As I approached my car, which was parked across the street from the Buffalo Bar, I noticed a light coming from the second-floor window above the bar. I knew that the bar was closed for the night, and that the second floor was filled with boxes and other storage items. I thought it was unusual for anyone to be in the storage room at that hour. I stood staring at the light in the window because it had a strange glow to it. It did not have the usual brightness of an electric lightbulb, but instead it had a warm glow. I stood there in the street below, just gazing for about a minute or so. It then struck me that the light was coming from a kerosene lamp, because I noticed the flickering, dancing light it cast on the wall inside the room. Now I was really intrigued. I thought to myself, "Who is in that room, at this hour of the night with an oil lamp?" No sooner had this thought occurred, when I saw the outline or shadow of a woman! She was wearing a long white-sleeved nightgown, and her hair hung long and loose. Not wanting to be noticed, I kept still. Then I saw and heard her push up on the window. When she opened the window, I was transfixed by her image. I decided to let her know I was watching her, so I yelled out, "Hello." She paid me no attention as she then leaped out the window! I was startled by this, because as she jumped and began her fall, she vanished in the air! The light in the room also disappeared at

"I stood staring at the light in the window."

that same moment. I didn't hear her scream or make any other noise.

After seeing this, I looked around, thinking there were others who had just seen what I had, but the street was empty. I quickly fumbled for my keys, opened the door, and drove out of the area as fast as possible! If there was ever a question in my mind about the existence of ghosts . . . well, I was convinced very quickly that evening.

CARRIZOZO

The small town of Carrizozo lies 20 miles north of the White Sands Missile Range and 30 miles northwest of Ruidoso. It's a junction site for Highway 54, North–South, and Highway 380, East–West.

The town took its name from *carrizo*, a reed native to the surrounding plain and foothills. There is a rumor that a ranch foreman embellished the name with an extra "zo" to indicate abundance. Carrizozo, county seat of Lincoln County, was established in 1899. The first governor of New Mexico, William C. McDonald, owned the enormous Bar W cattle ranch. His grave is located a few miles north of Carrizozo, in the ghost town of White Oaks. Billy the Kid and Sheriff Pat Garrett figured prominently in the history of the area.

Organized by Charles B. Eddy, the El Paso and Northeastern Railroad forged north of Alamogordo. Eddy's influence as a railroad pioneer had such an impact on the area that Eddy County was named after him. In 1905, Charles B. Eddy sold the railroad to the copper firm of Phelps Dodge, who then sold it to Southern Pacific in 1924. As the small town grew, eventually a railroad hotel was built. This construction was followed by a post office, a bank, a Baptist church, and a one-room schoolhouse. A doctor ran the only drugstore in town, while the local mortician doubled as a hardware dealer.

By 1909, the residents of Carrizozo voted to transfer the county seat from Lincoln to Carrizozo. As water wells were dug, irrigation transformed the dry, barren town into an oasis of green. Soon this was followed by the introduction of a modern sewage system and electric lights.

★   ★   ★

I interviewed Florecita at her home in Las Cruces. The day was very warm and, because of the heat, we decided to conduct the interview in her backyard. She located three wooden boxes, two of which we used as stools, and the third propped up my tape recorder. Under the shade of a large pecan tree, we sat sipping tall glasses of iced tea. Florecita's husband, Lorenzo, would quietly check up on us from time to time and refill our glasses. Thus was the setting in which Florecita told me the tragic, but beautiful, story of her two cousins, Irene and Lenchita.

AMPARO "FLORECITA" LUCERO'S STORY

I was born in Carrizozo in 1921. At that time, I remember, Carrizozo was just a little town without much excitement. I lived in Carrizozo until I got married at age 16 to my husband, who was from Las Cruces. The story I'm going to tell you is good, but it's also a sad one. It's a story about my two cousins, Irene and Lenchita.

I was 14 years old at the time, and my cousins lived a few streets away from our house. The little girls were eight and nine years of age and hung around each other all the time. Wherever one was, you could bet the other would be nearby. Our families were pretty close in those days.

One morning during breakfast, the sisters asked their parents, Josefa and Rodrigo, some unusual questions about two deceased relatives. They asked how the persons had died and what happens to people when they die. Josefa thought these were odd things for the girls to be curious about. She told them what she knew, but soon became upset. Such thoughts reminded her of her deceased loved ones, and she began to cry. Josefa instructed her daughters to leave such questions about death to God. After finishing their breakfast, the sisters went outside to play with the other children.

Josefa found it difficult to brush the girls' questions aside. She kept a close eye on her daughters that day. However, early that afternoon, the girls managed to disappear for a short time and then came into the house with their hands full of wildflowers. Josefa asked them why they had the flowers, and the sisters answered, "Mother, these flowers are for the Virgin. We picked them for the Virgin and we need a jar to put them in." Josefa located an empty pickle jar. After placing the flowers in the jar, the girls took the flowers to the parents' bedroom, where their mother had a statue of the Virgin on her dresser. The girls asked their mother to place the flowers before the statue and to join them both in prayer. Josefa was humbled by their actions and led them in the Hail Mary prayer. Satisfied, the sisters left the house to play with their friends. Josefa couldn't help thinking how strange the girls were behaving.

Later that day, Josefa discovered the family was out of milk. Not owning a car, she asked her husband to borrow a friend's car. He would need it in order to visit another family a few miles away, who owned several cows and had milk to sell. Cars had become a common mode of transportation at the time, although the usual way to get around was by horse and wagon. Unlike cars, which were always getting stalled or stuck in the sand or mud, horses were pretty reliable. Rodrigo borrowed the car, and the girls pleaded and pleaded for him to take them with him. The three of them got in the car, and off they went.

Not more than a few minutes later, the terrible sound of the Southern Pacific train hitting the car was heard throughout the town. With tears in their eyes, people came running to Josefa, telling her of the accident that had just occurred. Josefa ran to the railroad crossing, but the women held her tight, refusing to let her near the gruesome, and bloody, crash site. Apparently, the car Rodrigo was driving had stalled on the tracks; unable to stop in time, the train had hit the car with such force that the father and his two daughters were killed in an instant. It was so very sad. Josefa was hysterical.

The morning following the funeral, Josefa was sitting on the side of her bed with her eyes closed in deep contemplation. She was praying the Rosary before the statue of the Virgin. The wildflowers her daughters had gathered were still in the glass jar. Suddenly, an overwhelming scent of roses enveloped her bedroom. She slowly opened her eyes, and within two feet of her bed the ghosts of her two daughters appeared! Josefa put her hands to her heart and began to cry. Josefa asked the ghosts of her daughters, who were dressed in white dresses and holding each other's hands, "Why did you leave me?" They did not respond. Instead, they stood before her peacefully smiling. Then Josefa asked, "Where is your father?" The girls raised their arms and pointed in Josefa's direction, which indicated to her that he was right next to her. Josefa looked to her left and saw the ghost of her husband. Rodrigo reached out his opened hands to his daughters. At that moment, all three images of her family slowly disappeared.

Josefa felt comforted and was filled with a sense of peace and calm. In her words, "I am now able to be at peace, knowing that my family is together for all time."

Since the day of the peaceful apparition of her family, Josefa has always kept three fresh flowers in a vase by the statue of the Virgin in her bedroom. Josefa maintained her symbolic gesture of love until the day of her death in 1976.

A wooden grave marker was placed on the graves of the father and his two daughters. Hung on the marker was a religious medallion of the Virgin to whom the girls so lovingly prayed and brought flowers on the day of their tragic death.

Our family believes that, in some way, the girls had knowledge of their impending deaths. I know the story of Josefa's family has helped me throughout my own life. It is an inspiration to everyone who has heard it. I miss my cousins, Irene and Lenchita, very much. And I can't help wondering what their lives would have been like today. I know someday soon, I'll be with them as well.

WHITE OAKS

White Oaks is an old ghost town situated in the southeastern portion of the state. It lies in a valley at an elevation of 6,500 feet, surrounded by gently sloping mountains. These mountains are Lone to the north, Patos

to the east, and Carrizo to the south. Baxter Mountain, the least in elevation, contained the gold that was discovered in 1879 by John Wilson.
Long before the discovery, which led to the birth of White Oaks, there
is evidence that early Spaniards and possibly Native American people
worked these gold deposits. John Wilson sold his interest to his prospec-
tor friends, John Charles Baxter and John V. Winters, for a pistol and two
ounces of gold dust (approximately $38).

The Gold Strike was soon on! White Oaks was born and quickly
grew to a sizable town of about 2,500 people. Pat Garrett was the sheriff
in the early 1880s, and Billy the Kid rode into town on a few occasions.
In 1882, local Mescalero Apaches joined forces with other Apaches—
Geronimo, and Loco from Arizona—and killed more than 100 settlers
just south of White Oaks. The citizens of White Oaks were so concerned for their safety that all the women and children gathered
together in a rock house, located somewhere in the northern section of
town. The local butcher ran through town in a frenzy, with a meat axe
in one hand and a lantern in his other, proclaiming his protection for
the women and children of the town.

The gravesite of W. C. McDonald,
New Mexico's first governor.

The only sidewalks at the time were located in front of store buildings and were made of rough wood planks. In its heyday, White Oaks was a pretty civilized place. When the post office opened in 1879, there were four churches, a school, and a bank. The town's first newspaper was *The Golden Era*, edited by Major William Caffrey. Doctors A. G. Lane and Melvin Paden settled in and started medical practices, and Melvin Paden put in a drugstore. J. Howe Watts designed the business plan for the town, and two Chinese citizens, Wah Sing and Ah Nue, began a restaurant and laundry. Like all frontier towns at the time, White Oaks also had its share of bawdy houses. One of the largest was The Little Casino, operated by a cunning dealer named Bell LaMar, or Madame Varnish. She earned her "special" reputation because of her "slick ways" in dealing with the miners. A poem written by present-day White Oaks resident Ruth Birdsong conjures up a sense of the life of Bell LaMar:

Bell LaMar
was her name.
Fleecing the miners
was her game.

In White Oaks Town
lived this lady of pleasure.
With charisma and harlotry
as her treasure.

She came from St. Louis
her El Dorado to find.
It was at the Little Casino
she located her gold mine.

This house she operated
with cunning and style.
So devious her tactics,
so cold her smile.

There the music played
and the liquor flowed.
And the card games went
on for hours, we're told.

The miners wasted their dust
on the charms she sold.
And slick she was
as she took their gold.

As Madam Varnish
she became known.
Her slick, slippery ways
could not be condoned.

So one dark night,
out of town she rode.
Off in quest of
the mother lode.

White Oaks would have unquestionably been a flourishing little metropolis today had the leading men of the time not been so greedy. The El Paso and Northeastern Railroad had plans for the railroad to be built through town. The property owners were convinced that they had not merely the best route, but the only route. They refused to donate a right of way and priced land so high that the negotiators walked off, told the surveyors to forget White Oaks, and headed for the other town of Corona.

There is no denying the fact that White Oaks was on its way towards becoming a thriving town of excellence. Due to unforeseeable circumstances, however, it sank into oblivion.

★ ★ ★

I interviewed Fran in her kitchen. Both Fran and her husband are artists and currently live in a very huge and wonderful Victorian house. The house is impossible to miss as it sits on top of a prominent hill. The house is such a focal point in White Oaks that, although it is not a museum, the public is normally drawn to it. During the time of my visit, Fran had a plate filled with baked cookies to offer the public just in case someone happened to drop by. Fran was very open to discussing her experiences with ghosts in the house. Read on now as Fran tells of her personal experience in her home.

FRAN J. MACK'S STORY

I've lived in White Oaks for about two years. My first experience with something ghostlike took place a year ago during October. The house I'm currently living in is more than 100 years old. My husband and I had just recently moved into the house when we started hearing the odd sound of a ringing bell late in the evenings. We would be lying in bed when the soft ringing sound would start up. We didn't know what it could be, but we would get out of bed and search the house for its source. The sound was muffled and distant. It was as if the bells were ringing inside a box or were under blankets in another room of the house. The ringing would suddenly begin and then abruptly stop. This continued for three nights in a row. It became irritating for us, as we expected to hear this sound each night.

On the fourth night, the bells began to ring once again. I got out of bed and searched the bottom floor of the house. The ringing was loudest in the parlor room. I followed the sound to a wall of the room, and noticed the sound got louder when I placed my ear next to an old electrical wall socket. I brought my husband downstairs, and sure enough, he heard the sound as well, coming from the wall.

Just a few days later, we had the telephone company send a service worker over to investigate and to install a phone in the house. He told us that the company had no record of phone service ever having been installed in the house. He also gave us a strange look when we told him about the ringing bells we were hearing. However, he did search

"The house is more than 100 years old."

through the house. He reported that he could find no explanation for the ringing noises we had been hearing. Just about four months ago, we also started to experience another odd thing in the parlor. When we placed an object down on a table, within a few seconds it would disappear! On one occasion, I was getting ready to hang a picture and had the nails, hammer, wire, and picture hook on a table next to where I was seated. I picked up the hammer in one hand and then reached towards the table for the picture hook. It had just vanished! I looked under the table, on the floor, and it was nowhere to be seen. Frustrated, I walked into the kitchen, then turned around, walked back into the parlor, and sat down on the chair. To my amazement, the picture hook had reappeared on the table! There was no way I could have missed seeing this. Since then, we have had no further occurrence of the sound of ringing bells or missing things. I believe that tricks were being played on us, and as soon as we discovered the source of the trick, as with the ringing bells, the mischief stopped. You might ask, "A trick, by who?" Well, if you ever find out, please tell me and then we'll both know!

★ ★ ★

I interviewed John in his kitchen. As I walked into his simply decorated home, I was struck by the many beautiful paintings on his walls. I soon found out that John was an artist and, further, that his house doubled as both home and art gallery. After more discussion, I also discovered that Mr. Duncan has a degree in anthropology, and he amazed me with his knowledge of Californian Native American culture. John himself is truly an undiscovered walking treasure of southern New Mexico. I would encourage lovers of fine art and individuals in general to pay John a friendly visit. He's got a lot of tales to tell, and after all, he might even share a ghost story or two. The following is a short version of the visit I had with John not so many months ago.

JOHN W. DUNCAN'S STORY

I've lived in White Oaks for just over two years. I'm a landscape painter, and my home also serves as a small gallery. I had my first experience with a ghost when I first moved into the house.

The house was built by the Taylor family around the year 1885, and had not been lived in for more than 20 years. When I moved in, there was dirt everywhere. Bats had gotten in through the broken windows and were roosting in the ceilings. As you might imagine, it was a quite a job cleaning this place.

I was sweeping the upstairs bedroom one day when I decided to sit down on the bed and take a short break. As I sat there, I closed my eyes, and then suddenly I saw an image of a large man. The man was wearing a large black cowboy hat with a very tall crown. I don't know why I had this image. It just came to me. I immediately felt the sensation of someone standing to my left.

I opened my eyes, looked to my left, and saw nothing. Thinking that I was just tired, I thought nothing more of this. But after that day, I did begin to hear footsteps throughout the house. Even my small dog would bark at these sounds, day or night. I got used to the sounds and didn't give them any further thought. There have been times when visitors have felt a tug on their clothes, but have seen no one. I myself have felt my clothes being pulled on several occasions when I was alone in the house.

John and "Lulu."

A week later, I spoke to a friend who told me the strangest thing. She said she had been trying to get a hold of me for a week. I asked her why hadn't she phoned? She responded, "I've called your house and have left messages with someone who answers your phone. Your phone rings, and the person who answers says, 'I'll take a message for John.' I say, 'Tell John that I need to speak with him.' I give them my name and then I'll hang up." I informed my friend that I had never received her messages. Furthermore, since I live alone, it would have been odd to have someone answer my telephone. My home is very quiet, and if someone were to call, I would definitely hear the phone. We both didn't know what to make of all this. I must admit I did think that perhaps something supernatural was going on.

"The grandson had died in the house."

A few weeks later, while I was sitting in the kitchen with my little dog, Lulu, one evening, I decided to command the ghost, if there was one, to make its presence known to me. I know the name of the man who built the house, Napoleon Bonaparte Taylor. At the time, not knowing who the ghost might be, I decided to name it "Nappy," a name I thought might be a shorter version of Napoleon. I thought that perhaps the ghost in the house might be the original builder. I said, "Nappy, come out and talk to me. Nappy, if you are hearing me, come out. Let's talk!" Nothing happened. Maybe that was a good thing, because if I had heard something, I might have had a heart attack! Bored and sleepy, I decided to go to bed. While lying in bed, I was surprised when I heard a loud noise coming from the ceiling with a "bang!" My little dog, Lulu, was barking uncontrollably. Try as I might, she would not stop barking. I got out of bed and I felt my hair stand on end! I turned on the light and said, "Nappy, I was just kidding. Forget what I said. I don't want to talk with you." Luckily, I didn't hear anything further that night. Eventually,

Lulu calmed down and I felt drowsy enough to go back to sleep.

Sometime later, a descendent of the Taylor family came to the house to visit me. She was an older woman. I didn't wish to mention anything about ghosts, thinking she might humor me. But out of historical curiosity, I did ask her to give me information about her family and the house. She told me that the grandson of Napoleon Taylor had died in the house in 1917, and was buried in the local cemetery. I got to thinking that maybe he was the cause of the footsteps and all the other noise I had heard in the house.

There have been other little things that have happened here in the house, which make me wonder if I'm alone. I'll just save those stories for another time.

LA LUZ

La Luz was founded in 1863, when Juan Garcia led a covered wagon caravan of colonizers from the Rio Grande area. These pioneers each quickly built their one-story adobe houses in a small cluster, surrounded by a high wall that afforded them protection from the threat of an attack by the local Apache people. These pioneers risked being killed each time they left the comfort and security of their small, walled village in order to farm their fields. The warm rich soil of the area supported the perfect conditions for growing pears, pecans, apricots, and fig trees. They also had great success in growing grapes and vegetables.

These *rancheros* were always on guard against being attacked by the Mescalero Apaches. The Mescalero were masters of guerrilla warfare. U.S. calvary soldiers, who were sent to subdue them, were once lured up into the perilous Dog Canyon nearby where they were ambushed.

Huge boulders were rolled down the canyon walls upon the men and horses, crushing several to death. Fierce protectors of their ancestral lands, the Apache people were both feared and respected.

★   ★   ★

I interviewed Katie in her home on a warm sunny day in June. Her home is nestled among very tall and old cottonwood and willow trees, which sway their long green branches in the slightest desert breeze. Her comfortable home is filled with various pictures of her family, and especially of her deceased husband who she is very proud to mention at every opportunity. Katie has the great ability to remember minute details of her life and of La Luz's community events. It was not difficult for her to recall specific dates and people whom she and her husband had met throughout their many years of marriage, because she has put together a wonderful scrapbook of those years, which she shared with me that afternoon.

As I drove away from Katie's home that warm afternoon, I took one last look and saw her motherly image standing at her door, waving good-bye to me.

CATALINA "KATIE" GARCIA'S STORY

I was born in the town of Bent, New Mexico, located near Mescalero. My mother died on my sixth birthday. I got married in Alamogordo. I've lived in La Luz since the age of 17. I am now 82 years old. When I first arrived in La Luz, it was during the Depression, and I got a job at a small hotel/restaurant named The Lodge. I was paid three dollars a week, plus room and board. The Lodge is now named "Mi Casa," and has since been turned into an apartment complex. It sure doesn't seem like a lot of money now, but during that time, I was able to survive on the three dollars I earned. I worked from 6 a.m. until 9 p.m.

My house is an authentic adobe, over 250 years old. Although I remodeled the house a few years ago, I still have my bedroom looking as it did when I first moved into the house, many years ago. I plan to remain here until the day I die.

My experience with a ghost took place in this home, only two years ago. I was lying down on my bed one day, when I was awakened by the strange sense of the "presence" of someone else being in the room. I looked at the foot of my bed, and I saw a tall man covered in a long white cloth. A soft white, glowing light emanated from him. He seemed to be bathed in this light. He just stood there, without saying a word. When I said, "Who are you?" he didn't answer. Once again, I said, "Who are you? Do you want to talk to me?" Again, he did not answer. Then I asked him, "Oh, I know who you are; you're Jesus, aren't you?" Again, no answer. So, I got quiet. He just stood there, when I said, "Please answer me, who are you?" Then he spoke. But, his words did not come from his mouth. The words seemed to come from his energy, if you can understand what this would be like. In other words, the sound of speaking came from his light. He said, "I want you to do a favor for me. I know that you pray a lot, and I want you to complete a task for me." I answered, "Oh, yes, of course. What is it?" He said, "I want you to give a message to each of your children. Will you do this for me?" I asked, "What kind of message? What do you want me to say?" He answered, "When you get a visit from the first son to visit you, I want you to explain that you have a message to tell him. When this is done, I will give you the words to speak. I cannot tell you what these words will be until that time." As soon as this spirit finished speaking to me, he disappeared.

Well, the next day, my oldest son, Johnny, and his wife came to visit me. He must have noticed something was on my mind because he asked me, "Mother, is something bothering you?" I told him I had something to tell him and asked him to have a seat. We sat facing each other. I described the strange, but beautiful, visitor, and the odd task I had been told to complete. We became silent at that moment and bowed our heads. After a few minutes, my son slowly raised his head and said with amazement, "Mother, I just received the message, but I was told to keep it to myself." My son never told me the specifics of his message, and I respected his decision to keep it a secret. Only he knows what the message was.

A few weeks later, I was asleep in my bedroom when suddenly I was awakened by a loud noise. I opened my eyes, got out of bed, and walked to the kitchen. I walked all around the house. I didn't see anything, so I went back to bed. The next night, I was again in bed, when suddenly the sweet smell of flowers surrounded me in the room. I was so surprised by this scent, I turned on the bedroom light and just sat on the bed enjoying it. After a few minutes, my phone rang. It was my best friend, Vidie Morgan. Vidie called me to say that she had just had a dream about me. She said in her dream, I was in my bedroom, and an angel was watching over me. It was a beautiful dream, and the angel was covered in a bright light. It was so peaceful. Then she said in this dream, there was an abundance of flowers that had an overpowering, beautiful scent. When the angel waved his hands, this caused the beautiful perfume to get stronger. Because of the strong scent, it caused my friend to wake up from her dream. Her dream made such an impression, she knew she had to immediately phone and describe it to me. We spent the next several minutes comparing our experiences and describing our joy.

I believe that I was visited by an angel. I know I am safe and protected by this beautiful visitor. As long as I live, I will never be afraid of anything again. To this day, I always pray with all my heart. Although I don't pray as often as I would like, when I do, I put my heart in my words. I don't light candles or kneel down; I just sit on the side of my bed and open my heart. That's all.

TULAROSA

In 1860, several Spanish settlers decided to leave their settlement in the Rio Grande Valley, and seek out a new settlement to the east. They came upon a beautiful and fertile land, where many wild roses and tule grass grew. They decided to settle in this area, and named the town Tularosa, after the tule and roses that grew in profusion.

On April 17, 1868, Sergeant Edward Glass and his four-horse wagon train from Fort Stanton came under attack from 200 Mescalero Apaches. Twenty-six settlers from Tularosa soon heard word of the ambush, and armed with axes and other crude instruments, they headed out to aid the soldiers. While en route, the settlers prayed to their patron saint, Saint Francis. They made a *promesa* (promise) to the saint, that if he would answer their prayers, they would make an annual pilgrimage to him. Arriving at the scene of the ambush, the settlers soon won victory over the Apaches. Not long after, some of the townspeople claimed to have seen a vision of the saint riding a white horse. On the exact spot where this apparition had been seen, a church named Saint Francis de Paula was erected. The church was built entirely of adobe bricks that had been made by the women of the community. With the help of the men, the church was completed within only one year. For the following 42 years, this was the only church in Tularosa.

Every year since its construction, the community of Tularosa fulfills the *promesa* made by the settlers of 1868 with a fiesta honoring Saint Francis.

★   ★   ★

The day was cloudy and a few raindrops were falling the afternoon I came upon Señor Candelaria's home. Antonio (mi tocayo) was in his driveway talking with a neighbor, who was behind the wooden fence that divided their two properties. After I had introduced myself, Antonio quickly, but politely, excused himself to his neighbor and showed me into his humble home. I could not help but notice the various armed forces mementos that were arranged about the kitchen and living room. Also prominent among his collections were religious pictures and paintings of Catholic saints and Jesus Christ. After speaking with Antonio, I knew he was very knowledgeable regarding the history of his community. He immediately struck me as being a well-read man.

When my short interview with Antonio was over, he asked pleasantly if I would like to see two of his own literary works. Then he inscribed and presented two books to me entitled Juan Cibola, *a legendary narrative, and* The Valley of Peace, *a story about the first settlers of Tularosa.*

Antonio and I have since become "pen pals." It is such human gifts as these that make the project of my books so much more than mere work.

ANTONIO SERNA CANDELARIA'S STORY

I'm 72 years old and have lived in Tularosa all my life. However, in 1942, I did leave the town for three years when I was in the U.S. Marine Corps. I've seen many changes in this little town. The most obvious and negative influence has been the breakdown of the family structure. In my opinion, due to the introduction of illegal drugs, the traditional way of life among the Hispanic people has suffered. Television has also put an end to communication among the older Hispanic people. It used to be that folks would gather together and talk. We would spend hours at a time, just talking about anything. There was joy in conversation; now television has taken away everything! Everybody is looking at television. Everybody is also speaking English. English is spoken everywhere. What about Spanish? Who speaks Spanish these days? Not many people do. Years ago, everyone spoke Spanish, or Spanish and English, but these days Spanish is considered old fashioned. Our language is Spanish, and it hurts me to see how so few of the young people know it.

When I experienced my encounter with a ghost, I was 13 years old. I was with a group of friends at the time, and we were hanging around outside of the two-story red-brick school building. I remember the evening very well. The sun had just gone down, and the sky was deep purple. We

The school building in Tularosa.

were standing in the middle of the unpaved street. Suddenly, in the distance, we heard the sound of a horse's galloping hooves. We turned in the direction of the sound and saw the shadow of a man on an invisible horse! We were terrified! This ghostly, horseless rider kept bouncing in step with the galloping sounds of the horse. We were scared. The darkness only made this ghost even more frightening! The last thing I remember was the dust clouds that our feet made as we rushed off to our homes. I'll always remember that experience with the ghostly rider, and I'm sure all my friends will too.

LINCOLN

Lincoln began as a small Hispanic farming community more than 100 years ago. Considering the history of settlement of New Mexico, this was rather late. Considering also that the southeastern area in which Lincoln was to be located was the homelands of the warrior Apache people, it is easy to understand why non-native people were late in settling here. With the establishment of Fort Stanton, just nine miles away, more families came to stay. Farmers and sheepherders built *placitas* up and down the river, which were known as *las placitas del Rio Bonito* (the little plazas by the pretty river). When Lincoln County was created in 1869, La Placita, the largest of *las placitas del Rio Bonito*, was designated the county seat, and its name was officially changed to Lincoln. When the county was doubled in size, in 1878, it was the largest county in the United States.

During this time, the seeds that led to the Lincoln County War were being sown. Two men, Colonel Fritz and Major Murphy, former officers at Fort Stanton, formed a mercantile partnership and soon gained control of the county, politically and economically. By mid-1877, John Tunstall, a young Englishman, and attorney Alexander McSween, his business associate, had opened a rival store and challenged the establishment. Tunstall was killed on February 18, 1878, and shooting started, which led to the Five Days Battle in Lincolntown. When McSween was killed and his home burned to the ground, the war was about played out. But, as always with war, neither side won; the economy was ruined and lawless elements, brought in to carry on the war, were set loose. Billy the Kid, who worked for Tunstall and had made good his escape from the burning McSween house, became the leader of his own little band of cattle and horse rustlers, until he was captured and sentenced to hang right here in Lincolntown. He made his escape by killing his two guards, only to be tracked down and shot by Sheriff Pat Garrett two-and-a-half months later, on July 14, 1881, at Fort Sumner, and a legend was born.

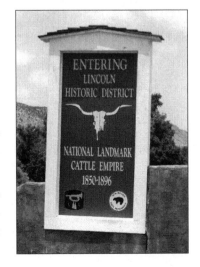

After this bloody interlude, Lincoln went back to its quiet and relatively peaceful existence. Fort Stanton was a major deterrent to the

Apaches, and the people went about the business of making a living, raising a family, and building a proud and law-abiding town.

Present-day Lincoln is both a national and a state monument, and is part of an architecturally zoned area one mile wide by ten miles long. Lincoln remained the county seat until the coming of statehood in 1912, when the seat was moved to Carrizozo, a young and growing railroad town.

THE ELLIS STORE AND COMPANY

Sabino Gonzales, one of the first Hispanic settlers of the area, was the original builder and owner of the "Ellis" store. The property was home to the Gonzales family until sometime in the mid- to late-1860s. Currently, the house is more than 140 years old!

In May 1, 1993, owners David and Jinny Vigil opened the historic property as a wonderfully quaint bed-and-breakfast. The relaxing, tranquil, pampered environment of the B&B has become a haven for those weary of the "rat race" out in the real world. There is much more to the interesting history of the Ellis Store, a history of events that even includes a ghost!

DAVID A. VIGIL'S STORY

Within two months of moving into the house, my wife, Jinny, and I began to experience strange things. Unexplained ghostly happenings convinced us that something out of the ordinary was dwelling in the house. Beginning my research on the property, I discovered that the house is the oldest standing structure in the town of Lincoln!

A corner room and the kitchen were built by the original owners, the Gonzales family. In 1861, the Gonzales family sold the house to Elisha Dow, who added another room. In 1876, Elisha Dow resold the house to the Ellis family who came to Lincoln from Colfax County, New Mexico. The Ellis family added the front wing to the house, which they used as a general store. They also built the dining room and rooms in the rear of the house, which my wife and I currently use as our personal living area. The Ellis family lived in the house until 1904, at which time the house was once again sold. Doctor James Laws purchased the house and added the large, beautiful *portal* (porch), as well as the pitched roof. He used the front of the house for his office and examination room. He also used a portion of this area as an operating room. Within the main structure, he added what we call the great room, which includes a large fireplace. During the time he lived in the house, it was known as the "Tuberculosis Ranch." In 1918, the E. P. & N. W. Railway (later Southern Pacific) bought the property from

Dr. Laws and had every intention of building a railroad to Lincoln. Since water was needed for the steam engines, the railroad dispatched Mr. Bert Pfingsten to the Bonito Valley to acquire all water rights. In this way, the Bonita Dam could be built and used as the primary water source. However, federal regulations allow railroads to be built only in county seats, and since Lincoln was no longer a county seat, this dream was abandoned. The management of all the property was turned over to Pfingsten, who later bought most of it from the railroad. He sold the house to James "Red" and Sophronia "Froney" Ramey, who lived in the house until 1976. After James died, Sophronia sold the house to the Martin family, who immediately started restoring the house. In 1993, my wife and I became the new owners, after purchasing the house from the Martins.

My first strange experience took place two months after having purchased the house. At about 11 p.m., I was in the kitchen preparing coffee for the following morning. Friends were staying with us and helping us to paint the inside of the house. Later that evening, after dinner, everyone left to go to their rooms and were soon asleep in their beds. Suddenly, I heard a woman singing a beautiful opera-like song. I listened closely and followed the music. The singing woman quickly ended her song and began to laugh. I went into our living quarters and asked my wife if she had heard the singing woman. She was totally surprised and responded she had heard a similar voice, singing at the rear of the house. Thinking it might have been one of our friends, we decided to ask them about this in the morning.

The following morning, Jinny and I were seated at the kitchen table enjoying our coffee, when our friends entered and greeted us. They wasted no time in asking, "Were you and Jinny in our room last night?" Surprised by their question, I answered, "No, not at all. Why do you ask?" They gave each other a puzzled look and then told us what they had experienced. As they were lying in bed, someone opened and closed their door, walked around the room, and once again opened and closed the door. Jinny and I could not explain it. All we could say to them was, "We didn't go into your bedroom and we don't know what's going on. Jinny and I heard a woman singing in the house last night, and we thought it might be you." The subject was dropped and never mentioned again during their visit.

Five months after that first incident, we opened the B&B business. Jinny was waiting in the living room for guests who were expected to arrive. I was away from the property, taking some workers home who had helped us out with tasks around the property. Jinny decided to turn on a lamp in the living room. As she reached for the lamp switch and turned it, she saw the electrical plug was lying on the floor, out of the wall socket. Jinny remembered one of the workers was using that socket for a power tool. She walked to another lamp and turned it on instead. She walked into the adjoining kitchen for a glass of water and returned to the living room. As soon as she entered the living room, she noticed both lamps were on, including the lamp that was disconnected. The cord had been plugged back into the wall! Jinny was the only person in the house. She definitely would have heard or seen someone in the room with her. The floorboards to the house are quite old and always creak whenever someone walks on them. She heard nothing. After this last incident, we both knew that there was something more to this house than just its old-fashioned charm.

Guests began to tell us they had experienced a person in their rooms who would open and close doors. Others described voices, singing or laughing in the middle of the night, which would wake them from their sleep. At this point, I decided to give the ghost a name, in order to refer to her as something other than just "the ghost." I decided on the name Veronica. I don't know why; the name just "felt" appropriate for a female ghost.

A week or so after our last guests had left, we had a single guest, a woman, who was a return visitor from the first year we had opened our B&B. This woman knew nothing of our ghost, Veronica. Not wishing to scare any potential business away, Jinny and I chose not to mention our ghost for obvious reasons. Well, this woman approached us the following morning after spending a night in her room, with a story about a woman's singing voice and the slamming of doors in her room. We both pleaded ignorance and left it at that.

Soon after, Jinny's personal items began to mysteriously disappear. Kitchen knives would disappear from where Jinny had laid them and days later reappear in guest rooms that were vacant. The knives appeared in other areas of the house as well. There was no explanation for this, since several times during these occurrences Jinny and I were the only "living souls" in the house for days! One day, my wife's cake cooling rack disappeared. We looked everywhere for that thing. We thought, "What would a ghost want with a wire cake rack?" A few days later, I walked into the kitchen and spotted the darn rack on the table. I asked Jinny where she had found it. She was as surprised as I was to see it.

A guest, Albuquerque artist Steve Reyes, painted this portrait of Veronica, which hangs in the Vigils' living room.

Another time, we had guests who arrived late one evening. I proceeded to accompany them to their room, and as I pulled on the doorknob, I could tell it was locked. The door had been locked from the inside! The latch was fastened tightly. Minutes before I had personally gone inside to inspect it, having made sure that the room was clean and ready to receive guests. I turned to the couple and explained that the room was somehow locked from the inside. I tried once more to open the door, and without much effort, it opened very easily! I believe that Veronica was having fun with me that evening.

We had an Albuquerque artist, Steve Reyes, visiting us a year ago. He also heard the singing that the other guests had heard. He asked us about it, and we felt comfortable enough to tell him about Veronica. He was inspired to paint the picture of Veronica that now hangs in our living room.

I decided to ask the previous owner, Tony Martin, about his experiences with any ghosts in the house. He said that his only experiences had been with a pair of horseshoes. While sitting on a chair one day, he had gotten up, turned around, and seen two horseshoes lying on the chair! He kept the shoes, and now has them hanging on his wall as a reminder of that strange experience.

"People in the town of Lincoln tell me they are familiar with the ghosts of the barrack . . ."

On the property, there is one old barrack that was brought over years ago from Fort Stanton. The barrack was removed from the fort and brought to the property for use as a storage shed. My ghostly experience with this building took place one day. I was outside, just a few yards away from the barrack. I heard a man's voice call out my name. I listened closely, and sure enough, I heard my name being called out. As I approached the small barrack, I heard the muffled voices of men in conversation. Try as I might, I was unable to make out their speech. I looked inside and saw no one. This has been a long-standing phenomenon, which has happened to me several times. People in the town of Lincoln tell me they are familiar with the ghosts of the barrack, and in fact, the stories of it being haunted began when James and Sophronia Ramey owned the property many years ago.

The Mill House on the property is also haunted. The Mill House was originally built in the 1880s on the Rio Bonito River to grind corn from the Ellises' fields. In 1906, Dr. Laws dismantled and moved the Mill House to its present location, in the back of the main house. The house was then used as quarters for the nurses who assisted Dr. Laws in his practice. After Dr. Laws had left, it was used as a bunkhouse for the railroad workers and a lodge hall for The Woodmen of the World.

"The Mill House on the property is also haunted."

Not long ago, six women who were staff from the University of New Mexico rented the Mill House. They informed my wife and me about the sound of footsteps they kept hearing throughout the house. However, one major incident frightened them the most. A large, mounted deer head that I had very carefully hung on top of the stairs mysteriously came off its hook, and rolled all the way down the stairs! When I went to investigate, I found the deer head on the floor with the hanging hook still attached to the back of its head. I inspected the wall where it had hung undisturbed for weeks before. The large nail I personally had hammered into the wall was still there! I can't explain why it fell off the wall. The only way it could have fallen was for someone, with a lot of upper-arm strength, to have actually lifted it off the nail. The women had much better things to do, I'm sure.

The story does not end there. A few weeks later, we had a couple spending the night at the Mill House. They actually witnessed carefully stacked dishes and pots fly off shelves on their own and hit the floor!

It's been only five weeks since we last experienced or heard anything usual. Our B&B is a wonderful place to visit and relax. Jinny's cooking is well known throughout southeastern New Mexico. There is much tranquility to be gained from staying at our B&B. A ghost now and then, although not planned, is unique to the experience. Don't you think?

"They kept hearing the sound of footsteps throughout the house."

★　★　★

I interviewed Dori in her office at the Lincoln Museum. My initial impression of Dori was that sitting before me was a quiet and reserved person. As I started my interview, her personality soon changed. Dori became spirited and very open about the strange and unique experiences that both she and her family had encountered at their home. There have been times during my interviews when I have had the impression the person being interviewed is having fun with me or not even telling the truth. Then I have ended the interview and, having thanked them for their time, I have moved on. My interview with Dori left me in no doubt that she was more than honest and sincere. She invited me to visit her home and to follow up by interviewing her mother, if I felt the need to do so.

Interviewing people for their personal encounters with ghosts can sometimes be surprising and scary. Interviewing Dori proved to be one of those moments that caused me to pause and think about the evil that lurks just beyond the short reach of sanity.

I asked Dori, "Why do you still choose to live in the house, after all that has happened to you and your family?" I'm sure Dori's answer will surprise you as much as it did me.

DORI W. SALAZAR'S FIRST STORY

I've lived in Lincoln for more than 15 years, and am currently employed at our local town's museum. My title is Historical Interpreter. My personal experience with a ghost, or ghosts, took place at my home here in Lincoln. What I experienced at the house really upset me and my family. But, before I go any further, I'd like to share a bit of the history of the house with you.

The house is located about three miles west of the center of Lincoln. The dirt road, which leads off the main paved highway, can be bumpy and, in wet weather, slippery. The original first floor of the house was built in the 1850s and is made of adobe brick. The second level was added on seven years ago and is wood-frame construction. The house and 40-acre property belonged to my great-grandfather, Yginio Salazar. He was known to have fought with Billy the Kid, and his is the house my family now lives in. We know there are Native American burial sites on the property and all over the general area. On our property, we found an Indian Pit House that dates from AD 900. An archaeologist came from the state of Delaware and did the investigation and research. Having finished, he returned to Delaware with a Native American skeleton.

When we were living on the original first-floor portion of the house, there was no electricity or running water. One day, my sister and I were alone in the house when we heard the doors to our bedrooms open and close on their own. Sometimes, we were in the living room and could hear the springs of our beds making noise, as if someone were jumping or lying on the beds. We also heard the sound of footsteps walking across the floor. We had no idea who, or what, this was about. These incidents took place about three or more times a week, and we noticed the sounds always began at sundown. We told our parents about the things that my sister and I were experiencing. They just took it in stride, I guess, because living in an old house, my parents assumed it must have a ghost or two, so why give it much thought. The noises lasted for several months, but as soon as the construction had begun on the second-story addition, the sounds ceased. However, this was not to last. Numerous other things began to take place.

After the new addition had been completed, I was alone one evening when I suddenly heard the kitchen faucet being turned on. I cautiously walked into the kitchen. As I entered the kitchen, the sound of running water stopped. I got up to the sink and it was dry. I didn't see water anywhere, not even a drop! Many times my family would be in the living room watching television, when suddenly we'd hear the chairs in the kitchen moving. My father was standing in the kitchen one day and actually saw the drawer that

Yginio Salazar, one of the last survivors of the Lincoln County War. He died in 1936 at the age of 78.

held the silverware open and close on its own. At other times, we heard the loud ticktock of what sounded like an antique windup clock. We did not own a clock like that.

My father, who tended to rationalize a lot of the strange occurrences, had a quick change of mind one night. He was awakened by the spirit of his grandfather, the original owner of the property, who was standing by his bed. My father described the spirit as wearing a dark coat, and on his head he wore a rounded hat. The spirit just stood there, staring at my father. When my father made a move towards the ghost, the spirit moved suddenly away, and eventually faded. After this experience, my father took the other examples of ghosts in our house much more seriously.

It wasn't long before I heard more footsteps walking about the house; only this time, I also heard the sound of a heavy fabric being dragged across the floor, something resembling a woman's skirt. When I ran to my bedroom, the footsteps followed right behind me! At the time, I had a small poodle, and my dog ran from me and hid in the closet. After this experience, my sister and I both heard the footsteps, and often, we actually saw a woman's long skirt move around the rooms and then disappear! It was a white skirt. We tried to keep this to ourselves, but soon we decided to tell our mother.

My sister and I were out in the backyard one day, when our mother came running out the door. She was excited and had a terrified look on her face. We asked her what was wrong; she explained she had just seen a ghost standing in the doorway of the kitchen. It was a tall woman, wearing a long skirt. The whole figure was glowing in a white light. It frightened her so much she ran out of the house. My sister and I explained our own encounters with the ghost to our mother, and right then, we knew we were not imagining things.

"It frightened her so much she ran out of the house."

I have also seen the spirit of a young girl in my room. She has appeared as I was walking up the stairs in front of my bedroom door. I looked up and there she was! She appeared to be about seven years old and was wearing a white dress. I couldn't make out her face because it was a blur. I also had a little stuffed teddy bear, which I kept in my bedroom on a shelf. Whenever the little girl's ghost appeared to me, I found my teddy bear off the shelf and lying in the middle of my bedroom floor. To this day, I still have the teddy bear, but I haven't seen the little girl's ghost.

A couple of years later, when I was a young woman, the ghosts in the house got so bad that I had to move out of my bedroom for about a year and share my sister's room. We didn't have a door to our bedroom. In place of a door we strung a cord between the doorjambs and draped a blanket over the cord to serve as a curtain. There were times when we sensed movement and saw the impression of hands or fists hitting the blanket. We stared in terror as the blanket visibly shook with each blow the ghostly hands delivered.

One night, I woke up to discover a large painting lying on top of me! The painting originally hung on the wall in my bedroom, and now here it was on top of me! It was a large, heavy painting I had painted on 3/4-inch plyboard. This startled me. Who did this to me, and how could this happen without my noticing it? To this day, I have not been able to explain it.

Another night, I awoke from a sound sleep to the noise of loud footsteps by my bed. I got out of bed and turned on the light. As I stood there looking around the room, a large artist's eraser I kept on a table with my other art supplies suddenly came flying towards me. Luckily, I saw it coming and managed to move out of the way, so it hit the wall next to my head.

My sister had frequently seen the figure of a woman entering her bedroom. This ghost woman, dressed in dark clothing, would approach her bed and begin to tuck the blankets in around her. My sister sat up in bed, and as soon as the figure was close enough, she reached out to touch the ghostly woman. The ghostly figure pulled away and disappeared! As my sister further explained, she didn't feel the least bit frightened by this ghost. In fact, she felt a sense of motherly love emanate from her.

On the other hand, one night, both my sister and I got the fright of our lives. During the time I was sharing my sister's room, we experienced a very evil thing. While asleep in our separate beds, we were suddenly awakened by the presence of a hand on our throats. A powerful force grabbed hold of both our throats and yanked us up into a sitting position! Both of us were violently lifted upright at the exact same instant! We were left speechless and terrified! We remained in this invisible hold for a few seconds and then, just as suddenly, we were released. It would be impossible to try to describe the thoughts in our minds. We knew then there were definitely two opposite forces in the house. One force was loving and protective, which needed to tuck us into bed, and one wanted to cause terror and mischief.

Another night, about four years ago, my sister and I were in our bedroom when suddenly I saw a flash of metal. An old, brass, antique oil lamp appeared out of nowhere, suspended above my bed. I reached out to touch it, but it disappeared! This happened while all the bedroom lights were on.

"A powerful force grabbed both of our throats . . ."

Before I forget, I want to tell you about the experiences my family has had with our dogs.

Our dogs were kept outdoors, and they had the most unusual reactions to the ghosts. Sometimes, they just gathered outside my parents' window and barked at something that only they were able to see. We thought at times something was attacking them because of the excitement and intensity of their barks. Apparently, the ghost in particular hated one of our dogs, a Saint Bernard. Each evening at four, this dog would bark and bark. Almost immediately, he would cry out as if something was attacking him. Then, our dog would chase this invisible thing around and out the yard. My family witnessed this on numerous occasions. We never saw anything that made us believe our dog was chasing "anything living." It was the strangest thing to witness.

We knew our house had evil spirits and some nice ones. The nice ones were like the little girl I saw from time to time. But there was no mistaking the evil ones. We felt the presence of a big, dark entity. This "thing" would physically move us out of its way, as it moved around the inside of the house. At times, it would prevent us from leaving out the front door! It would block the doorway with a heavy, cold presence. We had to walk around this presence that felt ice-cold to the touch. We also knew it was evil because it had an aversion to religious things.

In our house, we had an antique statue of the Virgin Mary, which my mother had placed on a shelf. When we returned from church one Sunday afternoon, the sense of the dark, cold presence was everywhere in the house. Then we found the statue broken into pieces on the floor. The feeling of evil had been strongest in the house right before we left for church. One time, when we had returned from church, the rosaries my sister and I had hung on the wall above each of our beds had been removed. We found them tied into knots on the floor! Prior to this happening, my sister's rosary had disappeared from its place on the wall. For several weeks it was missing. Then, one day, I was in the bedroom and right from out of nowhere it was thrown at me.

Today, I am an artist, and I recall the time when I had several completed paintings stored in my bedroom closet. I decided to look at one particular painting of a little boy and a dog. I opened the closet door, and as I brought out the first canvas, I saw a large red blotch of something on it. It was a red powdery substance, which I was not familiar with. Luckily, the other paintings were untouched. I took a wet towel and as hard as I tried, the red stain would not come off. I went back to the closet and searched for the source of this pigment, but I was not able to find it. I looked once again at my other paintings, and was I in shock! The rest of the paintings were now covered in this red substance! Just a few minutes before they had been as clean as could be. I knew that this was just another example of the ghosts in the house.

I remember one Christmas we had a nine-foot Christmas tree in our living room. It was decorated with beautiful glass ornaments with sparkling rhinestones. We left one evening to attend a Christmas celebration. Returning to the house, as we opened the door and entered, we immediately felt the now-familiar presence of something evil. Entering the living room, we saw all the beautiful decorations scattered on the floor! Something had not only removed the ornaments, but broken them all over the house!

About three years ago, my parents decided to contact a local priest from the nearby city of Carizozo to perform an exorcism. The priest

"A woman friend saw a dark shadow on the stairs . . ."

told us to document our experiences by keeping notes of our encounters. We kept these written records in a notebook in the kitchen. One day, the notes disappeared. We searched the house and found them, all crumpled up, in a trash can! No one knows how the notebook with the torn, crumpled pages ended up in the trash can, but we suspect it was the ghost.

We were all present when the priest arrived to conduct the exorcism. My family and followed the priest around the house as he blessed every wall and closet with incense and Holy Water. Nothing unusual happened during the exorcism. But, I remember the priest saying, "Sometimes a house blessing makes the spirits angrier, and makes things worst!"

Although lately we haven't experienced the ghosts that I have already mentioned, my father did see a ghostly dark dog appear to him in the house. This dog leisurely walks from room to room, then disappears. We also have friends who have been frightened by shadows of people. We were having a Christmas party one evening, and a woman friend, who lives about 30 miles away, saw a dark shadow on the stairs leading up to the second floor. She nearly had a heart attack! Other friends who have also seen the shadow refuse to visit our home after dark.

I know this might sound weird, but I do miss all the activity in the house. I guess I got used to having the ghosts around. My father also thinks the same way I do; he says they kept him entertained. My sister, however, wants nothing more to do with them.

DORI W. SALAZAR'S SECOND STORY

I'll tell you about another house in Lincoln that I personally know to be haunted. It's called the Ellis Store and Company. I experienced things in a house on that property named The Mill House. The current owners are the Vigil family, but I used to take care of the building before they moved into town. In fact, I used to live in The Mill House. I would hear, on numerous occasions, the voices of women laughing and talking in the kitchen. I would be in other rooms of the house, and these voices were so obviously loud that I would walk into the kitchen and expect to see someone. Of course, the kitchen would be empty. At the same time, I would hear several doors throughout the house open and slam closed on their own. One night, my mother came to stay with me at the house. The owners had gone on their vacation to Europe, and my mother had decided to spend a few days with me on the property.

It was about five in the evening when my mother and I decided to take a walk outside. We had been walking the property when suddenly I spotted smoke coming out the top of the chimney. I knew no one else was on the property, so we both assumed it had to be illegal trespassers. I went to the next property, and asked the man if he would go inside the house and investigate. We all walked into the house, and it was empty.

There was no hint of a fire being started in the fireplace; it was cold to the touch! As we walked through the empty house, I noticed that down the hallway, where the stairs to the second floor began, was the long light cord hanging from the ceiling. I noticed it because it was swinging vigorously, as if someone had just pulled on it. We checked the house from top to bottom, but found it empty. When the owners returned from their trip, I asked them about the smoke we had seen, and if there had been any recent construction to the chimneys, which would have caused smoke to be vented in an unused fireplace. They were surprised to hear about the smoking chimneys we had all seen. He said, "Dori, the fireplaces have been cemented and rocked up now for more than 20 years. You couldn't have seen any smoke; the fireplaces are unusable!"

★   ★   ★

I interviewed Walter at his home, which he shares with his pleasant wife, Nora. After a short conversation with Walter, I was able to sense that he is very well versed in the history of southeastern New Mexico and the town of Lincoln. Both Walter and Nora are well-known locals in their small historic town. Nora had the good fortune of being recently interviewed for a Public Broadcast Television documentary about the life of Billy the Kid, and, no wonder, since she currently conducts walking tours of Lincoln. Both Walter and Nora granted me the pleasure of interviewing them one late rainy afternoon in their adobe home. What follows is that interview.

WALTER HENN'S STORY

My wife Nora and I have lived in the little town of Lincoln for 30 years. Because of the town's strict zoning ordinances regarding new buildings, there have not been any noticeable major changes in the town. It still retains the charm and character of the Old West. When we moved into Lincoln, the first house we lived in was located right in the center of town. The building was made of old adobe bricks and constructed around 1890. In this house I had my experience with a ghost.

One evening, as my wife, Nora, and I were getting ready to go out for dinner, I gathered some clean clothes, arranged them on the bed, and jumped into the shower. Nora was in another part of the house. After finishing my shower, I dried off, and wrapped a towel around my waist. I turned off the bathroom light and walked into the bedroom. I reached for the bedroom light switch and clicked it on. Suddenly, some activity in the corner of the room caught my eye. I noticed the clear figure of an elderly woman, rocking back and forth on a rocking chair! She was wearing a Victorian-style, dark green, long dress. Her dress had long sleeves and a high collar, trimmed with white lace. I was obviously startled to see this strange woman in our bedroom. As I held my towel tightly around my waist, I called out to my wife, Nora. There was no answer. I turned once again to look at the figure on the chair. As the ghostly woman stopped rocking, she turned her head slowly in my direction. Our eyes met and I froze. She seemed startled. Apparently, she was as surprised to see me as I was to see her! In an instant, she had disappeared! This whole experience caught me off guard, and I sat on the bed trying to compose myself. Just then, Nora came into the room and I explained to her what had just taken place.

Shortly thereafter, I asked some of the old-timers in town if they knew some history about the house and, in particular, anything about an older woman. They described a woman who fit the description of the ghost I had seen in my bedroom. This woman lived in the house and was the sister of the original owner, Dr. Wood. Dr. Wood's sister came to live in Lincoln after moving from her home in Michigan. That's all I was told. My own personal belief is that this woman is the ghost I saw in my bedroom.

These days, I'm not interested in seeing any more ghosts. The town of Lincoln has had such a violent past, I'm sure a few ghosts will continue to turn up now and then.

ARTESIA

The "Valley of the Pecos" was discovered by settlers over 100 years ago. There was a meadow-like oasis called the *Bosque Grande*, or the valley of the "Big Trees." In this valley, near the edge of the great *Llano Estacado*, were New Mexico's Thousand Hills, land that was known for perhaps the best cattle grazing in the state. John Chisum, a Texas cattle king, along with his drivers, pushed thousands of wild Texas Longhorns across the Staked Plains and up the Pecos Valley. This was the beginning of New Mexico's cattle industry.

The railroad, too, played an important part in the development of this area. In 1889, the charter for the first railroad that was to come through Artesia was procured by J. J. Hagerman, a Pecos Valley pioneer who did much to promote development of this area of New Mexico.

Prior to the influx of the "strange men with blue eyes," this land was the ancestral domain of both the Comanche and Apache peoples. The area also witnessed the footprints of the notorious outlaw Billy the Kid, and other outlaws who were "as common as rattlesnakes."

The first settler, Union soldier John Truitt, homesteaded along the famous Chisum Trail at Chisum Springs Camp, which is now just three blocks from the heart of Artesia's main business district. When the Pecos Valley Railroad was completed in 1894, Artesia was known as Miller's Siding. The community had another name change when promoter Baldwin Stegman settled in Miller's Siding and married Sallie Roberts, the niece of the famous cattleman John Chisum. Together, they established a post office, naming the town Stegman.

In 1903, the town adopted a new name, Artesia, for its artesian wells. That same year the Artesia Townsite Company joined with the Artesia Improvement Company to drill the first Artesian well in the community. By November, a well 830 feet deep with a six-inch casing was completed three miles outside of town, making it the world's largest artesian well at that time. The age of the big water well had come, and each week saw a new well surpassing the previous one in size. From 1905–1907, ample water for irrigation brought over 1,200 people to the area's farms.

For Artesia, 1923 was a record year, when two men from Robinson, Illinois, hearing of the oil traces in the Artesian well, brought a steam-powered, cable-tool oil rig to drill a well, Illinois No. 1. After several dry holes, Van Welch and Tom Flynn were ready to pack up their drilling rig, when Martin Yates II acquired state leases east of the Pecos River. Yates talked the two into drilling one more well, Illinois No. 2, which was more promising. The next well produced gas. While not marketable then, it supplied energy for the equipment on future wells. By April of 1924, the company brought in the well Illinois No. 3, which was the first producing well in New Mexico's oil-rich Permian Basin.

The first urban renewal project in New Mexico, the Eagle Draw, was turned into a 35-acre city park, which today continues to catch excess water in times of heavy downpours and provides an added recreational facility.

★ ★ ★

I interviewed Phyliss behind the waiter's station at the local K-Bob's restaurant one afternoon. She lit a cigarette, and quickly described the ghost experiences that she had had in her Artesia home. "I was a little disturbed," she said. "I knew there was definitely something going on that was not right in the house." Thirty minutes and two cigarettes later, our interview ended. Phyliss returned to her waitressing job, and taking customers' food orders. It would be interesting to witness her customers' reactions if they were told they had just been served by a haunted-house survivor!

PHYLISS A. WILLIAMS'S STORY

I've lived in Artesia for 21 years, and have been working as a waitress at our local K–Bob's restaurant since the day it opened, three years ago. I had my first experience with an unfriendly ghost about 17 years ago, at a little house located at 606 Washington Street. I was renting the house at the time, and, let me tell you, my roommate and our children experienced some strange things in that house!

Early one evening, my female roommate and I were in the living room of the house, relaxing and drinking iced tea. Our children were in their beds, sound asleep. We had eaten dinner an hour or so before, washed the dishes, and were now relaxing. Suddenly, we heard a loud crashing, and the sound of breaking glass coming from the kitchen. We both rose from our chairs and rushed into the kitchen. We saw all of our water glasses had been broken and were in a pile of sharp pieces in the sink. The cupboard door, located about five feet away from the sink, was wide open. The dishes stacked within the cupboard, next to where the glasses had been, remained undisturbed. Who could have done this and why? The kitchen door was locked and the kids, who were at the opposite end of the house asleep, could not have caused such a mess. It was a mystery to us. As we carefully cleaned up the broken glass, we considered the possibility that there was a ghost in the house. What else could have, in just a few seconds, carried all our glasses from the cupboard, broken them in the kitchen, and then gotten away without being seen?

It was then that we began to notice other strange goings-on in the house. We heard the sound of footsteps at all hours of the day and night throughout the house. Very soon after, other unusual things began to convince us that our house was haunted.

With a baby in the house, we had toys and clothing, rattles and blankets, which were strictly for the baby's use. We noticed that some of the baby's items were disappearing for no reason. I remember having placed a box of clothes on a top shelf in a closet. A few hours later, I returned and discovered that the box had just disappeared! Also that day, I recall storing the baby's blanket in a drawer and, when I returned for it, it too had disappeared. It was the strangest thing. I noticed that none of the other children's belongings had been disturbed, only the baby's. Of course, I asked the children about the missing blanket and box of baby clothes. They answered that they were innocent. The baby's items disappeared so often that I had to go out and purchase more of the same items. Then, these newly purchased items would also disappear! Not only was this becoming weird, but it was costing me money.

One evening, I was outside talking to a neighbor. I told her of my experience in the house with the disappearing baby clothing. She told me about something that had taken place at the house prior to my moving in. I was so disturbed by what she told me, I decided to speak with a friend of a friend who worked for the local police department in town. She was a dispatcher for the department and gave me added details, which supported my neighbor's story. Apparently, there was a married couple who had occupied the house before I moved in. There was an argument between the husband and his pregnant wife about infidelity. The husband became so angry he killed her in the kitchen of the house. Along with her death, their unborn child was also murdered!

Everything came together for me when I heard this. It occurred to me that perhaps the violent energy of the murders still remained in the house! I also believe that the disappearance of the toys and clothing might have been caused by the spirit of the murdered woman, who missed the baby she never had given birth to.

"He killed her in the kitchen of the house."

My experiences in that house made a ghost believer out of me. Since I moved out of that house, I've had no other ghostly experiences. As far as I know, the manifestations might still be going on. The ghost who took my baby's clothes was a mother, like me, wanting to share her love with her baby. What more can I say?

ROSWELL

Roswell, located in the Pecos River Valley, is the largest city in southeastern New Mexico, with a population of over 50,000. In the 1860s, this valley, at the confluence of the Rio Hondo and Pecos Rivers, was abundant with grama grass and water. Thus, it was a favorite stopover for cattlemen from neighboring Texas. On their journey north, these cattlemen drove their livestock on the Goodnight-Loving Trail. John Chisum, a Texas cattleman, enjoyed this area to such a degree, he chose a site six miles south of present-day Roswell to build a ranch. (The Chisum Ranch, now owned by Cornell University and maintained as it was in the 1870s, may be visited by appointment.) From this ranch he drove his cattle west. The trail he used became known as the Chisum Trail. Eventually Chisum became a well-known cattle baron and controlled the territory from Fort Sumner to the Texas border.

The name Roswell can be attributed to Van C. Smith. Smith was one of the town's first businessmen, who named it in honor of his father. Agriculture played a major role in Roswell's beginnings, but in the 1940s and 50s Roswell's economy changed, when the U.S. government established the Roswell Army Flying School. In 1948 the school was renamed, and officially designated Walker Air Force Base (named after Brigadier General Kenneth Walker, of Cerrillos, New Mexico, who lost his life in the South Pacific during World War II).

Among the weird and wonderful attractions that present-day Roswell has to offer the public, are two museums dedicated to Unidentified

Flying Objects (UFOs). The International UFO Museum and Research Center maintains a growing collection of UFO material. (Material related to this interesting subject can be viewed at the museum by way of displays, videos, and written background histories.) The second museum related to UFOs is the Enigma Museum. This museum has a large display that is dedicated to the 1947 "Roswell Incident." (Allegedly a UFO was recovered near Roswell, and the bodies of the aliens were also retrieved.) This museum also contains numerous information on the study of UFOs.

★   ★   ★

I interviewed Mr. Agustin Nevarez at his home, where he and his family had experienced the ghost of a man. Although the Nevarez family experiences took place 12 years ago, Agustin remembers all the details very clearly. Agustin made me promise not to reveal the location of his home. It's currently for sale, and he would not wish to have a potential buyer scared away. What follows is one of the scarier ghost stories of southern New Mexico.

AGUSTIN NEVAREZ'S STORY

My family consisted of two brothers and four sisters. At 20, I was the oldest child. Soon after my parents had purchased the house, my mother noticed that my younger, eight-year-old brother's behavior had changed. It was increasingly difficult for her to wake him each morning for school, and his teacher told her he frequently fell asleep at his desk. One morning at the breakfast table, she decided to ask him his reason for being so tired.

My brother hesitated, and then told us that a "scary man" had been visiting him at night. His reply caught us off guard. I asked him, "What man are you talking about?" He said, "I don't know who he is, he just comes into my room and hangs around." My mother cautiously asked, "Does he have a name?" He answered, "I don't know who he is, but he scares me and doesn't let me sleep." We could see what my brother was describing was affecting him enough to make him uncomfortable. My mother attempted to comfort my brother by telling him that she would stay the night with him in his room. She promised that the man would not bother him again.

That night my mother kept her word. She did not intend to spend the entire night with him, only to reassure him. With the bedroom light turned off, she lay next to him and stroked his hair. Not long after, comforted by his mother's presence, he fell asleep. Just before she was about to leave my brother's side, a noise by the bedroom door caught her attention. She looked towards the door and noticed something moving. Then the shadowy silhouette of a man slowly appeared in the doorway. She was terrified! This ghostly figure took a few steps towards the bed. My mother lay motionless. The figure moved closer, and just before it got within arm's length of the bed, she whispered, "I don't know who you are, but leave my baby alone, and get out of my house!" The figure slowly backed away, and then disappeared.

The following morning, not wanting to alarm my brother and the rest of her children, my mother kept the experience of the night before to herself. However, she wasted no time in speaking to her *comadre* (girlfriend) about the ghost, who advised her to seek the help of a priest. After discussing the matter with my father, my mother and her *comadre* visited the church in town, and asked a priest if he would bless the house. The priest agreed and blessed the house within a few days. The following night, all seemed at peace in our house. My brother did not experience any more visits from "the visitor."

About three days after the house blessing, my father's brother and his wife came over for dinner. After dinner, at about 8 p.m., my father and uncle were playing a game of poker in the kitchen; everyone else was in the living room watching television. Suddenly, there was a knock at the kitchen door. My uncle, who was sitting nearest the kitchen door, reached over and opened it. There was no one there. My father said, "It must be a neighbor's kid playing a joke." They returned to their card game, but once again there was another knock at the door. Again, my uncle opened it, and again, no one was there. Becoming irritated, my father called me into the kitchen and told me his plan to catch the mischievous kid. I was to go into the backyard and climb onto the roof of the house. He thought the reason they had not seen anyone at the door was that the mischievous child doing the prank must be on the roof, knocking on the door below with his arm extended. I took a flashlight, shined it all over the roof, and found no one. When I got back to my father with this information, they told me that while I had been on the roof, there had been another knock at the door, and they asked if I had seen the kid. I told them I had searched all over the roof, and I hadn't seen anyone. They seemed puzzled.

My uncle was not going to let this kid get away with his prank. So, he placed his hand on the doorknob and twisted it until it unlocked with a "click" sound. He didn't open the door; he just held the knob, ready to pull it open. I was told to have a finger on the light switch, and at my uncle's command, I would turn on the outdoor light.

Sure enough, there came another knock on the door. My uncle gave the command, and I turned the light on. He swiftly pulled the door open. My father went outside and looked around, but there was no one to be found. He returned to the kitchen doorway, scratching his head in puzzlement. All the while, my uncle was still holding on to the knob of the opened door. Suddenly, we heard three knocks on the door! We looked at each other in amazement and disbelief. It was knocking by itself! My father's eyes opened wide, and then he dashed into the kitchen. We just about died with fright! My uncle slammed the door shut. After much discussion, our parents knew that we were dealing with something supernatural, something that didn't want to leave our house.

The next day, my father phoned and spoke to a *curandera* (traditional faith healer), who lived in El Paso, about our situation. He informed her about the incidents with the shadowy ghost in my brother's bedroom and about the knocking door. She reassured my father she would pay us a visit in two days.

The following night, my parents decided to go to the grocery store. I went along with them, but my 17-year-old sister decided to stay at home and care for my other siblings. My mother told her we would return in about two hours.

After purchasing the groceries, we returned to the house at about 7 p.m. As we drove up to our house, we immediately noticed all the lights were out. This seemed odd, because it was early in the evening, and usually the kids would be watching their favorite television program. When we got to the front door and turned the knob, we discovered the door was locked. My father whistled to the kids inside to open the door, but there was no response. Everything about this situation seemed odd. I crawled in through the open kitchen window and returned to the front door to let my parents inside.

As we turned on the lights, we immediately noticed that the living room was in complete disarray! The television was on with no one watching it. But the strangest thing was that our large 9' x 12' living-room rug was haphazardly gathered against one wall of the room with the love seat pushed up against it! We quickly walked through the darkened house, opening doors and turning on lights as we went.

When I reached my parents' bedroom, I attempted to open the door, but there was something on the other side, blocking me from opening it. Suddenly, I heard my brother and sisters scream! I managed to open the door a bit and looked inside. I noticed my parents' dresser drawer was blocking the door. Hearing their children's screams, my parents came running to the bedroom, and with the three of us pushing, we opened the door.

The bedroom was also a disaster! My brother and sisters were crying and huddled together. After realizing who we were, the children began to calm down, while my older sister told my parents what had happened.

She said it was not long after my parents and I had left for the grocery store that the children gathered in the living room to watch television. My sister noticed an empty rocking chair that was next to the television had begun to rock on its own! At that same moment, my three sisters and brother were sitting on a five-foot-long love seat, which had also suddenly begun to move. The rug and love seat were being dragged by some unseen energy, while carrying my brother and sisters to one side of the living room! When the love seat came to a stop, they heard a man's wicked laughter! The laughter was so loud it drowned out the sound of the television. My older sister ordered everyone to run to our parents' bedroom, where they barricaded the door with the dresser drawer. The next thing they did was remove the mattress from my parents' bed and lean it up against the wall. They used the mattress as a shield to hide behind. Then they waited, anxious and afraid, and hoped for our quick return.

The next day, the *curandera*, whom my father had recently contacted, came to our house. Accompanying her was her friend. This friend was introduced to us as an apprentice *curandera*, and was carrying a large paper bag. As soon as the *curandera* entered our front door, she said, "*Aye una cosa muy mala en este hogar. Bendito seya Dios; vamos a quitar este demonio!*" ("There is something very bad in this house. Blessed is God; we will remove this demon!") Each woman made the sign of the cross, then the *curandera* told my parents it would be best to start right away with the house blessing.

They had us close all the windows and curtains. Then, we were instructed to gather in the living room. Each of my family members took their turn sitting in a single chair that the *curandera* had placed in the center of the dimly lit room. She asked her *curandera* friend for the paper bag she was holding, reached inside, and gave the seated person a small black crucifix to hold. While each person was seated, prayers were recited, and a bowl of burning incense was passed over, around and under that person. A branch of a strong-smelling herb, *ruda* (rue), was also brought out of the paper bag. With this branch, the *curandera* ritually "whipped" us, all the time praying the Hail Mary. I know that there were other "things" that she did, but I've forgotten them. She closed her eyes and said, "*Aye halgo arriba en el techo; yo lo siento que esta entremedio de el techo y la pader.*" ("There is something in the ceiling; I 'feel' that something is between the roof and the ceiling.") My father handed me a flashlight and instructed me to go up into the crawl space of the ceiling. I was not told what I would find, but I was told to report anything unusual I might see.

I was crawling all over the ceiling, being very careful not to drop the flashlight, when suddenly the light beam in front of me landed on a small cardboard box. I grabbed the box, and handed it to my father.

Having placed it on the kitchen table, we noticed that it was wrapped in red tape. The *curandera* took a quick look at the box and then spitefully spat on it, saying, "*Esto es!*" ("This is it!")

She told everyone to have a seat. She asked my mother for a kitchen knife and then with the knife, opened the box. The box was filled with black-and-white photographs. Since I was the oldest, I was permitted to view the pictures, but we

"Each woman made the sign of the cross . . ."

were told by the *curandera* not to touch them. The *curandera* held them up for us to view. They were pictures of a naked Anglo couple in all types of obscene poses. We did not recognize these people, and didn't have a clue as to why they had posed for such photos. Most of the pictures were of the woman in a kitchen scene. As we looked at the pictures more closely, my father stated out loud, "That woman is in our kitchen!" Sure enough, the photographs were taken in our kitchen! It was not difficult to make out the pattern of the sink tiles, and the position of the window in the photos. It was definitely our kitchen in those pictures.

Immediately, the *curandera* asked me to build a small fire in the backyard. When I had finished with this task, we followed her to the backyard as she carried the dusty box. Her assistant *curandera* located two large stones in the yard, and then presented them to the *curandera*. As the fire was burning brightly, the *curandera* placed each photo on top of one of the stones, and with the other, hit the photo, saying, "*El poder del Senor, es como esta pierda. En el nombre del Espirito Santo, vete de esta casa, Santanas!*" ("The power of God is like this rock. In the name of the Holy Spirit, leave this house, Satan!") Having recited this, she tossed the photos into the fire, one by one, and within an instant, they were consumed. It was as if the photos were made of gunpowder, or gasoline. As soon as they got close to the flame, "poof," they disappeared. Not even a trace of ash was left!

About a week later, a neighbor came to our house and spoke to my mother about another neighbor who lived two blocks away. Apparently, this second neighbor had heard about the trouble we had experienced in the house by way of the neighborhood grapevine. The woman wanted to tell my mother about our house's previous owners. My mother was obviously curious to hear what this woman had to say, so she made contact with her and invited her to the house. The woman seemed to be very honest and sincere.

She informed my mother that roughly 10 years prior to our moving into the house, a couple from Texas had occupied it. The husband was a photographer. These people didn't speak any Spanish, so they kept to themselves. They lived in the house for about 11 months. One evening, the police arrived and found the murdered body of the man. He had been killed in the living room from a gunshot to the head. The wife had disappeared, so the police suspected she was the killer.

This was basically all the information the neighbor told my mother. She had received this information from her brother-in-law, who happened to be working for the Roswell police department at the time the crime took place. This new information definitely shed light on the possible cause of our ghostly experiences. Just the knowledge that a person had been murdered in our living room was disturbing enough! It also explained the pictures we had discovered in the roof of the house.

Since that time, we have not had any further disturbances in the house. My whole family knows of the power in the spiritual faith of *curanderas*. Some people might think that because these faith healers use herbs, incense, and candles, they are old fashioned. I know better. Believe me, I know better!

CARLSBAD

The Spanish explorers visited this area in 1534. This area in New Mexico remained the domain of the Comanche and Apache Native Americans until after the Civil War, when the first great Texas cattle herds moved in. Then, in the late 1880s, the era of irrigation began, and Carlsbad became the center of a rich agricultural and ranching industry.

From the city's south and northwest boundaries, roads pass the natural brown Ocotillo Hills, which are the start of the rugged Guadalupe Mountains. From the east or the southwest, roads travel over the blue Pecos River, which forms the twisting eastern border of the city. Carlsbad's hills break the high plains of the rest of the region. Because of the city's both abundant water and history, Carlsbad's location is different from its neighbors.

The city was founded on September 15, 1888. Lillian Green, the daughter of one of the area's early promoters, made it official when she bashed a bottle of champagne against the bank of the Pecos River, to christen New Mexico Territory's newest city: Eddy. Charles B. Eddy, after whom Eddy County is named, sought to use the life-giving Pecos River as an investment magnet. He sought funds from a Swiss bank and, through various advertisements, tried to attract European settlers to Eddy's clean air and sunny climate.

Eleven years later, by a vote of 83 to 43, the city residents voted to rename their community Carlsbad, after the famous European health resort, Karlsbad, in Bohemia (then Czechoslovakia). The mineral content and healing properties of the water in the two cities, continents apart, were virtually identical. Carlsbad Spring still flows today, in the northern corner of the city near the Pecos Flume. When rebuilt in 1902, the flume was the largest concrete structure in the world, and today it still carries vital irrigation water.

In 1922, an organized expedition explored a large cavern southwest of the town. The cavern was so impressive that President Coolidge proclaimed it Carlsbad Caverns National Monument the following year. In 1930, it was designated as a National Park. Internationally famous Carlsbad Caverns National Park makes the city a location that is annually visited by hundreds of thousands of tourists.

★ ★ ★

I interviewed Nicolas in one corner of the Carlsbad City Library. Nicolas is an 86-year-old man who has lived in Carlsbad all his life. He told me about his experience with the ghost of Stanley Meeker. Mr. Meeker, a dwarf, lived in Carlsbad for a short time, until his untimely, terrible death in 1914. Nicolas values the memories of his friend Stanley Meeker and said, "He was a good little man; too bad he had to die the way he did. I've always thought of him over the years." What follows is the story of friendship and hope in the desert land of southeastern New Mexico.

NICOLAS HOLGUIN'S STORY

Stanley Meeker came from Austin, Texas, in the year 1908. He was on his way to Tucson, Arizona, where he planned to start a fabric and mercantile business. Stanley arrived in Carlsbad one windy, dusty afternoon on the train from Pecos, Texas. Meeker always spoke about the day being the dustiest day on earth. "My belly filled with sand, before the dinner bell. Good thing; it kept me from blowing back to Texas!"

As soon as he had settled into his hotel room, Stanley Meeker took a short stroll around the town. He was so impressed with the local community and economic possibilities that he decided to stay in Carlsbad. He told me that the mountains and the Pecos River sold him on the land. I spent a lot of time with Meeker, helping him to communicate with the Spanish people in town. He bought a small lot of land on the southern portion of the Pecos River, right off of Guadalupe Street. Gradually, stone by stone, board by board, Meeker's new store began to take shape.

Before long, the mule-drawn freight wagons came into town and emptied their contents of colorful bolts of cloth and supplies into Stanley Meeker's new fabric mercantile. In one corner of the building was a large iron stove. This stove was to be the primary source of heating for the store. It was the end of December when the last freight wagon arrived with his supplies.

Meeker's living area was below the store, in the basement. Being a dwarf, he didn't have much need for high ceilings, so I'm sure the basement served him well. An additional smaller wood stove was installed to warm the basement. The basement also served as a storage area for the extra supplies of cloth.

I'll never forget the tragic night of Meeker's death. It was a cold moonlit December. I was deep in sleep, when suddenly I was awakened by the town's church bell. Very soon after, the alarming sound of pistol shots could be heard. That only meant one thing: fire! Whenever there was a fire in town, the quickest way to alert everyone to action was to ring the church bell, and then the men would fire their pistols in the air. The town's people quickly left their warm houses and gathered by the church. We followed the fire's blazing light, and sadly it led to Meeker's new store. An attempt to form a bucket brigade was made, but failed. The closest water source, a well, was too far away to be of any help. We stood helplessly, watching as the fire quickly consumed the fabric store. Meeker was not among us; we knew he was trapped in the basement! I hoped the fire would not reach my friend. We desperately wanted to go inside the burning store, but the fire was raging with too much intensity. It would have been useless for any of us to try. We stood in silence.

As the morning sun slowly lit up the sky, one by one we sadly returned to our homes. Later in the day, a few of the men, including myself, returned to the charred remains of what was left of the store. With shovels and rakes, we carefully combed through the remains. As we searched among the smoking embers of the store's foundations, we discovered Meeker's body among the ashes. Some of the store's floor timbers had fallen on top of him. His body was in bad shape. We placed his remains in a regular-size coffin and then buried him in the cemetery. All that remained of the store he was so proud of was its stone foundation. The likely cause of the

Stanley Meeker.

deadly fire was a flying ember from the wood stove, which had ignited nearby cloth.

In the basement, a storage trunk and a few other personal possessions survived the fire. Looking through the trunk, I found a picture of Meeker among some items. I assumed that the picture must have been taken in Texas. Since I spent a lot of time with him, I decided to keep the picture as a memento of our friendship.

Just a few nights after his burial, two men in town began to speak of a ghostly image they had seen at the site of the fire. They were on horseback passing the site, when suddenly, the horses seemed uneasy. One of the men looked in the direction of the soot-covered, stone foundation, and caught sight of Meeker! The rider spoke to his partner,

"Look, do you see what I see?" Sure enough, Meeker's ghost was definitely walking about his burned-out store! Both men stared as the ghost walked back and forth on top of the snow-covered rubble. The ghost paused, then looked at the two men, and with a thankful gesture, raised his fingers and touched the brim of his hat. In just a few seconds, Stanley Meeker's ghost simply vanished!

A few months later, Stanley Meeker's brother came to Carlsbad, had his brother's remains exhumed from the cemetery, and took them back to Texas. Since then, Stanley Meeker's ghost has not been seen. I know that Meeker was very happy to have had the opportunity to spend a few months in Carlsbad. It's a shame that things did not work out as he had planned. He had made friends, and I'm happy to know that he would have appreciated our attempt that cold winter night, so long ago, to save him and his store.

DOÑA ANA

HISTORY OF DOÑA ANA
by Senator Mary Jane M. Garcia

By 1920, there were two cemeteries in Doña Ana village, one Catholic and one Methodist. This social split was created with the introduction of the Methodist religion into the established Catholic community through marriage. During the Civil War, Methodist Anglos moved into the area from other states and married Hispanic women. Not only was a new religion introduced, but the new Anglo

husband could now own these traditional, large Hispanic lands. This arrangement favored the newcomers, who soon amassed virtually all the valuable farmland in Doña Ana.

In 1842, Doña Ana was settled by a group of 33 male colonists from Old Mexico. They fought both a lack of resources and the Apache people in the area. The first major task these men were required to complete was the construction of an *acequia* (water irrigation ditch).

These colonists had traveled north from Old Mexico, across the border crossing known as El Paseo del Norte, or the Northern Passage (present-day Juarez). Eventually, they settled in this fertile area where they established a small village that would be known as Doña Ana. The men petitioned the governor of Chihuahua, Mexico, for the land grant in 1839. One of the original men of the colony was my great-grandfather, Jose Ines Garcia. In 1850, when this area became a territory, 60 men, under the direction of Rafael Ruellas, moved part of the colony south and settled the town that is now Mesilla. A few remained in Doña Ana village, which was by then eight years old.

"I was born and raised in the house . . ."

During the U.S. Civil War, a famous Polish Catholic named Sam Geck (whose last name has most likely been shortened from Geckovich) was supplying the Confederacy with arms. He was arrested, found guilty, and sent to prison. Sam Geck's home was located directly across from the Garcia family home in Doña Ana. Another influential man in Doña

Ana's early history was John D. Barncastle. During the Civil War, he arrived in Doña Ana with the first California Battalion Column.

The first *alcalde* (mayor) of Doña Ana was Pablo Melendrez. His daughter, Josefa, married John D. Barncastle. I was born and raised in the house that had been the mayor's house. This house remains the Garcia family home to this day. The house is filled with history, but to me it is just home.

★ ★ ★

Senator Garcia wrote the first documented history of Doña Ana village, An Ethnohistory of Doña Ana Village: Hispanic Catholics vs Hispanic Methodists, *for her master's thesis in anthropology. Her study, published in 1986, is an analysis of the religious and political drift that occurred between these two religious groups during the turn of the 20th century.*

THE OLD CEMETERY
When Mary Jane Garcia was doing the research for her thesis, she brought four historical anthropologists from New Mexico State

University (NMSU) to the original cemetery of Doña Ana. The professors were overwhelmed by what they discovered. Among the overgrowth of desert shrubs, water-starved mesquite trees, and debris were 75 tombs, presumably the graves of the original settlers. The professors immediately realized the significance of the old cemetery and in particular Doña Ana. Doña Ana's history was literally at their feet!

Sadly, in the 1960s, while Mary Jane Garcia was working overseas, an outside land developer bought and completely developed an area that was part of the original cemetery. The developer built a trailer park on top of much of this original cemetery, directly over the graves! The Antiquities Act, which protected such sites of historical and cultural significance, had yet to be enacted. By the time the residents of Doña Ana, including Mary Jane Garcia, had discovered what had taken place, the damage had been done. The land was completely flattened, and a trailer park now stood where, only months before, the rich history and remains of some of the original settlers of Doña Ana had once rested. The remains of these people were never removed; instead, the heavy earth-moving machinery simply tore apart and unceremoniously erased a major part of Doña Ana's past! The tombs discovered in the 1980s remain covered beneath the mesquite bushes.

The developer built a trailer park on top of the cemetery.

A woman resident, who now lives in the trailer park, described a strange experience she and her family once had at about 5 a.m. one day. The family was abruptly wakened by the loud voices of people in prayer just outside their trailer. The whole family rose immediately out of their beds and gathered together in one room of their trailer home. They looked out a window and saw three ghostly old women, wearing black lace veils over their heads. These ghostly women were rubbing their hands together. The manner in which these women were chanting gave the family the impression that the women were reciting the Rosary Prayer. Who were these women? Were they the ghosts of the disrespected graves that had recently been disturbed? Answers to these questions might be found in the following personal interview with Doña Ana's very own historian, *mi manita*, New Mexico Senator Mary Jane M. Garcia.

★   ★   ★

Ms. Garcia is currently the State Senator for District 36, a diverse district that begins just east of Las Cruces and ends in the north valley, in the town of Hatch. Made up of extreme economic latitudes, her district includes the village of Doña Ana at one end, and an upscale country club at the other. Senator Garcia is, at the time of this writing, in her second term of office and will be seeking a third term. Although the senator is very approachable and good-hearted, I also had the impression that she can be as tough as a tiger when it comes to safeguarding her district from inequities on the political front.

SENATOR MARY JANE M. GARCIA'S STORY

I was born in the village of Doña Ana in 1936. It's difficult for me to express the love I have for the residents of my small community. As you know, my family's history is embedded in this place since the town's inception many, many years ago. The stories I'm about to tell you are true.

I definitely believe in ghosts because of my own personal experiences. I will tell you what I have experienced, both as a young girl and as an adult.

My first ghostly experience happened when I was only six years old. A friend and I were playing in her backyard one bright sunny day. Something caught my eye. I turned to see a strange woman walking across the yard; she was dressed in a brightly colored skirt. Her skirt was made of bright blues, yellows, reds, etc. At the bottom of this skirt was a large ruffle. I thought she was strange, not only for her skirt, but because of the way she wore her hair. Although I only saw her profile, I could see that she wore her dark black hair in bangs, not unlike the pueblo women had done many years before. What really scared me about this woman was that, as she approached the back door, she floated up and over the stairs into the house! I screamed because, even as a child, I knew people did not walk in this manner. Many years later, as an adult, I spoke to the people who lived in the house. They told me of their own experiences with that same ghostly woman, who wore the colorful skirt.

This family kept their newborn baby in a cradle by their bedside. On several occasions they would wake to find the baby and cradle had mysteriously moved into the next room. At other times, the husband would attempt to open a closet door, only to find a force behind the door pulling it shut! Ultimately, the husband would win this tug-of-war by using both hands to pull with all his strength. When the door opened, he saw, floating right before him, a brightly colored skirt with a large ruffle. No sooner had he seen the skirt appear than it disappeared! After a few more of these strange experiences, the family moved out of the house. The house now sits empty and alone with its windows and doors boarded shut.

My second experience happened one night in my own home when I was 10 years old. My home is very old, and was part of a type of fortress built to protect the original inhabitants from the Apaches. I went to use the bathroom; I turned on the light, and closed and locked the door behind me. As I turned to face the mirror, I saw a strange woman, whom I did not recognize, dressed in white in the room with me! I was so frightened, I ran out of the bathroom straight into my mother's bedroom. My mother comforted me and reassured me that everything would be all right.

Years later, as an adult, I went to visit my sister in San Francisco. During one of our conversations, we reminisced about our childhood in Doña Ana. I was shocked when she told me that she too had witnessed the woman dressed in white in our bathroom. All these years, and neither of us had known about the other's ghostly experience!

Another time, while I was sleeping, I heard beautiful music. It sounded as if an old Victrola was playing. The sound was very loud. I got up to investigate the source of the music and walked from room to room. The rooms were dark, and the only radio we owned was turned off. As I walked into another bedroom, I was immediately hit with the loud sound of a full orchestra! The music was so loud that I had to cover my ears. I slammed the door shut and ran to my parents' bedroom. My parents heard nothing and thought I was dreaming. The music I had heard was very old and had a melody I did not recognize. I went back to bed and eventually fell asleep. The next morning, a neighbor came by and spoke to my mother. She asked my mother, "Were you playing some music last night on an old Victrola? It was after midnight. Where did you get that music?" I immediately spoke up and said, "Oh my God! I was about to ask you the same question!" We discussed what we each had heard the night before, but could not come up with an explanation. She said that other family members in her home had not heard the music. I was glad to hear that someone else besides me had heard the music. I was beginning to think that I was going crazy.

I recall one night, when I was 18, being awakened by my mother pacing back and forth. I asked her what was wrong. She said, "Oh, nothing. Go back to sleep." I closed my eyes, and as soon as I had started to fall back asleep, I woke again. This time, my mother got into bed with me. I was so sleepy I didn't have the energy to say anything. The next morning, I asked her why she had come to sleep in my bed. The reason she gave did not satisfy me. But I decided to drop the subject. Later that afternoon, my sister told me the reason for my mother's odd behavior. She said, "Last night, Mom heard a noise coming from your room and it woke her. She got out of bed and went into your room to check up on you. She looked inside your room and saw the ghostly figure of a woman in a white dress. It was moving all around your bed. As Mom entered your bedroom, the ghost woman backed away and disappeared! That's why she decided to stay the night in your room, to protect you from the ghost." Of course, I was frightened by this story, but at the same time I felt protected by my mother's concern for me. Not long after that, my brother Jerry had his own frightening experience with a ghost in my bedroom.

Jerry was 19 years old at the time. He woke up in the middle of the night to see the strong presence of someone standing in the room. His eyes were drawn to the doorway where he spotted the image of a dark figure. This ghostly figure raised one arm and proceeded to make its way towards his bed. My brother was frozen with fright as the ghostly figure moved closer and closer to him. Just as the ghostly hand was inches away from his face, he let out a loud scream and covered his head with the blankets! Hearing the scream, my parents came rushing into the bedroom and saw my brother trembling with fear. Needless to say, my brother was a believer of ghosts after that experience.

Another personal ghost encounter I had took place in 1970. I was staying in another bedroom in the house. I had just turned the lights off and had gotten into bed. It was a very hot July night, and because of the heat I was unable to fall asleep. I lay in bed with my eyes opened. Suddenly, the bedroom door swung open with a loud whoosh! As I looked, I saw that no one was at the doorway. Immediately, a tremendous whirlwind filled the room, and I knew something was about to happen . . . something ghostly. I reached for my crucifix and began to pray. I was screaming so loud, I must have woken up the whole neighborhood! This wind moved quickly and forcefully about the room. Then it stopped! My mother came running in. I kept screaming, "It's in here! It's in here! This thing won't leave me alone!" Mother held me close to her and reassured me that everything was going to be all right. I prayed so hard and with such sincerity that night that I believed nothing was going to bother me again.

Several years later, I remember talking with a woman who had rented a portion of the house next to ours. She told me about a similar experience she once had with a whirlwind and something about her cat. All this stuff just gives me the creeps talking about it. I'll now tell you about the time when these ghostly encounters turned evil.

My older sister, Elodia, was asleep in the bedroom where I experienced the ghost. I was asleep in the adjacent bedroom and I had shut the door. Suddenly, I awoke with the sensation that something was sitting on my feet at the end of my bed. At the time, I thought it was Elizabeth, our family cat, who had jumped on me. Then I thought, how could she have entered my bedroom with the door closed? With my eyes half open I said, "Elizabeth, Elizabeth, what do you want?" I started to feel something heavy crawling up towards my upper body. With one arm I reached down towards my leg, expecting to touch my cat. Without warning, something grabbed a hold of my neck! I was terrified because I couldn't see anyone. I could feel the grip of this ghostly hand slowly squeezing my throat. I was never so afraid in my life! With both my hands, I somehow managed to take hold of whatever demonic force was wrapped around my neck and throw it off me. I screamed for my sister, "Elodia, come here quick!" Elodia came running into my room and took hold of my shoulders. She asked, "What's wrong? Tell me what's wrong!" After I had told her what had happened, she said I must have had a nightmare, but I knew better.

Five years after this terrifying experience, a dear friend of mine, Joan, came to visit from England. We had met while I was in Europe, and had become good friends. I loaned her my bedroom during her stay in Doña Ana. She told me she was having a wonderful time in New Mexico. After Joan had returned to England, we kept in touch by phone and frequent letters. In 1978, while I was in Spain, Joan joined me for a portion of my trip. At one point, Joan confided to me something that had happened to her in Doña Ana while in my home. She said, "You're my best friend and I hope not to hurt your feelings, but something terrible happened to me one night when I slept in your room." I got a lump in my throat as I responded, "Joan, you won't hurt my feelings. Tell me what it is!" Joan proceeded to describe the horrible feeling of being slowly strangled in her bed by an invisible force. She said, "I felt this 'thing' come up, grab my throat, and smother my whole face. I was so terrified, I wanted to scream. I didn't know what to do and was afraid to wake everyone up." I felt so bad for my friend. I knew the courage it had taken for her to confide in me. I was overwhelmed with sorrow and emotion for what she had gone through. I told Joan of my own similar experience. This honest dialogue strengthened our friendship, and we have been the best of friends ever since.

When I remodeled our house some years ago, we had the opportunity to dig in the ground below my bedroom. In some cases of ghostly activity, people believe that money or something else of value may be buried, which can cause spirits to linger on after death.

I also have my own theory: perhaps a woman encountered a violent death and was buried beneath the house. Perhaps she was the ghostly woman we've witnessed all these years. My brother dug a deep trench in the hope of discovering something. He dug and dug but, unfortunately, nothing unusual was uncovered.

I am aware of three deaths that have taken place on this property. In the 1940s, two men, playing a game of dice, began to argue. The argument escalated to the point where one man shot the other with a bullet to the head. Not too long ago, a cousin of mine was killed by his best friend, not far from the spot where this previous murder had taken place. They had been drinking, things got out of hand, and sadly my cousin was murdered. Just recently, in my backyard, an old man was stoned to death by some of his acquaintances. People in the neighborhood know well the ghostly history of my house. Ghost encounters in Doña Ana are not unusual. Almost everyone has a story to tell.

Finally, something else you might be interested in knowing relates to the old church that is located across the street from my home. The church, Nuestra Senora de la Candelaria, is now on both the State and Federal Registry of Historical Sites. The old Camino Real runs directly alongside the church. This church is now being lovingly restored by the community of Doña Ana. About four years ago, during the beginning of the restoration, a grave including a tall skeleton was discovered inside the church right in front of the altar. I suspect it might

"During the beginning of the restoration, a grave including a tall skeleton was discovered inside the church . . ."

have been a priest, or even the founder of Doña Ana, Pablo Melendrez! You will notice the windows of the church are set high up on the walls. I'm told by the old-timers in the community that this was to guard against Apache raids.

Doña Ana is a beautiful village with beautiful people. I know who my neighbors are, and I love our sense of community. You won't find gift shops or galleries in Doña Ana, just old adobe, and what I call, "the historic poor." It's my home and I love it!

★   ★   ★

I interviewed Yetta one afternoon in her thrift shop, which she manages in downtown Deming. Yetta moved to Deming nine years ago from Doña Ana. As you are about to read, Yetta had quite an interesting experience in her rented home. Coincidentally Mary Jane Garcia, whose own story precedes Yetta's, was Yetta's landlord! As I soon discovered during my interview with Yetta, with or without ghosts, she proved to be quite an interesting individual in her own right. I can guarantee that if the "spirit" ever moves you to visit Deming and to seek out her store, you'll be in for some good conversation and hospitality. I'm sure she wouldn't have a strong emotional attachment to one of her "treasures," if you chose to purchase one.

YETTA M. MCCORKLE'S STORY

In 1987, I lived in the town of Doña Ana, which is located just 12 miles north of Las Cruces. I lived in Doña Ana for a year, and in that short time I experienced some strange things that I will never forget.

I lived in an apartment located directly across from the old Catholic church. From what I know, my apartment used to be part of one big house that was later converted into smaller apartments. The complex is made of very thick adobe walls, and was quite comfortable for me when I lived there.

One morning, about 3 a.m., I was awakened by a sudden chill. It was such a cold that enveloped me, I felt as if I were sandwiched between two blocks of ice! I'm talking COLD! I reached for the light, and turned it on. As my eyes grew accustomed to the bright light, I felt and saw wind blowing things around in the room. It was as if someone had turned on a large wind-generating fan that was causing papers, curtains, and clothes to be blown about. My cat jumped in the air, ran back and forth, and clawed at the whirlwind. I got out of bed and walked through the kitchen, down the hall, and into another bedroom. As I did this, the mysterious whirlwind followed me through the house and into the bathroom! I returned back to my bedroom and crawled under the covers. I could hear the whirlwind approach the side of my bed, and when I stuck my hand out to touch it, my arm felt as if it had been covered in an ice-cold frost. I jerked my arm back under the blankets!

I thought about what was happening and couldn't come up with a logical explanation. I knew that every window was locked, because I had locked them myself. Eventually, I just fell asleep, and when I woke in the morning, the whole house was a mess.

One night, two months later, a friend and I were spending a nice quiet evening. We were in the living room. I was sitting on my couch reading a book, and my friend Howard was sitting in a chair. Suddenly, Howard said, "Someone just came in the back door." I answered, "No, they didn't." Howard insisted that someone had entered the house, because he had heard the back door open and close. I told him, "Oh, Howard, it's just my ghost; just leave it alone." Then Howard said I was crazy. He got up from the chair and went to check the back door. When he returned, he said the door was locked. "I told you so," I said. "It's just my ghost come to pay me a visit." Howard sat down and said, "There is no such thing as ghosts." Then, without warning, the cold whirlwind I had experienced two months before returned at that moment. Howard sat still and silent. Having experienced this before, I asked Howard to hand me a thermometer that was on my bookshelf. The thermometer registered 78°F. When I extended it into the whirlwind, it immediately dropped 30 degrees! There was no way we could explain this.

Just as before, my cat jumped frantically and ran about the room. Just as quickly as it had started, the wind stopped. I told Howard about my previous experience with this strange wind, and that it was harmless. The ghost would come in the form of a cold wind. It never did anything dangerous to me, so I was not afraid. And after I had moved out of the apartment, it didn't follow me to my new home in Deming.

Later, I found out that the people who had built the house in the year 1850 had had a child who had died in the house. I was never able to confirm this. I was also told that the mother of the family who had bought the house in 1929 had died of a heart attack in the living room. Soon after, this family sold the house to the Garcia family. I also discovered an old cemetery adjacent to the house. I have walked around the property and stumbled upon old wooden crosses and headstones. I believe that what I experienced in the apartment is a result of it being built so close to this cemetery. Some kind of energy must be moving around that area. It would make sense.

LA MESA

La Mesa translates into English as "tableland." It's primarily a farming community located six miles south of Las Cruces. La Mesa is named after the nearby lava flow called Black Mesa. The town was founded in 1854 by Spanish and Anglo-American pioneers. The Gadsden Purchase became effective on November 16, 1854. Before that time, this area of the Rio Grande Valley remained part of Mexico. To the pioneers, La Mesa was a desirable place to settle because it was above the flood level.

Today, La Mesa remains a small community, surrounded by fields of corn, chile, squash, and pecan orchards. This little village is dear to my own heart because it was my mother's place of birth, and numerous relatives of mine still live here. What follows is my late uncle Luis Ramirez's account of something that happened to him many years ago in La Mesa.

TIO LUIS RAMIREZ'S STORY

One summer night, in 1930, seven friends and I were playing hide-and-seek in a grassy field. I was 10 years old. The field was, for the most part, level with the exception of a few small clusters of tall weeds. Surrounding the field were several old, tall pecan trees. A dirt road passed along one side of these trees.

As we played our nighttime game, I remember running and hiding behind some tall weeds. Suddenly, I saw the figure of a very tall man walking towards us. We remained hidden as the figure approached. The man was wearing a big cowboy hat. Because of the darkness, we were unable to recognize who he was. This stranger came walking closer towards us. I noticed that my friends were also watching the man.

Suddenly, I recognized who he was and whispered to my friends, "*Es el senor que se cava de murir, Vamonos!*" ("It's the man who just died! Let's get out of here!") Just a few days before, the figure of the man before us had been laid to rest. We scattered to our homes like scared quail, running this way and that!

The memory of that night has lingered with me for a long time. I know that my friends have never forgotten it either. There are many more ghost stories about La Mesa; unfortunately, most of those people who experienced ghosts are no longer living.

CLOUDCROFT

The peaceful mountain village of Cloudcroft was founded in 1898, when a group of surveyors reached the summit of the Sacramento Mountains. The sight of a single white cloud nestled among the towering pines inspired the men to name the spot Cloudcroft, "croft" being an Old English word for meadow.

A lodge for the railroad workers was erected on that summit, and over the years the lodge, and the village that grew up around it, has been a favorite vacation spot.

The greatest attraction in the Cloudcroft area is the 215,000 acres of the Lincoln National Forest. Here, a wide variety of recreational activities are available: bike riding, camping, fishing, hiking trails, and picnicking. In season, the mountains are filled with hunters pursuing bear, turkey, elk, deer, antelope, and mountain lion.

The village of Cloudcroft itself, located both north and south of Highway 82, is a charming collection of shops that specialize in handmade items by many local artisans. The old-time atmosphere of the town is enhanced by the wooden barrels of flowers that line the main street, Burro Avenue. The Sacramento Mountain Historical Museum in the village is a must for those visitors interested in the history of the area. Antiques, historical artifacts, and photos illustrate an era gone by.

Fall is perhaps the most spectacular season in the mountains. The aspen leaves turn a lively gold and are highlighted by the intense scarlet of maples. Colorful fruit stands along the highway display local apples, pumpkins, corn, and ristras of red chilies. Many local farmers along Highway 82 open their orchards to those who want to handpick their own harvest.

HISTORY OF THE LODGE

Originally constructed in 1899, by the Alamogordo and Sacramento Mountain Railway as a by-product of the railroad's search for timber and railway ties, the resort of Cloudcroft became an immediately successful mountain retreat . . . a cool reprieve for thousands of overheated Texans. (Remember that New Mexico, Oklahoma, and Arizona were not states at the time.)

As the actual log-constructed lodge neared completion in 1899, an article in the *Albuquerque Journal-Democrat* reported, "This beautiful building will be known as Cloudcroft Lodge and its interior will be furnished with a lavish hand, yet in keeping with the character of the place. Fireplaces, with wide, hungry mouths, will sparkle and crackle and dart forth welcome tongues of flame to hundreds of merry guests, who will find a new pleasure in life during the long, sultry summer."

On June 13, 1909, a disastrous fire destroyed the Lodge. But by 1911, the Lodge had been rebuilt and reopened on its current, more scenic site. Since then, it has undergone numerous renovations, but the outside of the building remains almost unchanged.

During the 87-year history of the Lodge, thousands of Southwestern families have called the Lodge and Cloudcroft their second home. The Lodge has entertained and hosted hundreds of politicians, artists, entertainers, and business leaders, including such notables as Pancho Villa, Judy Garland, and Clark Gable. Both U.S. and Mexican government officials have long visited the historic hotel. And, in fact, the most famous hotelier in the world was once associated with the Lodge; Conrad Hilton managed it in the 1930s.

Today, the Lodge continues in the tradition of friendliness, hospitality, outstanding food, and unique lodging.

★ ★ ★

I interviewed Linda in the Lodge's bar. Originally from Texas, Linda is a recent arrival to Cloudcroft. She was a very pleasant person to talk to, so it is no surprise to me that she was hired to be the Lodge's public contact person. After my interview, Linda gave me a tour of the various rooms and restaurant she had mentioned to me. One particular thing she showed me, which I clearly recall, is the stuffed black bear displayed in the lobby. Standing upright on its two back legs and with raised front paws and an open, snarling mouth, the bear is quite "attractive." As Linda and I walked past the bear, she informed me that newlyweds enjoy taking pictures of themselves with this bear. Then Linda personally showed me the pose she is most fond of. She placed herself between the bear's raised paws and said, "See what a nice picture this would make?"

Linda was a joy to talk with. Her ghostly experiences at the Lodge were equally interesting to hear. If you ever decide to visit the Cloudcroft Lodge, do make it a point to speak with her. Aside from getting an excellent tour of the facility, you just might make a new friend!

LINDA GOODWIN'S STORY

I'm currently the Administrative Assistant of Sales at the Lodge. I recall a portion of my pre-employment orientation involved being informed about "Rebecca," the ghost of the Lodge. As the Assistant of Sales, it is my duty to know every aspect of the unique history of the facility, and if this includes a ghost, well, so be it. My knowledge of the ghost is the following.

The short but tragic, well-known story about the ghost began many years ago. A beautiful, young, flirtatious and mischievous woman, with striking blue eyes and shocking red hair, had a secret sweetheart unknown to her lumberjack fiancé. One day, her lumberjack came by unannounced and caught the two engaged in a romantic situation. His rage was so out of control that he took matters into his own hands and did away with Rebecca. Her body was never found; however, her room was covered in blood. People think he buried her body somewhere on the grounds. Apparently, her spirit still wanders throughout the lodge. Rebecca's ghost is most often seen by honeymooners. But I'll tell you more about Rebecca later.

My first strange experience at the Lodge took place about two months after I had started working there, and it involved, of all things, a typewriter.

One day, I needed to do some typing, so I borrowed an electric typewriter from our accounting department and took it to my office. I began to type on it, when suddenly it started to type out strange-looking symbols. To me, these symbols looked like hieroglyphs. Not having seen anything like this before, I decided to ask a woman who had used this particular machine to come and take a look at what was going on. She came to my office and tried to type something legible. It began to print out the same symbols for her as well. Thinking that something was mechanically wrong, we unplugged it and sent it off for repair. When it was returned from the repair shop a few days later, the note attached said nothing was wrong with it. I took it up to my office, plugged it in, and as soon as I began to type an A, once again the darn thing began to print out the same weird symbols. I was told a short time later that our offices are located where the original chamber rooms used to be, and that one of these rooms had been Rebecca's. That was enough for me; I knew Rebecca's spirit had something to do with the typewriter's strange activity. I wrapped the cord around the typewriter and set it aside for good!

One winter, about five years ago, while we were renovating portions of the hotel, a plaque that said "Rebecca's" was removed from one of our suites. Although Rebecca had never stayed in the room, for some reason unknown to me, it was named the Rebecca Room. The room was then renamed the Governor's Room, because of the different New Mexican governors who have stayed in the room while visiting Cloudcroft. In the reception area near the front desk, there is an old switchboard that is kept as an antique showpiece. The strange thing about this antique switchboard is that it is, and has been, unplugged for many, many years. As soon as the Rebecca Room was renamed, the old switchboard began to light up in the middle of the night. The indicator light for the old Rebecca Room, now Room 101, lit up as though someone was calling from the old

The entrance to the Governor's Room . . . formerly "Rebecca's Room."

room! The switchboard was completely inoperable. And whenever the light would go on, the room was completely empty. Knowing this, the staff would go and take a very, very quick look anyway. This happened so many times, that the Lodge lost several night auditors. They were hired, and before long they resigned, having had enough of the ghost.

I know of a guest who was convinced he had seen the ghost of Rebecca in his room. He was so shaken by her apparition,

A ceramic rendering of Rebecca.

395

he asked to be placed in another room. It so happened that every room that night was booked. Given this unforeseen circumstance, he decided to spend the night in the lobby area with a blanket on a couch.

Another ghostly incident happened to Nosi, one of our staff bartenders. We were having a very busy day at the bar, with lots of people ordering both food and drink. It's not difficult to imagine the bustling activity the employees must have had to deal with. Nosi needed to visit the ladies' room, but because of the full house, the only unoccupied bathroom was downstairs. Nosi told me she had entered the bathroom, had seen it was empty, and then had turned on the lights. She had entered one of the stalls and, after having completing her business, she had noticed there was no toilet tissue. She said, "Oh damn, there's no toilet paper in here." As soon as she had said this, a roll of paper had come rolling into her stall from the neighboring stall. She had been very surprised by this because she had thought she was alone. She had not heard anyone enter the bathroom or make noise. Being courteous, she had said, "Thank you" to whoever had been there. There had been no reply, and when she had come out, there had been no one else in the bathroom.

Rebecca's image in stained glass.

Another time, a very good waitress was in the process of serving coffee to a table of guests in the Fireside Dining Room. While addressing her guests, she suddenly felt a strong tug on the serving tray she was holding. She immediately froze! As she tried to steady the tray, the tugging increased in force until the cups full of coffee were thrown off the tray and fell to the floor.

The restaurant manager, Judy Montoya, also had an experience in the Fireside Dining Room with a newlywed couple. This couple was spending their honeymoon at the Lodge and were celebrating the joyous occasion with an intimate dinner in the Fireside Dining Room. With their glasses raised, filled with red wine, they were about to toast their love for each other when the glasses amazingly exploded, and they were left holding only the glass stems! The diners seated at nearby tables were equally surprised as glass flew onto their tables and plates. The manager quickly entered the dining room having heard the commotion. Judy hastily

"Rebecca created quite an expensive trick that evening . . ."

attempted to calm the patrons that evening by announcing that their meals would be "on the house." Rebecca created quite an expensive trick that evening, a trick which had cost the restaurant several free meals and a large cleaning bill for stained, white tablecloths! Apparently, couples, drinking red wine, frequently have their glasses shattered. Interestingly, Rebecca leaves couples who are drinking white wine, alone.

Although Rebecca is a very mischievous spirit, she has never hurt anyone and will not respond when called. She operates on her own schedule and will do things only to those persons whom she is attracted to, like newlyweds. Personally, I'm not scared by her presence, but I'm nervous about actually seeing her.

DEMING

Deming is located on I-10, in the southwestern portion of the state. The city was founded as a railroad town more than 100 years ago, and named for Mary Deming Crocker, wife of a railroad magnate. Much of the economy of Deming and Luna County relies upon the tourist-related establishments located along this route. Two major tourist attractions are Rock Hound State Park, a geologic phenomenon, and Pancho Villa State Park, a historical site commemorating the famous Mexican revolutionary's raid on the border town of Columbus, New Mexico.

★   ★   ★

I interviewed Dolly in the Deming Luna Mimbres Museum. In a quiet room that was filled with mementos and artifacts of the Old West, we sat facing each other with the tape recorder on top of an antique table that was between us. I was able to sense that Dolly was a little apprehensive about my visit and about my "ghostly" questions. But she came through graciously and coherently, although, I suspect she held tightly onto her purse with both hands for moral support!

DOLLY H. SHANON'S STORY

I've lived in Deming for 34 years, and have been associated with the museum as one of its archivists for six years. For a time, I was also an elementary school teacher here in the city.

My first ghostly encounter took place about 30 years ago. I was in my kitchen working one afternoon, when I noticed a large dark figure rush past me. Then I heard my teenage son's bedroom door open and close. I thought, "What is my son doing home so early from school?" I called out his name, and when I received no answer, I walked to his room and opened his bedroom door. The room was empty.

Of course I was concerned, but what could I do? Who could I go to with this experience? People would think I was strange, maybe even crazy! I did confide in my husband and two sons. They smiled at each other when I explained to them what I had seen, so I knew they thought I was imagining things. But one day, my son Tim came to me and said, "Mom, I know you saw something. I believe what you are saying." He never did tell my why he felt this way, but I know he himself experienced something. My husband said it may have been the reflection on the wall of a passing car's lights. His explanation did not convince or comfort me. I kept this experience quiet and hoped I wouldn't see the thing again. But I did.

Over the years, on several occasions, I have seen this shadowy figure run down the hallway or rush by an opened door. These encounters all have taken place during the day, never at night. I could never make out who this figure was. Each time I experienced it, I froze and just stood there. I tried to rationalize the situation and fix my mind onto other things. Sometimes this worked for me. But most times it didn't.

The last ghostly experience I specifically recall in that house was hearing the sound of jars in the kitchen being moved about, and jar lids being removed and then replaced. It occurred one afternoon while I was in the kitchen. Some neighborhood children were visiting me. I offered cookies to the children and sent them out to play. About an hour later, I was in the living room reading, when I heard the sound of the cookie jar lid opening in the kitchen. It had a distinct, unmistakable sound. I assumed a child had returned for more cookies. I walked into the kitchen to confront the little thief, but to my amazement the kitchen was empty. I found the back door locked and the cookie jar undisturbed. No one had been in the kitchen. I knew in my heart that the ghost had come for another visit.

"I saw this shadowy figure run down the hallway."

Shortly thereafter, we moved to another house, and since then I have had no other ghostly visitors. So far.

COLUMBUS

The Village of Columbus, a National Historic Site, was established in 1891 near the border, just north of Palomas, Mexico. When the El Paso and Southwestern Railroad built its depot in 1902, the town moved three miles north and grew to support two hotels and a variety of merchants. Camp Furlong at Columbus was one of a series of border military encampments.

On March 9, 1916, Mexican revolutionary General Francisco (Pancho) Villa's army crossed the border in a predawn attack upon Columbus. The town was sacked and burned by the estimated 1,000 Villistas. Eighteen residents and U.S. soldiers were killed before the Villistas were driven out. More than 100 of Villa's men lay dead in the streets at dawn amid the burning ruins.

General John "Black Jack" Pershing commanded the U.S. Punitive Expeditionary force from Camp Furlong to pursue Villa deep into Mexico. It was the first time in American history that motorized vehicles and aircraft were used in warfare. The first Aero Squadron flew from the first operational air base at Columbus. The pursuit, however, was in vain. Villa and his army successfully escaped into the Mexican mountains.

Villa continued his career as a revolutionary until July 1920, when he retired. On July 20, 1923, Villa was assassinated in the city of Parral, Chihuahua, Mexico.

Today, Columbus is an international port of entry serving as the border crossing between Columbus and Palomas, Mexico. Pancho Villa State Park, a 49-acre, 65-space campground, is located on the old Camp Furlong site. The park offers one of the most beautiful desert botanical gardens in the Southwest.

★   ★   ★

I interviewed Señor Pantoja at his sister's house in Columbus at about 8 p.m. My interview did not end until after 11 that night. Señor Pantoja is a large, heavyset man with a trimmed, graying moustache. After my interview, his wife, Delfina, brought him his guitar and asked him to entertain me with a few songs. He needed no further encouragement from his wife, so he straightened himself up on his chair and began to play several of his favorite, traditional Mexican corridos (ballads). It was not long before Delfina herself joined in and performed a duet with her husband. It was clear to me that Delfina wanted to entertain as much as he did. They seemed to be the perfect couple, both in marriage and as a singing combo. "So many of the old songs are not played and have been forgotten these days," he said. "Maybe they'll just die with us old folks." What follows is my interview with Señor Manuel Pantoja.

MANUEL PANTOJA'S STORY

Manuel Pantoja bought his 10-acre property more than 40 years ago. The property lies at the foot of the Tres Hermanas (Three Sisters) mountains. He had heard from people in the area that on the property there were the ruins of an old adobe house. The house used to belong to a man who was known on both sides of the border to be a *brujo* (witch). This witch was named *El Delgado* (The Skinny Man). This was not his real name, but due to his very thin body and wispy facial hair, it was a nickname given to him by the people of the area.

The "Tres Hermanas," or Three Sisters.

Manuel said, "People told me that El Delgado made his living out of catching, and then skinning, rattlesnakes. He would tan the skins and make belts, which he then took across the border to sell. However, he was best known for his ability to cast evil spells on people."

Apparently, people from both sides of the border knew very well of the mystical power that El Delgado was able to harness. Visitors who had heard of his power visited him at his home and asked him to cast spells. These requests were for the purpose of gaining a love interest or to cause an enemy harm. His knowledge of magic was so well known people would pay him whatever he asked. In addition to money, payments also included food, blankets, or jewelry.

Once the two parties had agreed upon a fee, the process of casting the spell would begin. The visitor would be instructed by El Delgado to sit on a chair in his small kitchen. He would bring out a small clay doll, then unwrap the dark blue cloth it was bundled in. He would carefully remove the doll, then place it on the table. He would turn the doll in order to have it face the person. The doll was made of hollow clay with a grinning, slightly open mouth. El Delgado would hand a small kernel of corn to the visitor, and then he would instruct the person to place the corn kernel into the doll's mouth. If the doll made a swallowing noise as the corn kernel moved down through its throat, El Delgado would be able to conduct the spell. However, if the doll made no sound, it would be useless to continue. Such was the process of elimination that El Delgado conducted with his clients.

He was also known for another peculiar trait. During the day, wherever El Delgado traveled, a large black raven was always in close proximity. As he would walk the unpaved streets, this mysterious raven would fly from tree to tree or simply hover in the air. People believed it was a symbol of his guardian spirit. It was also believed among the people that at night the raven transformed into a white owl. At any rate, El Delgado was always in the company of one of these birds.

"El Delgado made his living out of catching, and then skinning, rattlesnakes . . ."

One day, El Delgado was visited by a woman from Columbus. She wanted to have a love spell cast upon a man she desired to have for her own. Her problem was that the man was already married. El Delgado brought out the doll and gave the woman a corn kernel, which she proceeded to place into the doll's mouth. The doll made the swallowing sound as the kernel passed down through its throat. Thus, El Delgado could continue with his magic. He instructed the woman to return the next day with any type of clothing that the man she wanted had been known to wear.

The following day the woman returned with an old shirt that had belonged to the man. She had removed it from his clothesline during the night. She presented the shirt to El Delgado. He took the shirt and tore a small strip of cloth from the back and placed the strip on the table. He brought out a dead hummingbird he had had among his collection of "supplies," and placed it next to the strip of cloth. After this, he used a pair of scissors to cut a lock of hair from the woman. He folded the woman's hair under the hummingbird's wing, and with the strip of cloth, he wrapped the bird into a tight ball and then placed it into the woman's hands, saying, "Don't worry, this man will be yours!"

"Long rattlesnake skins hung like chile ristras, blowing back and forth in the dry wind."

Word reached the man about the spell that El Delgado had cast upon him. A neighbor in town had overheard the woman bragging about the spell. Upon hearing the news the man was in a rage. He was not about to be hexed by a witch, and decided to get on his horse and confront El Delgado himself!

As the man approached the witch's house, El Delgado, who was out in his yard, caught sight of the angry man, rushed inside, and locked his front door. El Delgado must have been surprised to have seen this man on horseback. The witch was in the process of drying, and preparing, snakeskins because, attached to the exposed *vigas* (beams) on the porch of the house were long rattlesnake skins. They hung like chile ristras, blowing back and forth in the dry wind.

The man yelled at the witch to come out of his house. El Delgado did not respond. The man yelled and yelled until finally El Delgado opened the door and said, "Leave my house or I'll make sure your death will come quickly!" The man threatened to burn down the witch's house, but after a few minutes, out of frustration, he pulled on his horse's reins and left in a rage! El Delgado would not be threatened by him or any man, and so that evening the witch cast a death spell.

That evening, the man was at home with his wife and child. He noticed that whenever he walked from one room to another in his house, he heard a strange noise up on the ceiling or roof. The noise sounded as though a large animal was stalking him. It would walk and then stop at the exact moment the man would. Whichever room the man would move to, the large beast moved there as well. And if the man stood in one spot for a few minutes, the animal on the roof began to scratch the area directly above him! It sounded like a large dog digging.

The man and his wife went outside to see if they could spot a dog on their roof. In the dark night, they saw an owl perched on one corner of the roof, the white owl of El Delgado! As soon as the man saw this symbol of the witch, he knew he had been hexed. He immediately decided to pay another visit to the witch. He got on his horse and galloped quickly away.

Arriving at the witch's home, he saw the yellow glow of lamplight shining through a window. The white owl, the one that the man had seen back at his house, was perched and hooting a loud warning in a nearby tree. The man noticed El Delgado's shadow at the window. He yelled to the witch to come outside, but the witch yelled back, "I told you, you would be sorry. Your death will be an example to all. No one disrespects me! No one!" The man was then gripped with anger and revenge.

He quickly gathered dried brush and sticks and piled them against the house on the wooden porch. Then he set fire to this material and watched as the flames quickly began to consume the house. From within the house, the witch's angry words could be heard, as he screamed obscenities at the man. Soon enough, the roof of the small house, ablaze in fire, came crashing in and put an end to El Delgado's life. News of the witch's death soon reached the people in town. Most were glad, but there were a few who were not. They believed El Delgado had chosen a life of evil, and that his death reflected his evil life.

The following day, after the fire, some people went to see the destroyed house for themselves. With rakes and wooden poles they searched among the ashes and debris, but, to their amazement, found no trace of the witch's body. What they did find were all sorts of carved dolls' heads made of stone. Some of the dolls still had portions of their wooden bodies attached. Most were heaped together in a burned, broken pile. The strange details of the dolls' carved faces shocked the people. Each of the crudely carved heads distinctly resembled a person in town! The people assumed that the witch was using these voodoo-type dolls to cast spells on the community. Immediately, these carved heads were gathered together and one by one were shattered to pieces and destroyed. El Delgado's property remained vacant for many years, until Manuel Pantoja bought the property.

At the time of his purchase, Manuel was unaware of its legendary history, but it did not take long for word to get to him. A neighbor told him the story of El Delgado and about the ruins of the witch's house being located on the eastern edge of Manuel's acreage. One day, out of curiosity, Manuel decided to search the property for the ruins.

Manuel told me, "I had to be careful where I stepped in and around the ruins, because it seemed there were rattlesnakes under every bush. I was more afraid of getting bit by one of these serpents than of seeing a witch."

He found the partial adobe walls of the witch's house.

He found the partial adobe walls of the witch's house. "As I turned over stones, kicking aside old burned boards, I found a small carved stone head, just like the ones I was told about.

"The first night I brought it home, I put it on a shelf above my kitchen sink. I placed the face of the head towards the window. I told my wife the entire story about the stone head from the witch's house. She seemed interested, but not at all frightened. That evening, as we were asleep in bed, I kept waking in the middle of the night. I could not get the image of the little stone head out of my mind. I decided to go into the kitchen and have another look.

As I turned on the light over the sink, I saw that the little head had moved from the position I had left it in and was now facing inwards, away from the window! My wife heard me get out of bed and followed me into the kitchen. I asked her if she had moved the stone head. She answered, 'No.' Without thinking any more about it, I turned the face of the head once again towards the window, and we both returned to bed.

"As you can see, it is an eerie thing."

"The following morning, I went to the kitchen to turn on the coffeemaker. I looked at the head and to my amazement, not only had it turned around towards the kitchen, but it was now at the far end of the shelf! I asked my wife again about moving the stone head, but she denied touching it and immediately demanded I remove it from the house. I took it outside and stored it in the toolshed, far from the house. Occasionally, I bring it out to show people. As you can see, it is an eerie thing to look at, especially if you know its history."

LORDSBURG

OFFICIAL SCENIC HISTORIC MARKER

LORDSBURG
Population 3,195 · Elevation 4,245

Lordsburg was founded in 1880 on the route of the Southern Pacific Railroad, near that used by the Butterfield Overland Mail Co., 1858-1861. It eventually absorbed most of the population of Shakespeare, a now-deserted mining town three miles south.

The town of Lordsburg, located on the old Butterfield Stage Route, was founded in 1880. It grew as a town because it was on the route of the Southern Pacific Railroad.

The Apache nation had made the area their home for many generations. Among the first white men to arrive were the soldiers of the Mormon Battalion in 1846. In 1853, the area became a U.S. Territory through the Gadsden Purchase, which established the borderline between the United States and Mexico. The new border created a southern route to the West Coast, which was established by the Butterfield Stagecoach Company, and traveled by the Pony Express in the late 1850s. Sometime around 1850, pioneers bound for California and the newly discovered goldfields followed an old Apache trail located two miles south of the town. There, Mexican Springs provided these travelers with precious water. Shakespeare Ghost Town (listed on the National Historic Register) is all that now remains of the town that grew at Mexican Springs. It was first named Grant, then soon changed to Ralston, and then finally Shakespeare. Sixteen miles west of Lordsburg, also located along the Butterfield Stage Route, is Stein's Railroad Ghost Town, founded circa 1870. Lordsburg has grown from being a small settlement on the stage trail en route to California, to a town of more than 5,000 people.

In the early 1920s the first airport in New Mexico was built at Lordsburg. This is where Charles Lindbergh stopped on his famous 1927 transcontinental flight. Amelia Earhart, Tom Mix, and other celebrities at the time also stopped at Lordsburg on their way to Los Angeles. Lordsburg is also the birthplace of New Mexico's state song.

★ ★ ★

Armando is a short man, with a jovial personality. I interviewed him at his home, south of town. Although he was more than willing to tell me all the details of his experience with ghosts, he requested that I not reveal the exact location of his home. He felt it would be best to keep the "energy" of whatever remained on his property undisturbed. Having neighbors, or sightseers, walking about might "start things up" once again. Armando has quite an interesting story to tell, as you'll read.

ARMANDO'S STORY

I've lived in Lordsburg for about 16 years. Prior to moving to Lordsburg, I lived in Silver City, a little more than an hour north of town. When I purchased my house, I knew it would be too small, so, with the help of friends, I immediately began to construct additional bedrooms to accommodate my family. The property was mostly undeveloped, with lots of large rocks and debris and various desert brush that needed to be hauled away. The work was difficult, especially during the heat of the day.

The foundation for the extra bedrooms was begun, and soon the walls went up. When we were done with the construction, I decided to build a small barn and chicken coop about 200 feet from the rear of the house. The following year I bought the materials for the job and soon was ready to begin.

I paced the area where the barn would be built and hammered wooden stakes into the ground, marking the corners. As I was doing my pacing, I noticed the unusual formation of some rocks within the area I had marked. The other rocks were scattered about, but these rocks were laid out in a perfect square! Well, I didn't pay too much attention, and just continued my work. Because of the intensity of the desert midday sun, I decided to end my chores and seek cool comfort indoors.

Later that day, I had a surprise visit from three relatives of mine, who were from out of town. They had brought along a friend of theirs, Juanita, from California. After dinner that evening, we were all gathered in the backyard, sitting and drinking cold beer. The evening was warm, the sun was below the horizon, and we were trying to catch any breeze that would blow in our direction. Suddenly, Juanita set her can down and said, "Armando, look over there, who is that?" I looked towards the rear of the property and responded, "I don't see anyone; where are you looking?" Juanita said, "Over there by that tree, there's a man standing there." We all stared in the direction of the tree, and sure enough, there was the dark figure of a man, who seemed to be walking around the area where I had discovered the formation of rocks earlier in the day. I yelled out, "Hey, can I help you?" The man did not respond. I told everyone that I was going to see who this person was and what he was doing on my property. As I walked closer to the man, I noticed he was tapping his foot on the rock formation. And then his image seemed to dissolve before me! As I took another few steps in his direction, he totally faded away! I turned around, and ran back to my guests. They all said, "What the hell was that? Did you see that guy disappear?" I responded, "Why do you think I ran back here? That was a ghost we just saw!" We turned on the back-porch light and arranged our chairs in a close circle, for reassurance.

Our conversation then turned to ghostly experiences. Juanita's grandmother once had told her about a ghost that had appeared to her and had given her a message about a future event. Juanita made the suggestion that perhaps *this* ghost might be a messenger of some kind. After all, for some reason he had been tapping his foot on the rocks.

The next day, in the "safety" of the morning light, we decided to probe around the formation of rocks, to find a possible reason for the apparition. Since there were plenty of us to do the heavy lifting, we moved the rocks in no time. Directly underneath the rocks, we found an old sheet of corrugated metal and underneath were slats of wood. We knew we were on to something. Beneath the wood slats was just dirt. With picks and shovels, we took turns digging. The width of the area under the rock formation was about six-by-six feet. We didn't know what to expect. Maybe this was someone's grave or perhaps there was buried treasure somewhere below. We dug like mad gophers!

After digging about four feet down into the earth, we found a large bone. Our imaginations went wild. Maybe it belonged to a horse, cow, or maybe even a dinosaur! We put the bone aside, and continued our "dirty" job. We had soon dug a pit about seven feet deep. The sun was getting too hot to continue, so we decided to take a break.

Later, I brought out a portable radio so we could listen to music. And then we continued our digging as the sun began to set. We used a small ladder to climb in and out of the pit. Our helpers lowered kerosene lanterns to my cousin and me in the pit. It was getting dark; we had dug about another two feet. I dug my shovel into the earth and came up with what looked like a ball of hair! I thought it was someone's head! To our relief, it turned out to be a ball of tree roots.

We continued to dig, and when we got down about another two feet, my cousin and I noticed that the music playing from the radio had stopped. We looked up at my two cousins and Juanita. We were terrified—standing among them was the ghostly figure of the man we

413

had seen the night before! Chills ran down our spines as we scrambled out of the pit. We ran past our cousins and Juanita, shouting, "Let's get out of here!"

We ran into the house, and locked the door behind us. Once inside, my cousin and I explained what we had seen. Our cousins and Juanita were shocked because they had been unaware of any ghost standing between them. I explained how we had clearly seen the man's eyes and yellow teeth in the glow of the lanterns! Juanita began to cry and shake with fear as she thought about the ghost standing next to her. We were so afraid that we decided not to continue our digging.

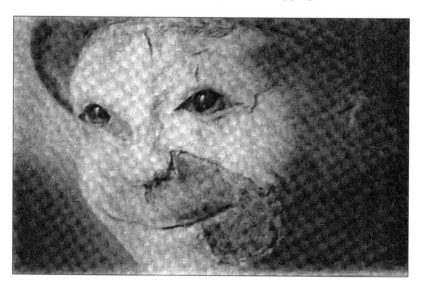

The following morning, we refilled the pit with the earth we had removed. I also chose another location, far away from the pit, to build my barn. What lies, to be discovered, in that pit remains a mystery to me. I have not seen the ghost on the property, but my dogs refuse to go anywhere near that side of the yard.

When anyone ever asks me if I believe in ghosts, I answer, "Damn right I do!" And then I tell them this story.

★　★　★

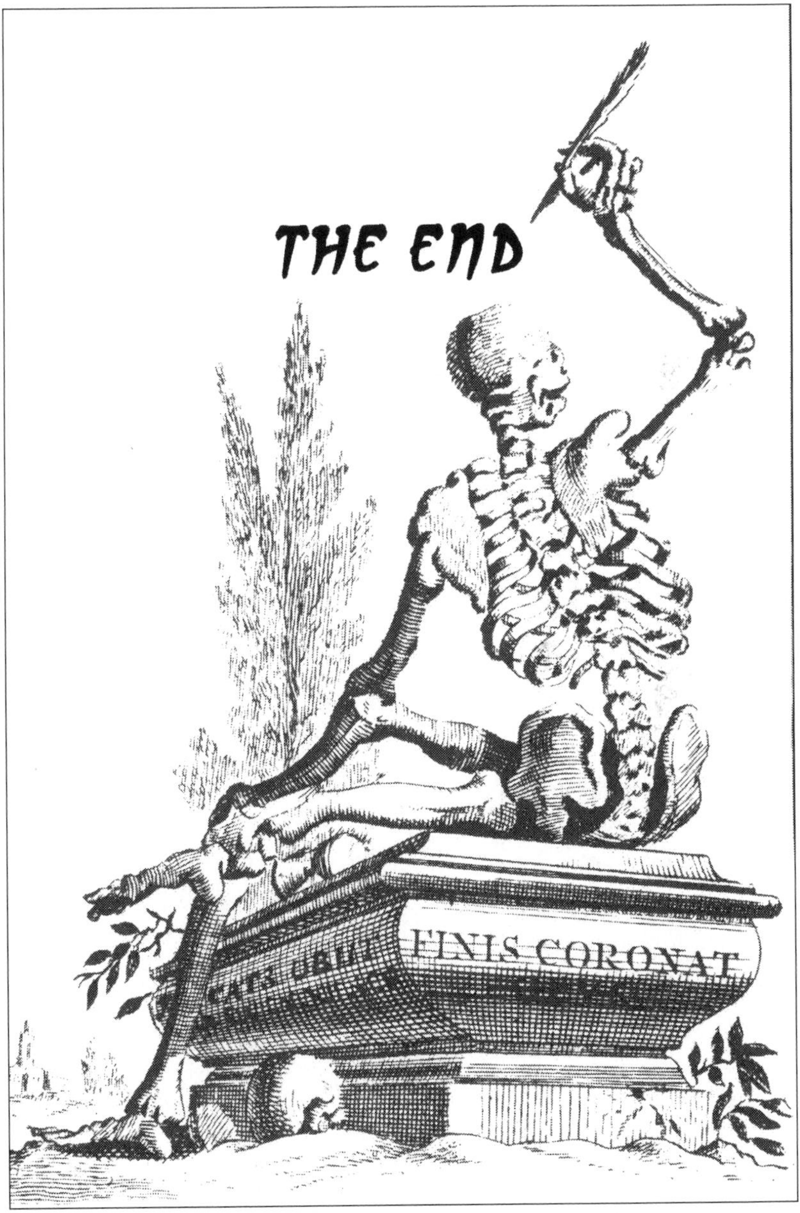

THE END

FINIS CORONAT

ABOUT THE AUTHOR

Antonio R. Garcez graduated with a BA degree from California State University at Northridge, then attended graduate school at the University of Wisconsin. Antonio resides, and continues to write from, his home in New Mexico.

Other titles by Antonio R. Garcez:
American Indian Ghost Stories of the Southwest •
ISBN 0-9634029-7-8
Arizona Ghost Stories • ISBN 0-9740988-0-9
Colorado Ghost Stories • ISBN 978-0-9740988-1-4
Ghost Stories of California's Gold Rush Country &
Yosemite National Park • ISBN 0-9634029-8-6
Ghost Stories of the Medical Profession • ISBN 0-9740988-2-1
Gay & Lesbian Ghost Stories • ISBN 0-9898985-0-8

The author may be contacted through:
Ghostbooks.Biz

Made in the USA
Columbia, SC
22 June 2019